PREPARATION AND PROCEDURE FOR BUSINESS MEETINGS
THIRD EDITION

PARLIAMENTARY LAW and PRACTICE for NONPROFIT ORGANIZATIONS

I0099796

HARRY S. ROSENTHAL

Parliamentary Services Publishing

Parliamentary Law and Practice for Nonprofit Organizations
Preparation and Procedure for Business Meetings Third Edition
All Rights Reserved.
Copyright © 2015 Harry S. Rosenthal
v4.0 r2.1

Parliamentary Services Publishing

ISBN: 978-1-4787-3403-1

Library of Congress Control Number: 2014943395

PRINTED IN THE UNITED STATES OF AMERICA

Disclaimer

This publication is intended to provide accurate and authoritative information on the subject matter discussed. All information found in this publication is general in nature and based on the experience and research of the author. The analysis is to be considered the opinion of the author.

This reference is offered and sold with the understanding that the publisher and author are not engaged in rendering legal, parliamentary or other professional service in specific situations. This publication should not be used as a substitute for obtaining professional service or in lieu of seeking legal or parliamentary advice in specific situations. All of the information contained in this text has been researched for accuracy, however, neither the author nor the publisher may be held liable for errors, omissions, misuse or misinterpretation. The author and publisher make no representations or warranties as to the accuracy of any information including any warranties of merchantability or fitness for a particular purpose. In no event shall the publisher or the author have any liability to any party for special, incidental, tort or consequential damages arising out of or in connection with the contents of this book even if advised of the possibility of such damages.

The statutory and case law in each state differs and changes over time. In addition, organizations use and rely on differing rules. Each situation is unique and must be individually researched by a qualified professional. The reader is urged to consult with an appropriate licensed professional prior to taking any action that might involve

Acknowledgments

I wish to thank my wife, Lynn, for her truly wonderful and ongoing support and encouragement throughout the research and writing of this book.

I also gratefully recognize and thank Nancy Kozlowski for her excellent secretarial work and many insightful comments during this project.

Special thanks to Michael S. Williams, J.D., LL.M. for his outstanding technical assistance and expertise.

And sincere thanks to Robert Faszczewski for his technical assistance with the editing of my manuscript.

Contents

Introduction

THERE HAS BEEN a significant upsurge in statutory changes and reported litigation in the field of parliamentary procedure since the first two excellent editions of this book were written by other authors. Parliamentary rule books have also changed. This third edition, with all new text, but with nearly the same chapter and section titles as before, will help nonprofit organizations when challenged to keep up with these developments before and during their meetings.

This text is not a standalone rule book but a valuable complement to them. It is a starting point for research and general reference on most parliamentary questions that may come up in preparation for or at an organization's formal business meeting. This includes nonprofit meetings of delegates, assemblies, members, boards, other governing bodies and large committees. Nonprofits have been defined to include a variety of organizations such as associations, foundations, condominium and other housing groups, religious bodies, museums, hospitals, universities, labor unions and many local governmental entities.

Although not a substitute for the presence and counsel of a qualified lawyer or professional parliamentarian, this book fills a large void for nonprofit organizations and others in the field of parliamentary practice and procedure. Two other advantages of this text are for its use in helping to write or amend bylaws and in undertaking a course of study of the subject.

What makes this book unique is simultaneous use of the three principal sources of parliamentary authority: selected state nonprofit statutory law, legal case law, and five of the principal parliamentary rule books.

Each of the five parliamentary rule books referred to in the text is quite excellent in its own right. (There are other fine rule books that are not included in this text that readers may wish to consult.) The nonprofit statutory law of five representative states, California, Michigan, New Jersey, New York and Pennsylvania were used. A sample of case law drawing from many more states was also selected. The cases illustrate how the courts at times get drawn into disagreements about business meeting procedures.

Each state in the United States has its own statutory provisions and body of case law which must be individually consulted. Understanding and applying statutory and case law is very state and fact specific and requires further research and analysis by a licensed local attorney in the jurisdiction.

The order of legal authority at a business meeting is as follows:

1. Statutes - most authority
2. Case law - next most authority
3. Parliamentary rules and their reference books - least authority

Most, but not all, provisions of the state nonprofit statutes delegate and allow a nonprofit that falls under its jurisdiction to decide procedural matters at a meeting for themselves through its articles of incorporation and bylaws. In turn, many organizations adopt in their bylaws a specific parliamentary reference book with its procedural meeting rules. One frequently adopted reference is <u>Robert's Rules of Order Newly Revised</u>. Another is the <u>Standard Code of Parliamentary Procedure</u>.

For example, the Pennsylvania nonprofit statute allows a board to meet by means of a conference telephone call <u>"except as otherwise provided in the bylaws"</u>. Another example from the Pennsylvania nonprofit statute that allows a corporation to decide certain situations for itself concerns the nomination of officers as follows: <u>"Unless the bylaws provide otherwise, officers shall be nominated by a nominating committee or from the floor."</u> An example in which a Pennsylvania nonprofit <u>cannot</u> change a nonprofit law through its bylaws concerns a general rule for quorums: <u>"A meeting of members of a nonprofit corporation duly called shall not be organized for the transaction of business unless a quorum is present."</u>

Readers should be aware that labor unions, condominium associations, governmental entities and health care organizations among others are also impacted by other specific statutes and regulations that affect their internal operation and meetings that are beyond the scope of this text. Occasionally, these other statutes are mentioned in the book, especially through the cited case law. Examples of meeting procedures in the context of these other kinds of laws are included in the book to further illustrate parliamentary principles. Some excerpts of the federal labor and health care laws illustrating points raised in the text are provided for general interest in the Appendix.

Situations that arise before and at a meeting often show consensus among the authorities on what procedures the organization should follow. In other meeting situations the authorities take very different positions. The applicability of each point of view must be determined. The particular facts and circumstances of a situation, relevant statutory and case law, and which rules have been adopted or relied upon by the organization must also be evaluated and applied on a case-by-case basis.

Comment about the Model Nonprofit Corporation Act (MNCA or Act)

A committee on nonprofit corporations of the American Bar Association has written revisions to the MNCA. State legislatures are invited by that committee to adopt the model Act. Some in the parliamentary community are concerned about certain of the Act's provisions believing that they differ from standard parliamentary procedure. The content, application and details of these changes and their impact on meetings are beyond the scope of this book.

Mr. Rosenthal's webpage is www.parliamentaryservices.us.

Harry S. Rosenthal
Philadelphia, PA

CHAPTER 1

Meetings and Notice

§ 1 GENERAL MEETINGS OF MEMBERS

Many state statutes require the meeting of members at least once a year for the election of directors.[1] However, others allow for a regular meeting less often - depending on the schedule of electing directors.[2] The bylaws should be specific on this subject. In at least two states an organization may hold its meeting in whole or in part electronically.[3] Many other states are following suit. The meeting may be held inside or outside its state of incorporation.[4] Non-election business also can be transacted at the meeting.[5]

All members in good standing have a basic parliamentary right to attend, participate in debate, make motions, and vote at the organization's membership meeting.[6] The bylaws should provide for both regular and annual membership meetings, and, if the bylaws and the organization's rules and customs do not provide for these meetings, the president or the president and secretary together can call the meeting.[7] In this writer's opinion it is good practice to hold an annual membership meeting to grant members an opportunity to participate in the governance of the organization even if some state laws do not always require such meetings.

The bylaws should include the place and month of these meetings. Many organizations hold an annual conference or convention and schedule the annual membership meeting in connection with it in its bylaws. The bylaws also should outline specific requirements for providing notices of meetings, including the fact that the organization should send notices via postal service or electronic mail to all members sufficiently in advance of the meeting.[8]

The organization should determine on a case-by-case basis whether announcements to the membership of scheduled reconvened meetings are sufficient. In this writer's opinion they should err on the side of caution. A reported Florida case upheld the validity of a reconvened homeowners association meeting because the president had announced the time, date and place of the meeting.[9] Stricter notice standards usually apply to governmental meetings.

In addition to elections, other kinds of business such as board, officer and committee reports are typically taken up at the annual meeting.[10] By state statute certain financial and other information must be submitted to the membership at the annual meeting.[11] This information may include, for example, the number of members in good standing, the organization's assets and liabilities, principal changes in assets and liabilities, and the expenses or disbursements.

A Michigan District Court in defining a "membership meeting" for a local union mentioned that it "requires provision to the membership of advance notice and of the agenda proposed by the chairman, conduct of the meetings by an officer elected by the membership, and transaction of all union business only by a vote of a stated majority of a stated quorum of the membership, after opportunity to present resolutions to the body and to debate all resolutions from the floor."[12]

Authorities differ on whether members attending a membership meeting can decide matters specifically reserved by the bylaws to the board.[13] In a Tennessee case, members at a general meeting may not reverse or change actions expressly reserved to the board under the bylaws.[14] There is room to debate the authority of the membership to overrule a board decision, even one reserved to it in the bylaws. That discussion is beyond the scope of this text. However, the membership cannot suspend the bylaws at the annual meeting.

Case opinions mention other activity at membership meetings. For example, in some organizations, especially small or local ones, all financial transactions must be approved at a membership meeting.[15] A general membership meeting in an Arizona case was used to consider adoption of a technical standard of a trade association of manufacturers and distributors.[16] At a general membership meeting of a nonprofit organization in Connecticut there was voting for approval of new members.[17] At another general membership meeting in California an appeal was heard for disciplinary action against a member of a professional organization.[18]

Minutes must be taken at all membership meetings. Prior meeting minutes must be offered for approval. If the minutes of more than one meeting need to be approved, the earliest minutes should be taken up first. In a reported union case, at a union's general membership meetings, disputes arose over the approval of minutes of the executive board used to approve salary increases.[19] At another union general membership meeting, the reading of the minutes of the executive board in a New Jersey case was not required.[20]

§ 2 SPECIAL MEETINGS OF MEMBERS

An organization may hold a special meeting of members between regular meetings to consider one or more specific and urgent matters. Only the business identified in the notice may be acted upon at the meeting. State statutes recognize such meetings[21] and they should be provided for in the bylaws.

Statutes or bylaws should set out who can call the meeting.[22] Under state nonprofit corporation statutes, which can be further qualified in the bylaws, among those who may be authorized to call a special membership meeting are the board, the president, other officers and the members.[23] State nonprofit corporation statutes provide how many members are needed to call a special meeting.[24]

Often the president with the approval of the board can call a special meeting at the request of a specific number of members.[25] Calling of a special meeting should not be abused.[26] A request for a special meeting may be refused if the request is unreasonable.[27] A Nevada court decided that members could call a special meeting if the president and the secretary refused to do so.[28] It has been held that a president of an international union has the authority to call a special meeting of a local union when the local president refuses to call one.[29] Some case law provides that members may call for a special meeting if the board fails to do so.[30] A special meeting also may be convened in the course of an annual membership meeting.[31]

Prior notice must be provided to all members stating the specific proposals to be considered and decided, and the subjects to be discussed.[32] The notice must identify the general nature of the business to be transacted,[33] although such a meeting can be called for "any lawful purpose."[34] Notice of a special membership meeting must be given in a fair and reasonable manner consistent with the bylaws.[35] A Connecticut court found the approval of a budget invalid at a meeting when the board failed to send out a summary 15 days in advance as required in the condominium declaration.[36]

To protect absentees unanimous consent cannot be used to waive notice requirements.[37] It has been held in a New Jersey case that a claim of lack of notice of a special union meeting was disallowed for failure to exhaust internal union remedies (and for other reasons).[38] Thus even if an otherwise valid claim is made that notice of a meeting was inadequate, a labor union member must first follow internal procedures in order to object to the notice.

Secondary motions that may come up, including but not limited to motions to amend, are permissible if they are germane to the business for which the special meeting has been called.[39] For example, it would be proper to make a motion to postpone a main motion which was the subject of the special meeting.

§ 3 MEETINGS OF DIRECTORS OR TRUSTEES

There should be at least one board meeting a year. Bylaws provisions determine procedure for notices of meetings of the board.[40] If the bylaws prescribe when meetings are to be held, prior notice is not required.[41] Special meetings of the board just like special membership meetings require more specific notice and must follow the requirements in the bylaws. At least one state statute provides that written notice of special meetings must be given at least five days in advance.[42] Some state statutes do not require notice specifying the purpose of special meetings[43] unless required in the bylaws. However, in this writer's opinion, it is good practice to give specific advance notice of the business to be transacted at a special board meeting even if it is not required.

In addition to those meetings established in the bylaws, the bylaws should specify who may call board meetings. Under the California state statute board meetings "may be called by the chair of the board or the president, or any vice president or the secretary or any two directors."[44] One court ruled that under an Ohio condominium act, two purported non-members of a condominium association were unable to call a board meeting. Only the chair of the board, the president, a vice-president, or any two directors could call such a meeting.[45]

All directors must receive proper notice of a meeting including the time and place of the meeting.[46] However, a New York court found that inadvertent failure to notify ex-officio non-voting members of a museum board did not negate a vote at a board meeting.[47]

The authority of the board is by virtue of collective action of directors at meetings, not as individuals outside of meetings.[48] A quorum
consisting of a majority of board members must be present, unless a
governing document [or statute] specifies otherwise.[49] The governing
document should avoid ambiguous language and specifically define
how a quorum is determined.

Large boards conduct meetings with the same formality and procedural rules as a deliberative assembly.[50] For smaller boards the rules
are considerably more informal and relaxed.[51] At least two parliamentary references take the position that board meetings of nonprofits should be closed - even to the rest of the membership.[52] In this
writer's opinion, there are many good reasons to do so. For example,
much like a business organization, a nonprofit may not want to reveal
its future plans and opportunities to a competitor.

The nature of the business to be considered may have a bear-
ing on which (if any) non-board members may attend. Minutes or a
similar record must be taken at the meeting. Under the Pennsylvania
nonprofit statute, if a director wishes to dissent to a board action he or
she may insist that his dissent be recorded in the minutes or promptly
file it with the secretary. If the director does not take one of these two
actions it is presumed that he assented to the action.[53]

Governmental meetings are subject to the state open meeting
laws.[54] There is a large body of statutory and case law concerning open
meeting laws and their related meeting requirements which are beyond
the scope of this text. A small sample of the case law is provided in this
text. For example, in a Pennsylvania case a state board did not violate
the open meeting law by holding a meeting held via telephone speaker
phone.[55] A Nevada court found that serial facsimile transmission and
telephone calls to members of a university board of regents constituted
a meeting that was subject to the state's open meeting law.[56]

The rules for a special board meeting are similar to the rules for
special membership meetings. As noted above, special meetings of

directors may be called to discuss and decide upon specific items of business.[57] A special meeting is to "transact the business for which the special meeting was called . . . ."[58] In a Wyoming case it was decided that a rescheduled regular meeting did not constitute a special meeting of a library board.[59]

A special meeting may also be held within a general board meeting.[60]

By statute, board meetings may be held in which one or more members are in attendance by telephone or similar electronic means if all attendees can hear one another at the same time.[61] Members of the board who attend by telephone must be able to hear one another and be present during the required amount of time.[62] A mixture of in-person attendees and telephone conference attendees at the same meeting can be awkward but is usually authorized.

Under relatively new provisions of the Michigan statute, "Unless otherwise restricted by provisions of the articles of incorporation or bylaws, the board of directors may hold a meeting of . . . members conducted solely by means of remote communication."[63]

The applicable state statute should be consulted to meet all meeting requirements.

§ 4 METHOD OF SERVING NOTICE
(TO MEMBERS AND DIRECTORS)

Proper and sufficient notice of meetings is essential to help assure good attendance and fair dealing and the subject should be addressed in the bylaws.

State statutes allow for organizations to serve written notice of members' meetings either personally or by mail to the address of the member in the corporation records.[64] Notice of members' meetings are now electronically permitted in some states by statute.[65] At least one parliamentary reference states that members receiving notice electronically or by fax must first give their consent to that method.[66] While electronic notice is a growing trend it is prudent to determine and comply with existing and applicable statutory and other legal requirements. The authorized use of electronic notice of meetings should not be taken for granted. However, California has liberally amended its statute to allow for electronic notices.[67]

Of course, the organization must abide by its bylaw provisions on meeting notices.[68] In an unreported Texas case email notice of a nominating committee was disallowed because it was not authorized in the community association's bylaws.[69]

Notice may be posted in the official newsletter or journal of the organization.[70] Convention notices are often issued in the form of a call to the convention.[71] There is no requirement that a new notice must be sent out for an adjourned meeting but it is usually advisable to do so.[72] If there are further changes after an adjourned meeting is scheduled, in this writer's opinion, a fresh notice should be sent to all prospective attendees. "A clandestine meeting . . . is obviously contrary . . . to parliamentary procedure . . . ."[73]

Courts have reviewed cases involving notices of governmental meetings. A Nebraska case found that stating the notice of a future governmental meeting in the minutes does not constitute proper notice to local citizens.[74] A New Jersey case held that there was insufficient notice for a township meeting requiring 48 hours of prior notice when the newspapers received, but were not able to publish, the notice within that time.[75] In a Wisconsin case, posting of a zoning board hearing at three public locations was sufficient especially when numerous members of the public appeared at the hearing offering their opinions.[76]

An Alabama ruling determined that the state's statute may set out the method of both regular and special meetings of a university board.[77] A Nebraska court ruled that a public body in that state had the authority to designate the method of giving public notice which should be recorded in the minutes.[78]

§ 5 WAIVER OF IMPROPER NOTICE

Even when notice of a meeting to attendees is inadequate, the improper notice may be waived either deliberately or unintentionally. Attendees should understand how this works and effectuate their wishes.

A member or director can waive an improper or lack of notice of a meeting by signing a waiver of such notice.[79] The written waiver can be signed "before, during, or after the meeting."[80]

In contrast, a common way a member, sometimes inadvertently, waives his or her rights regarding an improper or inadequate notice is by his attendance at the meeting.[81] In at least two state statutes, attendance waives inadequate notice.[82]

If a director attends a meeting only in order to object to the notice, this is not an admission that the notice was not defective.[83] The objection to the notice must be on the grounds that the meeting was not lawfully called or convened, not that it was run unfairly.[84]

Thus in this writer's opinion, if a member wishes to protest an improper meeting notice, he or she should clearly state this at the beginning of the meeting and further state that his or her presence is with objection. These events should be recorded in the minutes.

§ 6 ACTION WITHOUT A MEETING

State statutes allow for action to be taken by the membership and board of directors without the holding of a meeting.[85] It is good practice for the organization's articles of incorporation or bylaws to address this procedure. Bylaws often provide that if an annual membership meeting, especially a national one, cannot be held, a mail vote can substitute. Such a provision may prove helpful when significant decisions must be made in the face of a meeting being cancelled. However, an Ohio court mentioned that an action without a meeting cannot be combined with an annual meeting.[86]

When action is taken by a board without a meeting, written consents signed by all of the directors should be filed with the organization's minutes and describe the action taken.[87] In this event, the consent to the specific action must be unanimous.[88] If one member simply fails to vote or abstains, the requirement for unanimity is lost thus invalidating the action. Also, by unanimous consent a committee may issue a report that has been agreed to by all of its members.[89] A Nevada court ruled that the requisite percentage of members needed to pass an action validly gave their written consent to waive the meeting.[90]

Informal canvassing of members to determine their vote should be strongly discouraged. Under parliamentary reference, separate polls of individuals by telephone is disallowed since this eliminates the opportunity to debate and the opportunity to decide a question as a body is lost.[91] Separate telephone polls also eliminate the opportunity to offer other motions. Under at least one parliamentary reference such informal procedure resulting in this kind of decision must be ratified or confirmed at a later legal meeting in order to be binding.[92]

§ 7 ORGANIZATIONAL MEETING

State statutes contain provisions on the organizational meeting for a new nonprofit corporation.[93] While the details vary, such statutes typically provide for adoption of bylaws, designation or election of directors, and the "transacting [of] other business as may come before the meeting."[94]

Under the statutes, the meeting is commonly called by the original incorporators or directors named in the certificate of incorporation.[95]

Some statutes require that five days' notice must be given to other directors or incorporators for organizational meetings[96] and these notices must include the time and the place.

At the initial meeting to form an organization,[97] various motions are needed to get the group up and running.[98] They may include:

1. Recognition of a president, pro tem.
2. Recognition of a secretary, pro tem.
3. Adoption of a parliamentary authority. (This is optional at the start of the meeting).
4. A resolution creating the organization.[99]
5. Either adoption of a set of bylaws if already prepared or creation of a committee to return to the next meeting with a draft of proposed bylaws.

In a New York case, relocation of an organizational meeting was not ruled invalid when a change was unanticipated and reasonable.[100]

Other courts also have ruled that the right to vote at an organizational meeting can be challenged.[101] The date of the organizational meeting was recognized as the formal beginning of its legal existence in a Connecticut case.[102] A New York court noted that an organizational meeting should not begin until a quorum is established through the credentialing process.[103]

§ 8 ADJOURNED MEETINGS
(MEETING FOLLOWING A RECESS)

A meeting following a break in time - or recess - during the prior meeting is an adjourned meeting.[104] While many consider a recess any short period of time or intermission,[105] other parliamentary references contend that the break in time may mean any period of time until the next regularly scheduled meeting.[106] Cannon's Concise Guide to Rules of Order ("Cannon") calls the meeting following a short adjournment (a recess) a reconvened meeting.[107] The American Institute of Parliamentarians Standard Code of Parliamentary Procedure ("Standard Code of Parliamentary Procedure")[108] suggests use of the term "continued meeting" because an "adjourned meeting" is less confusing concerning the intent of the action taken.[109]

The meeting following the recess is a continuation of the prior, adjourned meeting.[110] A quorum must be established before continuing the adjourned meeting.[111] In this writer's opinion, a quorum count should be taken after every major adjournment at the start of the meeting. Robert's Rules of Order Newly Revised ("RONR") suggests reading the minutes from the prior meeting during the same session.[112]

Under the California statute, "[a]t the adjourned meeting the corporation may transact any business which might have been transacted at the original meeting."[113] A Mississippi case has commented that any business conducted at a regularly scheduled meeting of a city government could take place at the adjourned meeting after a recess.[114]

There has been much discussion about what notice must be given to hold a subsequent adjourned meeting. Unless the bylaws state to the contrary, some state statutes such as those in California only call for an announcement "at the meeting at which the adjournment is taken."[115]

Cannon recommends, out of fairness, that, if possible, new notice be provided of the reconvened meeting even if this is not required.[116] A motion temporarily adjourning a meeting should include the time and place at which the meeting will reconvene.[117] Good practice calls for erring on the side of prudence and issuing a fresh notice of an adjourned meeting. Some statutes provide that if a board decides after the meeting upon a new date for the adjourned meeting, then all members must be notified.

Governmental meetings are subject to formal notice requirements specifically set out in statutes and ordinances and must be carefully followed. In a sample of cases, a city council in Texas was required to provide public notice of an adjourned meeting following a two day recess between the original meeting and the adjourned meeting.[118] Yet an adjourned meeting in Florida of a community association following a recess did not require fresh written notice when details of the next meeting were announced at the preceding meeting.[119] In this writer's opinion, an organization is best served by re-offering meeting notices whenever in doubt.

---

[1]   *E.g.*, N.Y. Not-for-Profit Corp. Law § 603(b) (McKinney 2014); 15 Pa. Stat. Ann. § 5755(a) (West 2013).

[2]   *E.g.*, Cal. Corp. Code § 5510(b) (West 2013 & Supp. 2014); *see also* N.J. Stat. Ann. § 15A:5-2.b (West 2013 & Supp. 2014) (requiring a meeting at least every 25 months).

[3]   Cal. Corp. Code § 5510(f); 15 Pa. Stat. Ann. § 5708(a). Pennsylvania's statute was amended from allowing director participation "by means of conference telephone or similar communications equipment" to "by means of conference telephone or other electronic technology" effective September 9, 2013. 2013 Pa. Legis. Serv. Act 2013-67, § 35 (West). With respect to members the Pennsylvania statute now states,

> Except as otherwise provided in the bylaws, the presence or participation, including voting and taking other action, at a meeting of members, or the expression of consent or dissent to corporate action, by a member by conference telephone or other electronic means, including, without limitation, the Internet. shall constitute the presence of, or vote or action by, or consent or dissent of the member . . . .

15 Pa. Stat. Ann. § 5708(b).

New York recently passed the Non-Profit Revitalization Act of 2013, 2013 N.Y. Sess. Laws ch. 549 (McKinney) (effective July 1, 2014). However, while this act makes many changes, including allowing consents for actions in lieu of a meeting to be provided by electronic mail, the legislation did not provide for electronic participation and voting in meetings as permitted under Pennsylvania and California statute. *See id.* § 65 (to be codified at N.Y. Not-for-Profit Corp. Law § 614). See *supra* note 86-93 and accompanying text for a discussion of measures adopted in lieu of a meeting.

[4]   15 Pa. Stat. Ann. § 5703(a); Cal. Corp. Code § 5510; N.Y. Not-for-Profit Corp. Law § 603(a); N.J. Stat. Ann. § 15A:5-1.

[5]   *E.g.*, N.Y. Not-for-Profit Corp. Law § 603(b) (allowing "for the election of directors and the transaction of other business"); Cal. Corp. Code § 5510(b) (including the opportunity "to transact any other proper business which may be brought before the meeting"). For example, dissolution of a nonprofit corporation was a matter for the membership meeting to decide under Wisconsin state statute. *See* Feutz v. Hartford Cmty. Serv., Inc., No. 2006AP861, 2007 WL 754995, at *6 (Wis. Ct. App. Mar. 14, 2007).

6   SARAH CORBIN ROBERT, HENRY M. ROBERT III, WILLIAM J. EVANS, DANIEL H. HONEMANN & THOMAS J. BALCH, ROBERT'S RULES OF ORDER NEWLY REVISED 3 (11th ed. 2011) [hereinafter ROBERT'S RULES].

      For excellent summaries of the rights of members at a meeting, see FLOYD M. RIDDICK & MIRIAM H. BUTCHER, RIDDICK'S RULES OF PROCEDURE: A MODERN GUIDE TO FASTER AND MORE EFFICIENT MEETINGS 111 (1985) and GEORGE DEMETER, DEMETER'S MANUAL OF PARLIAMENTARY LAW AND PROCEDURE 305 (2001).

7   DEMETER, *supra* note 6, at 13. "If the annual or other regular meeting is not called and held within six months after the designated time, any member may call such meeting at any time thereafter." 15 PA. STAT. ANN. § 5755(a).

8   Westbury Condo. Ass'n v. Tashjian, 42 Conn. L. Rptr. 291 (Super. 2006); *see also* ALICE STURGIS, THE STANDARD CODE OF PARLIAMENTARY PROCEDURE 102-03 (4th ed., rev. 2001).

9   Lake Forest Master Cmty. Ass'n v. Orlando Lake Forest Joint Venture, 10 So.3d 1187, 1192 (Fla. Dist. Ct. App. 2009).

10   RIDDICK & BUTCHER, *supra* note 6, at 21. For nomination of candidates at a general membership meeting of a labor union, see *Herman v. New York Metro Area Postal Union*, 30 F. Supp. 2d 636 (S.D.N.Y. 1998).

11   *E.g.,* N.Y. NOT-FOR-PROFIT CORP. LAW § 519; 15 PA. STAT. ANN. § 5553.

12   Wade v. Teamsters Local 247, 527 F. Supp. 1169, 1174 (E.D. Mich. 1981).

13   For example, ROBERT'S RULES, *supra* note 6, at 353, suggests "standard" order of business which includes "New Business." Whereas, HUGH CANNON, CANNON'S CONCISE GUIDE TO RULES OF ORDER 81 (2001), recommends against including "New Business" as an agenda item.

14   *See* Dowdy v. Alexander, 51 S.W.3d 200, 206 (Tenn. Ct. App. 2001).

15   See, for example, *325 Bleecker, Inc. v. Local Union No. 747*, 500 F. Supp. 2d 110 (N.D.N.Y. 2007).

16   Heary Bros. Lightning Prot. Co. v. Lightning Prot. Inst., 287 F. Supp. 2d 1038 (D. Ariz. 2003), *aff'd in part, rev'd in part on other grounds* 262 F. App'x 815 (9th Cir. 2008).

17   Corcoran v. German Soc. Soc'y Frohsinn, Inc., No. 562775, 2005 WL 1524881, at *2 (Conn. Super. Ct. June 1, 2005), *rev'd on other grounds* 916 A.2d 70 (Conn. App. Ct. 2007).

18   Dougherty v. Haag, 81 Cal. Rptr. 3d 1, 12-14 (Cal. Ct. App. 2008); *accord* Kowaleviocz v. Local 333 of Int'l Longshoremen's Ass'n, 942 F.2d 285, 289 (4th Cir. 1991) (appeal allowed under union's constitution if in writing); *see also* McClernon v. Beaver Dams Volunteer Fire Dep't, Inc., 489 F. Supp. 2d 291, 294 (W.D.N.Y. 2007) (voting to impose disciplinary action during general membership meeting); Howard v. Weathers, 957 F. Supp. 165, 166 (N.D. Ill. 1997) (referencing a prior union membership meeting wherein a member "was expelled for life"); Elder v. Ferentz, Civil Action No. 97-5956 (D.N.J. Dec. 17, 1999) (allowing a union member could appeal a decision of the executive board at a general membership meeting).

19   Trerotola v. Local 72 of Int'l Bhd. of Teamsters, 957 F. Supp. 60 (S.D.N.Y. 1997).

20 Dzwonar v. McDevitt, 828 A.2d 893, 903 (N.J. 2003).

21 *E.g.*, CAL. CORP. CODE § 5510(e); N.J. STAT. ANN. § 15A:5-3; 15 PA. STAT. ANN. § 5755(b); N.Y. NOT-FOR-PROFIT CORP. LAW § 603(c).

22 RIDDICK & BUTCHER, *supra* note 6, at 183, notes that the bylaws should establish who can call special meetings.

23 *E.g.*, CAL. CORP. CODE § 5510(e); N.J. STAT. ANN. § 15A:5-3; 15 PA. STAT. ANN. § 5755(b); N.Y. NOT-FOR-PROFIT CORP. LAW § 603(c).

24 *E.g.*, CAL. CORP. CODE § 5510(e) (five percent); N.J. STAT. ANN. § 15A:5-3 (ten percent); 15 PA. STAT. ANN. § 5755(b) (ten percent); N.Y. NOT-FOR-PROFIT CORP. LAW § 603(c) (ten percent).

25 ROBERT'S RULES, *supra* note 6, at 92.

26 *See* Lynwood Redevelopment Agency v. Angeles Field Partners, LLC, No. B210165, 2009 WL 4690213, at *6 (Cal. App. Dec. 10, 2009) (stating the trial court found that notice for the special meeting violated state law before overturning the decision for lack of standing).

27 *Howard*, 957 F. Supp. at 166-67.

28 Eversole v. Sunrise Villas VIII Homeowners Ass'n, 925 P.2d 505, 508-09 (Nev. 1996).

29 Local 715 v. Michelin Ame. Small Tire, 848 F. Supp. 1397, 1399 (N.D. Ind. 1994).

30 Orange Landing Condo. Ass'n v. Paul, No CV-03-0476905, 2004 WL 2284302, at *2 (Conn. Super. Ct. Sept. 20, 2004); *see* Jackson v. Members of Calvary Missionary Baptist Church, 603 S.E.2d 711, 713-14 (Ga. Ct. App. 2004) (allowing members of a church to call a special membership meeting to elect new board members if the leadership fails to do so upon request). *But see* Federspiel v. Blank, No. 00-CV-0998E(SC), 2002 WL 31194563, at *4 (W.D.N.Y. Sept. 19, 2002) (stating that a non-member of a labor union was not authorized to attempt to organize a special membership meeting); Green v. Westgate Apostolic Church, 808 S.W.2d 547, 551 (Tex. App. 1991) (finding a special meeting called pursuant to a nonprofit corporation statute was invalid when contrary to specific procedures in the church bylaws).

31 Breezy Point Coop., Inc. v. Young, 842 N.Y.S.2d 150, 153 (App. Term. 2007).

32 AMERICAN INSTITUTE OF PARLIAMENTARIANS, STANDARD CODE OF PARLIAMENTARY PROCEDURE 113 (2012) [hereinafter STANDARD CODE]; *see also* Council of Dorset Condo. v. Gordon, 801 A.2d 1 (Del. 2002); *Breezy Point Cooperative*, 842 N.Y.S.2d at 153; ROBERT'S RULES, *supra* note 6, at 91.

33 *E.g.*, 15 PA. STAT. ANN. § 5704(c) ("[T]he notice shall specify the general nature of the business to be translated . . . ."); *see, e.g., Breezy Point Coop.*, 842 N.Y.S.2d at 153; ROBERT'S RULES, *supra* note 6, at 91.
    There must be sufficient detail in the notice for a special membership meeting to amend the Articles of Incorporation. Lain v. Credit Bureau of Baton Rouge, 637 So. 2d 1080, 1085 (La. Ct. App. 1994).

34 CAL. CORP. CODE § 5510(e).

35 Nguyen v. Tran, 652 S.E.2d 881, 884 (Ga. Ct. App. 2007); *accord Jackson*, 603 S.E.2d at 714.

36 Westbury Condo. Ass'n v. Tashjian, 42 Conn. L. Rptr. 291 (Super. 2006).

37 *Id.*

38 Wiggins v. United Food & Commercial Workers, 420 F. Supp. 2d 357, 363 (D.N.J. 2006). The court in *Wiggins* cited the U.S. Labor-Management Reporting and Disclosure Act (LMRDA) and quoted a union's bylaws: "No member shall institute an action outside the Union against the International Union, Local Union, or any of their officers or representatives without first exhausting all remedies provided by the Local Union bylaws and rules and the Constitution and laws of the International Union." *Id.* at 362-63.

39 ROBERT'S RULES, *supra* note 6, at 93.

40 *E.g.*, 15 PA. STAT. ANN. § 5703(b); N.Y. NOT-FOR-PROFIT CORP. LAW § 711(a); CAL. CORP. CODE §§ 5211(a)(2), 5151(c)(2).

41 *E.g.*, N.Y. NOT-FOR-PROFIT CORP. LAW § 711(a); CAL. CORP. CODE § 5151(b)(2).

42 15 PA. STAT. ANN. § 5703(b). CAL. CORP. CODE § 5211(a)(2), requires "four days' notice by first-class mail or 48 hours' notice delivered personally or by telephone, including a voice messaging system or by electronic transmission" and states that "[t]he articles may not dispense with notice of a special meeting."

43 *E.g.*, CAL. CORP. CODE § 5211(a)(2); 15 PA. STAT. ANN. § 5703(b); N.Y. NOT-FOR-PROFIT CORP. LAW § 711(b). Note that under 15 PA. STAT. ANN. § 5706, "Whenever the language of a proposed resolution is included in a written notice of a meeting required to be given under . . . the articles or bylaws of any nonprofit corporation, the meeting considering the resolution may without further notice adopt it with such clarifying or other amendments as do not enlarge its original purpose."

44 CAL. CORP. CODE § 5211(a)(1).

45 DiPasquale v. Costas, 2010-Ohio-832, 926 N.E.2d 682, at ¶ 90. In another Ohio case, two church trustees were authorized to elect a third trustee when the organization failed to create members through its organizing documents. Apostolic Full Gospel Church of Mansfield, Inc. v. Stair, 2007-Ohio-31, at ¶ 26.

46 RIDDICK & BUTCHER, *supra* note 6, at 29.

47 Dennis v. Buffalo Fine Arts Acad., No. 2007-2220, 2007 WL 840996, at *2 (N.Y. Sup. Ct. Mar. 21, 2007).

48 STANDARD CODE, *supra* note 32, at 196.

49 *E.g.*, 15 PA. STAT. ANN. § 5727(a); N.J. STAT. ANN. § 15A:6-7.b; *see also* ROBERT'S RULES, *supra* note 6, at 486-87; DEMETER, *supra* note 6, at 151 ("In meetings of organizations which do not prescribe a quorum, a majority of the entire membership constitutes a quorum.").

50 RIDDICK & BUTCHER, *supra* note 6, at 28-29.

51   *Id.* at 29. For an excellent summary of rules for a small board meeting, see ROBERT'S RULES, *supra* note 6, at 486-88.

52   RIDDICK & BUTCHER, *supra* note 6. at 28. Under Riddick, members may be invited to give information or advice. *Id.*

   Under STANDARD CODE, *supra* note 32, at 196, business transacted at a board meeting should only be discussed with other board members until the information is issued to all of the members.

53   15 PA. STAT. ANN. § 5714.

54   State open meeting laws are also sometimes referred to as "sunshine laws" or "sunshine acts". Throughout this text this writer uses these terms interchangeably.

55   Babac v. Pa. Milk Mktg. Bd., 613 A.2d 551, 553 n.4 (Pa. 1992). Similarly, a borough council met its responsibilities under the state sunshine act when an overflow crowd seated in a nearby room was able to hear the meeting via microphone and speaker in the meeting room at the appointed time. Sovich v. Shaughnessy, 705 A.2d 942, 946 (Pa. Commw. Ct. 1998) (citing *Babac*, 613 A.2d at 553 n.4).

56   Del Papa v. Bd. of Regents of Univ. & Cmty. Coll. Sys. of Nev., 956 P.2d 770, 778 (Nev. 1998). However, a committee of a university board of trustees that did not take any action on behalf of the board did not fall under the state's sunshine law. Auburn Univ. v. Advertiser Co., 867 So. 2d 293, 302 (Ala. 2003). An executive session of a university board of trustees which discussed the naming of a building or awarding of an honorary degree in the name of an individual was also not within the state's sunshine law. *Id.* at 302-03.

57   ROBERT'S RULES, *supra* note 6. at 91.

58   DEMETER, *supra* note 6, at 13.

59   Deering v. Bd. of Dirs. of Cnty. Library, 954 P.2d 1359, 1364-65 (Wyo. 1998).

60   *But see id.*

61   15 PA. STAT. ANN. § 5708; CAL. CORP. CODE § 5211(a)(6).

62   *E.g.,* Koprowski v. Wistar Inst. of Anatomy & Biology, 819 F. Supp. 410, 415 (E.D. Pa. 1992) (citing 15 PA. STAT. ANN. § 5708).

63   MICH. COMP. LAWS ANN. § 450.2405(3) (West 2013). Excerpts of the new provisions of Michigan law can be found in the Appendix of this text.

64   *E.g.,* CAL. CORP. CODE § 5511(b) (notice may also be sent to the address "given by the member to the corporation for purpose of notice"); 15 PA. STAT. ANN. §5702(a); N.Y. NOT-FOR-PROFIT CORP. LAW § 605(a); N.J. STAT. ANN. § 15A:5-4.
   Under 15 PA. STAT. ANN. § 5702(a)(ii), in addition to first class mail notice can be given "[b]y facsimile transmission, e-mail or other electronic communication to the person's facsimile number or address for e-mail or other electronic communications supplied by the person to the corporation for the purpose of notice."

65   *E.g.,* CAL. CORP. CODE § 5511(b); MICH. COMP. LAWS ANN. § 450.2404; N.Y. NOT-FOR-PROFIT CORP. LAW § 605(a), *amended by* The Non-Profit Revitalization Act of 2013, 2013 N.Y.

Sess. Laws ch. 549, § 65 (McKinney) (effective July 1, 2014); *see also* STURGIS, *supra* note 8, at 1-2 (approving of electronic notice).

66 ROBERT'S RULES, *supra* note 6, at 89.

67 CAL. CORP. CODE § 5511.

68 DEMETER, *supra* note 6, at 13. In, *Board of Managers of Honto 88 Condominium v. Red Apple Child Development Center*, No. 110827-07, 2012 WL 6971093, at *13 (N.Y. Sup. Ct. 2012), a notice of a board meeting to Unit Owners that "was neither mailed nor signed by an officer of the condominium" was upheld since such service was not in violation of the bylaws or the New York state statute.

69 Swonke v. First Colony Cmty. Servs. Ass'n, No. 14-09-00019-C, 2010 WL 2361691, at *13 (Tex. Ct. App. June 15, 2010), *reh'g denied*, 2010 WL 3583150 (Tex. Ct. App. Sept. 16, 2010). In an odd procedural twist, one justice while concurring with the decision to over-rule the rehearing motion, mentions that she has since changed her mind on the court's original decision with regard to the email notice. *See id.* 2010 WL 3583150, at *1-*2.

70 CANNON, *supra* note 13, at 87-88. CAL. CORP. CODE § 5511(b), allows for a meeting notice in a newspaper of general circulation in the county in which the principal office is located - if no address appears in the records.

71 STANDARD CODE, *supra* note 32, at 113.

72 DEMETER, *supra* note 6, at 14.

73 CANNON, *supra* note 13, at 88.

74 Wolf v. Grubbs, 759 N.W.2d 499, 518-19 (Neb. Ct. App. 2009) ("[T]rue notice of a meet-ing is not given by burying such in the minutes of a prior board proceeding, remembering that minutes and notice serve different purposes . . . .").

75 Lakewood Citizens for Integrity in Gov't, Inc. v. Lakewood Twp. Comm., 703 A.2d 1020, 1025-26 (N.J. Super. Ct. Law Div. 1997) (citing Worts v. Upper Twp., 422 A.2d 112, 114 (N.J. Ch. 1980)).

76 Step Now Citizens Grp. v. Town of Utica Planning & Zoning Comm., 663 N.W.2d 833, 849 (Wis. Ct. App. 2003). The complainant also claimed no prejudice by a failure to pub-lish notice of the meeting. *Id. See also* Jones v. Cnty. of Missoula, 127 P.3d 406, 410-12 (Mont. 2006) (looking at the collective circumstances to find sufficient public notice of a meeting was provided); City of San Antonio v. Fourth Court of Appeals, 820 S.W.2d 762, 764-66 (Tex. 1991) (finding sufficient notice for a city council meeting after looking at cumulative circumstances).

77 Dunn v. Ala. State Univ. Bd. of Trs., 628 So. 2d 519 (1993).

78 *Wolf*, 759 N.W.2d at 517.

79 *E.g.*, CAL. CORP. CODE § 5511(e); N.Y. NOT-FOR-PROFIT CORP. LAW § 108(a); 15 PA. STAT. ANN. § 5705(a); *see also* STURGIS, *supra* note 8, at 105.

80 STURGIS, *supra* note 8, at 105.

[81] See 15 Pa. Stat. Ann. § 5705(b); Cal. Corp. Code § 5511(e); Demeter, *supra* note 6, at 203; Standard Code, *supra* note 32, at 114; *see also* Silliman Private Sch. Corp. v. S'holder Grp., 819 So. 2d 1088, 1097 (La. Ct. App. 2002) (citing La. Rev. Stat. Ann. § 12:224(E)(6)) (applying Louisiana statute in finding attendance at meeting to waive notice); Badger v. Madsen, 896 P.2d 20, 24 (Utah Ct. App. 1995).

[82] 15 Pa. Stat. Ann. § 5705(b); Cal. Corp. Code § 5511(2)(e).

[83] See, e.g., Messina v. Klugiewicz, Civ.A. 2244-S, 2004 WL 1043793, at *2 (Del. Ch. April 30, 2004) (citing Del. Code. Ann. tit. 8, § 229) (holding that because plaintiff "did not attend for the sole purpose of objecting to lack of notice" there were no grounds to sue for failure to provide notice). The Delaware Code states:

> Attendance of a person at a meeting shall constitute a waiver of notice of such meeting, except when the person attends a meeting for the express purpose of objecting at the beginning of the meeting, to the transaction of any business because the meeting is not lawfully called or convened.

Del. Code. Ann. tit. 8, § 229 (West 2013).

[84] See, e.g., Zych v. Szczerba, No. 204323, 1998 WL 1988642, at *3 (Mich. Ct. App. Dec. 11, 1998) ("Mr. Szczerba was required to object because the meeting was not lawfully called or convened. In this case, Mr. Szczerba objected because he thought that the meeting was being run unfairly."). In *Zych* the court cited the state statute then in effect, Mich. Comp. Laws § 450.2404(3), which stated:

> Attendance of a person at a meeting of shareholders or members, in person or by proxy, constitutes a waiver of notice of the meeting, except when the shareholder or member attends a meeting for the *express purpose* of objecting, at the *beginning of the meeting*, to the transaction of any business *because the meeting is not lawfully called or convened.*

Zych, 1998 WL 1988642, at *3 (emphasis added by court). The current Michigan Compiled Laws Annotated section 450.2404(4) states:

> Attendance of a person at a meeting of shareholders or members, in person or by proxy, constitutes a waiver of objection to lack of notice or defective notice of the meeting, unless the shareholder or member at the beginning of the meeting objects to holding the meeting or transacting business at the meeting.

Mich. Comp. Laws Ann. § 450.2404(4) (West 2013).

[85] E.g., N.Y. Not-for-Profit Corp. Law § 614(a), *amended by* The Non-Profit Revitalization Act of 2013, 2013 N.Y. Sess. Laws ch. 549, § 65 (McKinney) (effective July 1, 2014) (requiring "consent of all members entitled to vote thereon" and allowing consent to be provided by electronic mail); Cal. Corp. Code § 5512(a) (allowing for action by members without a regular or special meeting, using electronic transmission and return of ballots); N.J. Stat. Ann. § 15A:6-7.c (allowing for action by the board or any committee of the board without a meeting upon written consent of all members of the board or board committee); *see also In re* Madison Cmty. Found., 707 N.W.2d 285, 288-89 (Wis. Ct. App. 2005) (showing a trust instrument that allows modification by unanimous written action without a meeting of board members).

86   Meadows Condo. Unit Owners Ass'n v. Blackey, 2010-Ohio-2437, at ¶ 36-38.

87   *E.g.*, N.Y. Not-for-Profit Corp. Law § 614(a), *amended by* The Non-Profit Revitalization Act of 2013, 2013 N.Y. Sess. Laws ch. 549, § 65 (McKinney) (effective July 1, 2014) (requiring written consent of all members entitled to vote to "set forth the action so taken"); *see also* Wellesley Builders, LLC v. Village of Cherry Glen Ass'n, No. M2002-03102-COA-R3-CV, 2004 WL 367646, at *4 (Tenn. Ct. App. Feb. 26, 2004) (holding board may only act without a meeting if all directors consent and action is evidence by one or more written consents describing the action taken) (citing Tenn. Code. Ann. § 48-58-202(a)); Levanger v. Vincent, 3 P.3d 187, 190 (Utah Ct. App. 2000) (holding actions taken by members of a homeowner's association without a meeting must be unanimous, have a consent in writing signed by each member entitled to vote, and set forth the action taken) (citing Utah Code Ann. § 16-6-33). The Utah statute cited by *Levanger*, 3 P.3d at 190, has since been repealed and replaced by a similar provision now located in, Utah Code Ann. § 16-6a-707 (West 2013).

88   *E.g.*, Cal. Corp. Code § 5211(8)(b) ("An action required or permitted to be taken by the board may be taken without a meeting if all directors individually or collectively consent in writing to that action and if . . . the number of directors then in office constitutes a quorum.").

89   *See* Robert's Rules, *supra* note 6, at 499 n.

90   Boulder Oaks Cmty. Ass'n v. B & J Andrews Enters., 215 P.3d 27, 34 (Nev. 2009).

91   Robert's Rules, *supra* note 6, at 487.

92   Demeter, *supra* note 6, at 270.

93   *E.g.*, 15 Pa. Stat. Ann. § 5310(a); N.Y. Not-for-Profit Corp. Law §§ 405, 602(a); N.J. Stat. Ann. § 15A:2-9.

94   15 Pa. Stat. Ann. § 5310(a); *see also* N.J. Stat. Ann. § 15A:2-9 ("[A]n organization meeting of the board named in the certificate of incorporation shall be held, at the call of a majority of the board named, to adopt bylaws, elect officers, provide for initial members if there are to be members, and transact all other business as may come before the meeting. The board members calling the meeting shall give at least 5 days' notice by mail to each trustee named in the certificate of incorporation, which notice shall state the time and place of the meeting.").

95   *E.g.*, N.Y. Not-for-Profit Corp. Law § 405(a); 15 Pa. Stat. Ann. § 5310(b) ("The meeting may be held at the call of any director or, if directors are not named in the articles, of any incorporator . . . ."); N.J. Stat. Ann. § 15A:2-9 ("[A]n organization meeting . . . shall be held, at the call of a majority of the board named . . . .").

96   *E.g.*, N.Y. Not-for-Profit Corp. Law § 405(a); N.J. Stat. Ann. § 15A:2-9; 15 Pa. Stat. Ann. § 5310(b).

97   This is sometimes called a mass meeting, especially before articles of incorporation and similar legal activities have been undertaken. *See* Sturgis, *supra* note 8, at 216-17 (describing an organizational meeting).

98   See Demeter, *supra* note 6, at 314-18, for an excellent description of meeting procedure to create both a temporary and permanent organization.

99   STANDARD CODE, *supra* note 32, at 254-55, shows resolutions to form either a temporary or permanent organization.

100   Morgan v. Lyman, 573 N.Y.S.2d 547 (App. Div. 1991).

101   McAnally v. Friends of WCC, Inc.. 113 S.W.3d 875, 879 (Tex. Ct. App. 2003). The challenge was unsuccessful. *Id.*

102   Simsbury-Avon Pres. Soc'y v. Metacon Gun Club, Inc., 37 Conn. L. Rptr. 726 (Super. Ct. 2004).

     When a "[f]und is not properly organized" under the state statute a court may order a new organizational meeting of the Fund's Board of Directors. White v. Carver, 622 S.E.2d 718, 719-20 (N.C. Ct. App. 2005).

     In an Ohio case, the state political party determined which of two competing organizational meetings to recognize Gallagher v. Lucas Cnty. Bd. of Elections, 2010-Ohio-4164, at ¶ 19.

103   Dinowitz v. Rivera, No. 260448/08, 2008 WL 5505514, at *12-14 (N.Y. Sup. Ct. Nov. 25, 2008). Lack of standing may be raised in a challenge to the validity of an organizational meeting. *E.g.*, Klein v. Garfinkle, 12 A.D.3d 604, 605 (N.Y. App. Div. 2004).

104   RIDDICK & BUTCHER, *supra* note 6, at 4.

105   DEMETER, *supra* note 6, at 112.

106   ROBERT'S RULES, *supra* note 6, at 93-94; *see also* CAL. CORP. CODE § 5511(d) ("No meeting may be adjourned for more than 45 days.").

107   CANNON, *supra* note 13, at 8.

108   The American Institute of Parliamentarians (AIP) Standard Code of Parliamentary Procedure is a principal parliamentary reference referred to in the within text. The AIP Standard Code is understood by this writer to be a successor to the Alice Sturgis 4th Edition, reference which is also mentioned on occasion in the within text.

109   STANDARD CODE, *supra* note 32, at 107.

110   *Id.* at 107.

111   *Id.* at 107.

112   ROBERT'S RULES, *supra* note 6, at 85.

113   CAL. CORP. CODE § 5511(d); *see also* N.J. STAT. ANN. § 15A:5-4.b ("[A]t the adjourned meeting only business shall be transacted as might have been transacted at the original meeting."); N.Y. NOT-FOR-PROFIT CORP. LAW § 605(b) ("[A]t the adjourned meeting any business may be transacted that might have been transacted on the original date of the meeting.").

114   Bailey v. City of Starkville, 807 So. 2d 465, 466 (Miss. App. 2001) (citing City of Biloxi v. Cawley, 278 So. 2d 389, 391 (Miss. 1973)); *see also* Underwood v. Ala. State Univ., 51 So. 3d 1010, 1014-16 (Ala. 2010) (finding a university board could adjourn a meeting and subsequently reconvene at the call of the chair and consider business not on the agenda under "other business").

[115] CAL. CORP. CODE § 5511(d). This includes notice of the adjourned meeting to those participating in the meeting through electronic means. *Id.* But if after the adjournment a new meeting is scheduled, all members must receive notice of the adjourned meeting. *E.g.,* N.Y. NOT-FOR-PROFIT CORP. LAW § 605(b); N.J. STAT. ANN. § 15A:5-4.b. The Pennsylvania statute provides that if directors are being elected, the next meeting must take place "only from day to day, or for such longer periods not exceeding 15 days each." 15 PA. STAT. ANN. § 5755(c). The Michigan statute, provides:

> If a meeting of the . . . members is adjourned to another time or place, it is not necessary, unless the bylaws otherwise provide, to give notice of the adjourned meeting if the time and place to which the meeting is adjourned are announced at the meeting at which the adjournment is taken.

MICH. COMP. LAWS ANN. § 450.2404(2). STURGIS, *supra* note 8, at 79, contends that "no additional notice is required unless provided for in the bylaws."

[116] CANNON, *supra* note 13, at 137.

[117] ROBERT'S RULES, *supra* note 6, at 244.

[118] Rivera v. City of Larado, 948 S.W.2d 787, 793 (Tex. Ct. App. 1997). Similarly, a Mississippi case held that an adjourned meeting of a board of trustees of a school district following a recess must be publicly posted within one hour after such meeting is called. Shipman v. N. Panolo Consol. Sch. Dist., 641 So. 2d 1106, 1115 (Miss.1994) (citing MISS. CODE. ANN. § 25-41-1).

[119] Lake Forest Master Cmty. Ass'n v. Orlando Lake Forest Joint Venture, 10 So. 3d 1187, 1192 (Fla. Dist. Ct. App. 2009).

CHAPTER 2

Mechanics of Meetings

§ 9 TIME AND PLACE OF MEETINGS

The bylaws sometimes designate where the meetings are to be held.[1] If the bylaws specify how the organization selects its meeting place then the organization must follow that procedure set forth in the bylaws.[2] Special rules or customs may also establish the time and place of meetings.[3] It is good practice for the board to pass resolutions scheduling or confirming future meetings.[4] Meetings may be called by the president or the president and secretary jointly if there is no other bylaw, special rule or custom dealing with the procedure for setting the time and place of meetings.[5]

Under both the California and Pennsylvania statutes meetings may be held electronically or by conference call.[6] California in particular has recently liberalized its corporate code to allow for electronic meetings.[7] The board may meet in or outside the state of its operation or incorporation.[8] Also under the New York statute, the bylaws may allow for a membership meeting within or outside of the state.[9] At least one parliamentary reference comments that the hour and place of meetings should not be included in the bylaws but established by a standing rule or be authorized by the board.[10]

The time and place of a meeting cannot be changed after notice is sent unless the organization also sends a notice of the change.[11] Notice should not be sent so late that it will affect the number of voters who will attend.[12] A New York court has held that a committee of a political party with authority to set the time and place of a convention cannot delegate that decision to someone who is not a member of the committee.[13]

It has been noted by a parliamentary reference that if the president is not present within 10 or 15 minutes after the meeting is scheduled to start, the secretary or other authorized officer can start the meeting and provide for the election of a presiding officer pro-tem.[14] Meetings cannot be started early unless all members attend and consent.[15] In another unreported New York case, the court held that, in the interests of fair play and justice, a meeting dealing with the election of board members that was begun exactly on time while a significant contingent of members was waiting in the next room required a new election of board members.[16]

Under Georgia's Open Meetings Act, when a regular meeting of a county board is cancelled, the new time, place and date of the replacement meeting must be publicly announced.[17] A government meeting that ran late into the night in California was unsuccessfully challenged.[18]

A meeting in which the organization has not finished the business scheduled for that meeting can be adjourned to a future time and place.[19] This is handled by a motion to adjourn to a specified future time[20] or by a motion to fix the time and place to which to adjourn.[21]

§ 10 QUORUM

A quorum is the number of members who must be present in order to transact business and to hold a legally valid meeting. Quorum requirements are determined by state statutes and the organization's organizing documents and bylaws. Virtually all states have statutes which cover quorum requirements for board and member meetings. For membership and delegate meetings of national organizations a realistic quorum, usually much smaller than a majority, should be set. Use of proxies, if authorized for this purpose, may help achieve a quorum.

Typically, a majority of the number of directors constitutes a quorum of the board.[22] Statutes also allow for bylaws which reduce or increase the size of a board quorum, but not less than a certain number or percentage.[23]

Parliamentary references note that if there are no pre-established quorum requirements, a majority of the entire membership must be present for a meeting of an organization to take place.[24] In a Maryland case it was noted that a quorum of a deliberative governmental body is at least a majority;[25] however, a bylaw that stated a fixed number even if that fixed number was less than a majority was upheld.[26] Under parliamentary reference, quorum requirements established in the constitution or bylaws cannot be suspended.[27]

As noted, state statutes address quorum requirements for membership meetings and, although this usually is a majority, it may vary.[28] The corporate articles or bylaws may alter the statutory requirement if the statute allows for it. Under the New York statute, the articles or bylaws may not allow a quorum to fall under a certain level but this number may be greater than a majority.[29] State statutes may also allow for less than the standard quorum required to conduct business at an adjourned membership meeting.[30]

Under parliamentary references, a quorum is all those in attendance at a mass meeting;[31] all those who attend when there is no reliable list of members;[32] and, in a body of delegates, a majority of those who have registered even if not present at the meeting.[33] Organizations differ in what they consider the effective date of delegate registration when this is used in calculating a quorum.

Those who abstain on a vote are still counted in determining the presence of a quorum.[34] Members behind in their dues are a part of the quorum (unless there is a rule to the contrary) but not those who have been disqualified, suspended or expelled.[35] A quorum may be based on the votes of each class of membership.[36] A Florida court determined that the number of condominium units in foreclosure was counted in determining the total number of units for establishing a quorum.[37] The court in the same Florida case noted that under the condominium association's bylaws owners may sign meeting minutes after a meeting is held and still be counted in determining a quorum.[38]

A quorum is assumed when the chair calls a meeting to order.[39] Under a Minnesota case "Once established, a quorum remains established until the adjournment of the meeting or until a member calls for a quorum count and one is found lacking."[40] The presiding officer can point out a lack of a quorum or a member can raise a point of order.[41] The point of order should be raised during the meeting - not after it has concluded. Without the presence of a quorum, no business can be transacted.[42] (This may have, in this writer's opinion, the unintended consequence of allowing for a deliberate effort to undermine a meeting by having members leave.) However, under some state statutes the meeting can continue even if less than a quorum remains after some members leave.[43] The requirement to hold a meeting would have been fulfilled even if there was no quorum.[44] Matters not requiring a vote such as the presentation of informational board, officer and committee reports, in this writer's opinion, are permissible without a quorum.

With the absence of a quorum, the attendees have various options[45] and several available motions: fix the time to which to adjourn, adjourn, recess, and try to obtain a quorum.[46] Thus during the recess an effort can be made to seek out other members to attend to create a quorum if they are nearby. The assembly can take its chances (not recommended by this writer) when there is no quorum and continue to vote on business, requesting ratification of the actions taken at the next meeting.[47] In a Colorado case, a town board of trustees was allowed to appoint a new trustee to a vacant position in order to achieve future quorums.[48] Another option when there is no quorum is to proceed with the business motions and seek their major ratification at the next meeting with a quorum. There are major risks with this procedure and this effort is not recommended by this writer.

In a Florida case, lack of a quorum at a board meeting negated the sale of real estate.[49] In another case, a vote purportedly approving bylaw amendments at a Wisconsin property association meeting was rejected by the court for not having a quorum - where a quorum was defined as a majority of the members.[50]

An organization which is unable to obtain an unrealistically high quorum to amend its bylaws may seek judicial relief. Similarly, if an organization is unable to obtain enough members to vote by mail because of an impractically high number of voters required, judicial relief may be sought. The "Rule of Necessity" was used in a Pennsylvania case to try to obtain a city council quorum which would otherwise not be possible due to voluntary recusals.[51]

§ 11 ADOPTING RULES FOR CONDUCTING MEETINGS

Nonprofit corporations are given broad state statutory authority for their internal procedural operation. This is granted through provisions in a corporation's articles of incorporation and bylaws.[52] In a somewhat unusual example of the above, Pennsylvania's nonprofit corporate law grants the president a large amount of discretion regarding meeting rules unless the bylaws provide otherwise.[53] It should be noted that bylaws cannot be suspended except for procedural provisions - when the bylaws themselves allow for such suspension.

Organizations often adopt in their bylaws the use of a parliamentary reference for conducting their meetings. Standing rules are also commonly adopted by organizations to cover the nonprocedural rules such as what time the meeting starts and how delegates check into the meeting. More specific rules that partially override the parliamentary reference, called special rules of order, may be adopted by the organization to meet its special needs.

RONR is the leading source of parliamentary procedure in the United States,[54] although other references are well respected and used. Another highly regarded reference is American Institute of Parliamentarians Standard Code of Parliamentary Procedure. When drafting for the bylaws, in this writer's opinion, it is advisable to adopt the parliamentary reference only for use in meetings and not collateral organizational activity.

Demeter's Manual of Parliamentary Law and Procedure ("Demeter") notes that if there is no applicable rule available in the "bylaws or parliamentary authority, the assembly has the "inherent power to create its own rule or provision - if it is not inconsistent with the organization's purposes or the existing rules of a superior body."[55] Under a Nebraska case there is no required procedure for taking of a vote if it is not stated in the bylaws nor required by state statute.[56]

In a sample of case law, even when the internal rules of an organization have not been followed, courts have been reluctant to second guess the organization.[57] In a Texas case, the court was especially loathe to intervene in the affairs of political parties with certain exceptions.[58] In another Texas case, the court accepted the procedural decision of a county Republican Party when the meeting had a quorum present and a majority vote was taken.[59]

Governmental entities are bound by statute or regulations for meeting rules. Some also adopt RONR. However, even when they have been adopted for governmental meetings, the applicability of RONR and how binding the rules are is far from clear.

"[C]ourts do not concern themselves with whether parliamentary rules are followed; instead courts are concerned with whether the law of the land is followed."[60] Overall, courts tend to be most concerned about whether a meeting is conducted in a fundamentally fair manner. In a Connecticut case, a failure to follow <u>RONR</u> by a zoning commission did not constitute a defect.[61] As mentioned in an Ohio case, "[P]arliamentary rules, even when adopted as board policy, are intended merely to assist the board in the orderly conduct of its business, and cannot operate to invalidate otherwise lawful actions of a duly elected board."[62]

In this writer's opinion, for a variety of reasons every effort should be made by the organization to comply with the procedural rules to which the organization is committed. A failure to do so can harm the long term health and welfare of the nonprofit. The leadership and members must be fully committed to following the procedural rules or risk alienating large segments of the organization.

Governments must look to and comply with applicable statutes and ordinances that control their meeting procedure. A Colorado court ruled that a local government could abide by its own rules to hold an emergency meeting without notice to the public if actions were ratified at the next regular meeting or noticed for the next special meeting.[63] Parliamentary procedure in the operation of council meetings in a Louisiana case was first examined in the context of compliance with statutory and constitutional requirements.[64] <u>RONR</u> does not dispense with statutory requirements.[65] In an Iowa case, parliamentary rules may be waived during a meeting as long as the waiver is not inconsistent with the statutory provisions.[66]

Courts have varied when deciding the consequences of a governmental body that does not follow its own rules.[67] When the rules are too impractical or impossible regarding the holding of a meeting or amending its bylaws, states may provide a mechanism for relief.[68]

Customs practiced over a long period of time may be binding as a rule unless a member raises a point of order objecting to the practice. Under an Arkansas case, when bylaws are not applicable an organization may rely upon its customs.[69] If a point of order is raised, in this writer's opinion, the adopted written rules must prevail over custom.[70] Challenging a long-held custom can cause internal confusion and dissention and it is best that the organization's customs are consistent with the bylaws and written rules.

§ 12 AGENDA AND ORDER OF BUSINESS

The agenda sets forth the schedule and order of business at a meeting.[71] Some nonprofits establish agendas in their bylaws[72] and the bylaws must be followed depending, of course, on how mandatory the wording of the bylaw. Other organizations set out the agenda in their rules of order.

After determining the presence of a quorum,[73] the agenda,[74] if it is not already mandated, is approved at or near the beginning of the meeting by a majority vote. It is a main motion and, is debatable and amendable.[75] Early in the meeting the minutes of the prior meeting should be considered and approved. Unanimous consent is sometimes used to approve a non-controversial agenda.

In this writer's opinion, the chair should be open minded and flexible when members offer requests and suggestions about the agenda before approval of the agenda is voted on. The meeting is owned by the attending assembly.

Often the president and the secretary, with the help of the organization's staff, will prepare the draft agenda. It is good practice, but not mandatory, for the assembly to receive the draft in advance of the meeting.[76] After the initial agenda is approved, it can be changed during the meeting by a two-thirds vote. Unanimous consent is often used for non-controversial agenda changes during a meeting. In this writer's opinion there should almost always be an opportunity to present new business near the end of the meeting so that members can formally bring important matters to the organization. The term "old business" is archaic and misleading; the term "unfinished business" should always be used in its place.

Agendas should fit the organization's needs including the goals of a particular meeting. The parliamentary references offer samples. RONR suggests the following:

1) Reading and Approval of Minutes
2) Reports of Officers, Boards, and Standing Committees
3) Reports of Special (Select or Ad Hoc) Committees
4) Special Orders
5) Unfinished Business and General Orders
6) New Business[77]

However, governmental organizations must exercise special care when they adopt or change an agenda for one of their meetings. The order of business may be already established by statute, ordinance or other regulation. Citizen rights are at stake and sunshine laws may apply. Complying with public notice requirements of a scheduled government meeting and its business is paramount. In a California case, an argument was made that a consent agenda item should be rejected by the court as a violation of a governmental code.[78] (See Section 53 for a discussion about Consent Agenda.)

Some procedural flexibility during a governmental meeting is recognized. In an Alabama case, matter not included in the preliminary agenda may be considered and voted on under "other business" even if it was not specifically advertised and agreed to by a majority of those present.[79] A governmental meeting scheduling public comment late at night at the end of a meeting was unsuccessfully challenged in a California case.[80]

General and special orders, also called orders for the day, are used to determine in advance the specific time certain business items must be brought up. Special orders under parliamentary authority usually require a two-thirds vote for approval or change.[81] Special orders may be included in an approved agenda or obtained by motion during a meeting. Implementation of special orders can interrupt other business at the appointed time.

§ 13 MINUTES OF MEETINGS

Minutes are the official written record of what takes place at a meeting (usually taken by the secretary) as the meeting takes place. The taking of accurate minutes is critical for the well being of an organization. State statutes require the taking of minutes.[82] In one reported California case, a failure of a city council to keep detailed minutes for a multimillion dollar bank loan caused complications.[83]

A sample of cases show the following. Minutes carry legal importance.[84] When litigation arises, they are frequently made a part of the court record and can significantly impact the outcome of a case. When the minutes record an action, such minutes are prima facie evidence that such minutes cover the action[85] - and the facts contained therein.[86] One court in Mississippi supported a chancellor's finding that corporate minutes were the best evidence of whether a nonprofit had members.[87] Failure to keep a record of its actions in a Wyoming case did not invalidate the action taken.[88]

There is disagreement on whether a meeting can and should be tape recorded.[89] RONR notes that a secretary may wish to record a meeting as an aid to taking minutes. Recording can cause unintended legal consequences and it is good practice for an organization to give this considerable advance thought. In any event, those attending a meeting should always be informed at the beginning of a meeting if it is going to be recorded. A reminder would help for late arrivals.

Minutes should primarily include what actions were taken at a meeting, not what was said.[90] They should be clear, concise and accurate.[91] Ambiguous records may be completed or clarified by parol evidence.[92] There is some discretion on what other information can be included in the minutes.[93] The minutes do afford an opportunity to include other information about what took place at a meeting but this should be done with care.[94] A trial court in Tennessee remanded a matter to a county board of zoning "for the purpose of amending and approving the minutes" of a prior meeting because "the minutes did not include enough information to determine what the grounds for denial of the [zoning] exception actually were."[95]

Members have the right to approve or correct minutes at the next meeting.[96] A Florida court mentioned that condominium minutes could be signed by members who did not attend the meeting to join in and ratify an action.[97] In a North Carolina case, minutes of a vote at a membership meeting were required to authorize a subsequent merger of two associations.[98]

Some contend that the secretary should sign the minutes[99] but it's been noted that this is not required.[100] Minutes should be read and approved, read and corrected, or their reading dispensed with.[101] In a reported New Jersey labor union opinion, a failure of the union to read the minutes of its executive board to the members at their membership meeting was not actionable as a violation of federal law.[102] For executive sessions, separate minutes should be taken and securely stored and they should be approved at the next executive session.[103] Executive session minutes are not approved at the next regular meeting unless there is a separate executive session therein. If there is no executive session held at the next regular meeting, then approval of the prior executive session minutes must wait.

§ 14 INSPECTION OF RECORDS

A nonprofit organization has a legal duty to maintain records of the organization including the minutes of meetings.[104] The secretary has the responsibility for maintaining the organization's records unless this duty is assigned to others.[105] The availability of an organization's records for inspection is an area strongly controlled by state statute. For example, statutes will often specify what records may be inspected, where, and what prior notice must be given. The records must be available to members for inspection upon reasonable request.[106] Directors should have access to a broader range of records (virtually all of the records) than other members given a director's legal oversight responsibilities.

Courts have ruled that the right to inspect records accrues at the time of membership and under a Louisiana case even if the membership is later terminated, a former member may still have the right to inspect.[107] Monetary damages were allowed in a Florida case in which a country club was required to provide a member with access to club records when the court found willful failure by the club to comply.[108] In a New Jersey case, a member of a local labor union was permitted the opportunity to inspect the collective bargaining agreement to which his local union was a party.[109]

The right to obtain access by a member is rather broad although it is not unfettered and a proper purpose is required.[110] The following was noted in a sample of cases. One court ruled that the burden of proof was on the association to show an improper purpose - including accessibility to a copy of prior legal bills.[111] A condominium unit owner in a New York case was entitled to inspect the records showing the names and addresses of all unit owners and the owner's opposition to a proposed bylaw amendment was deemed a sufficient reason to allow the inspection.[112] A homeowners association in a Florida case was required to make available for inspection recall petitions and related documents used to remove a director.[113]

There are various exceptions to member accessibility under statutory and case law. Intellectual property records are not available for inspection under the state (Ohio) Public Records Act.[114] Some nonprofits may be subject to their state open records act.[115] In a Louisiana case it was held that inspection of church records by a member was not a First Amendment violation.[116] A Pennsylvania court barred discovery of discussions he d in executive session at a board of commissioner's meeting as attorney-client privilege.[117]

Medical records may be protected from inspection by statute. Nursing home records may be protected by the medical committee and medical peer review privilege.[118] A hospital in an Iowa case was allowed discretion to deny public disclosure of certain infection data notwithstanding a state statute requiring disclosure of public records (Public Records Act).[119]

Courts engage in a balancing act and at times reach a compromise in weighing the rights of a member to see records versus the need to maintain record confidentiality. For example, competing interests were weighed between a director's right to see election ballots versus the right of privacy of a voting member of a California homeowner's association.[120] A New Hampshire court struck a compromise in protecting the privacy of condominium owners and a member's access to membership information.[121]

---

[1]   HUGH CANNON, CANNON'S CONCISE GUIDE TO RULES OF ORDER 4 (2001).

[2]   GEORGE DEMETER, DEMETER'S MANUAL OF PARLIAMENTARY LAW AND PROCEDURE 13 (2001).

[3]   Id.

[4]   SARAH CORBIN ROBERT, HENRY M. ROBERT III, WILLIAM J. EVANS, DANIEL H. HONEMANN & THOMAS J. BALCH, ROBERT'S RULES OF ORDER NEWLY REVISED 575 (11th ed. 2011) [hereinafter ROBERT'S RULES]. RONR notes some organizations "prefer" such practice. Id.

[5]   DEMETER, supra note 2, at 13; CAL. CORP. CODE § 5211(a)(1) (West 2013 & Supp. 2014) ("Meetings of the board may be called by the chairman of the board or the president or any vice president or the secretary or any two directors.").

[6]   CAL. CORP. CODE §§ 5211(6), §55'.0(f) ("Directors may participate in a meeting through use of conference telephone, electronic video screen communication or electronic transmission . . . ."); 15 PA. STAT. ANN. § 5708 (West 2013). As noted in Chapter 1, Pennsylvania's statute was recently amended from allowing participation "by means of conference telephone or similar communications equipment" to "by means of conference telephone or other electronic technology" effective September 9, 2013. 2013 Pa. Legis. Serv. Act 2013-67, § 35 (West).

[7]   For example, CAL. CORP. CODE § 5510(a) provides,

      Unless prohibited by the bylaws of the corporation, if authorized by the board of directors in its sole discretion and subject to the requirement of consent in clause (b) of Section 20 and those guidelines and procedures as the board of directors may adopt, members not physically present in person (or, if proxies are allowed, by proxy) at a meeting of members may, by electronic transmission by and to the corporation (Sections 20 and 21) or by electronic video screen communication, participate in a meeting of members, be deemed present in person (or, if proxies are allowed, by proxy), and vote at a meeting of members whether that meeting is to be held at a designated place or in whole or in part by means of electronic transmission by and to the corporation or by electronic video screen communication, in accordance with subdivision (f).

CAL. CORP. CODE § 5510(f) further states,

A meeting of the members may be conducted, in whole or in part, by electronic transmission by and to the corporation or by electronic video screen communication (1) if the corporation implements reasonable opportunity to participate in the meeting and to vote on matters submitted to the members, including an opportunity to read or hear the proceedings of the meeting substantially concurrently with those proceedings, and (2) if any member votes or takes other action at the meeting by means of electronic transmission to the corporation or electronic video screen communication, a record of that vote or action is maintained by the corporation. Any request by a corporation to a member pursuant to clause (b) of Section 20 for consent to conduct a meeting of members by electronic transmission by and to the corporation, shall include a notice that absent consent of the member pursuant to clause (b) of Section 20, the meeting shall be held at a physical location in accordance with subdivision (a).

[8] *E.g.*, 15 PA. STAT. ANN. § 5703(a); CAL. CORP. CODE §§ 5211(a)(5), 5510(a); N.J. STAT. ANN. § 15A:6-10.a (West 2013 & Supp. 2014); N.Y. NOT-FOR-PROFIT CORP. LAW § 710(a) (McKinney 2013).

[9] N.Y. NOT-FOR-PROFIT CORP. LAW § 603(a).

[10] ROBERT'S RULES, *supra* note 4, at 575.

[11] AMERICAN INSTITUTE OF PARLIAMENTARIANS, STANDARD CODE OF PARLIAMENTARY PROCEDURE 112 (2012) [hereinafter STANDARD CODE].

[12] *Id.*

[13] Brouillette v. Cerio, 865 N.Y.S.2d 730, 731 (App. Div. 2008).

[14] FLOYD M. RIDDICK & MIRIAM H. BUTCHER, RIDDICK'S RULES OF PROCEDURE: A MODERN GUIDE TO FASTER AND MORE EFFICIENT MEETINGS 38-39 (1985).

[15] STANDARD CODE, *supra* note 11, at 106.

[16] Hong v. 384 Grand St. Hous. Dev. Fund Co., No. 0101607/2008, 2008 WL 2328934, at *9 (N.Y. Sup. Ct. May 19, 2008).

[17] GA. CODE ANN. § 50-14-1(d) (West 2013); *see also* EarthResources, LLC v. Morgan Cnty., 638 S.E.2d 325, 328 (2006) (citing GA. CODE ANN. § 50-14-1(d)).

18   Holbrook v. City of Santa Monica, 51 Cal. Rptr. 3d 181, 184-86 (Ct. App. 2006) (decided on other grounds).

19   *E.g.*, 15 Pa. Stat. Ann. § 5702(b); Cal. Corp. Code § 5211(a)(4); N.J. Stat. Ann. § 15A:6-10.b (reference is made to an adjourned meeting).

20   Robert's Rules, *supra* note 4, at 233.

21   *Id.* at 242.

22   *E.g.*, Cal. Corp. Code § 5211(7); N.J. Stat. Ann. § 15A:6-7.a; 15 Pa. Stat. Ann. § 5727(a) ("[A] majority of the directors in office . . . ."); N.Y. Not-for-Profit Corp. Law § 707 ("[A] majority of the entire board shall constitute a quorum . . . .").
      When a labor union's constitution and bylaws fixes the exact number of executive board members required for a quorum, the fact that there is one permanent vacancy does not alter that number. N.Y. State Corr. Officers & Police Benevolent Ass'n v. Hinman Straub, P.C., 14585/04, 2004 WL 2889761, at *6 (N.Y. Oct. 18, 2004).

23   *E.g.*, Cal. Corp. Code § 5211(7) ("The articles or bylaws may not provide that a quorum shall be less than one-fifth the number of directors . . . or less than two, whichever is larger . . . ."); N.J. Stat. Ann. § 15A:6-7 a ("[A] quorum . . . in no case shall be less than the greater of two persons or one-third of the entire board or committee, except that when a committee of the board consists of one trustee, then one trustee shall constitute a quorum."); N.Y. Not-for-Profit Corp. Law § 707 ("[I]n the case of a board of fifteen members or less the quorum shall be at least one-third of the entire number of members and in the case of a board of more than fifteen members the quorum shall be at least five members plus one additional member for every ten members (or fraction thereof) in excess of fifteen.").

24   Riddick & Butcher, *supra* note 14, at 162; Robert's Rules, *supra* note 4, at 346; Demeter, *supra* note 2, at 151.

25   *See* Floyd v. Mayor of Baltimore, 946 A.2d 15, 38 (Md. Ct. Spec. App. 2008) (noting that Maryland's Open Meetings Act defines a quorum as "a majority of the members of a public body, or 'any different number that law requires'" (citing Md. Code, State Gov't § 10-502(k) (2004))).

26   *See id.* at 38-42. The Court in part cited, Robert's Rules, *supra* note 4. *Id.* at 38-39.

27   Robert's Rules, *supra* note 4, at 255; Alice Sturgis, The Standard Code of Parliamentary Procedure 85 (4th ed., rev. 2001)

28   *E.g.*, N.Y. Not-for-Profit Corp. Law § 608(a) ("Members entitled to cast a majority of the total number of votes entitled to cast thereat shall constitute a quorum . . . ."); N.J. Stat. Ann. § 15A:5-9.a ("[T]he members entitled to cast a majority of the votes at a meeting shall constitute a quorum at the meeting."); Cal. Corp. Code § 5512(a) ("One-third of the voting power, represented in person or by proxy, shall constitute a quorum at a meeting of members . . . ."); 15 Pa. Stat. Ann. § 5756(a)(1) ("The presence of members entitled to cast at least a majority of the votes that all members are entitled to cast on a particular matter to be acted upon at the meeting shall constitute a quorum . . . .").
      15 Pa. Stat. Ann. § 5756(b) provides two exceptions to its rule on quorums, including for "those members entitled to vote who attend a meeting of members . . . [a]t which directors are to be elected that has previously adjourned for lack of a quorum, although less than a quorum as fixed in this section or in the bylaws, shall nevertheless constitute a quorum for the purpose of election of directors."

29   N.Y. NOT-FOR-PROFIT CORP. LAW § 608(b) ("The certificate of incorporation or the by-laws may provide for any lesser quorum not less than the members entitled to cast one hundred votes or one-tenth of the total number of votes entitled to be cast, whichever is lesser . . . .").

30   *E.g.,* 15 PA. STAT. ANN. § 5756(b)(2).

31   ROBERT'S RULES, *supra* note 4, at 345.

32   *Id.* at 346.

33   *Id.*; RIDDICK & BUTCHER, *supra* note 14, at 162; DEMETER, *supra* note 2, at 151.

34   *See, e.g.,* Alvarez Family Trust v. Ass'n of Owners, 221 P.3d 452, 461-62 (Haw. 2009).

35   DEMETER, *supra* note 2, at 151.

36   *E.g.,* N.Y. NOT-FOR-PROFIT CORP. LAW § 608(a); CAL. CORP. CODE § 5512(a); *see also* La. Bureau of Credit Control v. Landeche, 6 So. 3d 935, 938 (La. Ct. App. 2009).

37   Chateau DeVille Condo. Ass'n v. Mikhail, 583 So. 2d 358, 360-61 (Fla. Dist. Ct. App. 1991).

38   *Id.* The court stated, "Under the particular by-laws of this condominium association then, the subsequent signatures could be used to establish a quorum. This being so, [the Florida statute] . . . [is] inapplicable and the use of the subsequent signatures to establish a quorum . . . was permissible . . . . " *Id.* at 360-61 (citing FLA. STAT. § 718.112(2)(b)). Note: In this writer's opinion this unusual ruling may be dependent on the presence of a specific bylaw provision.

39   CANNON, *supra* note 1, at 90.

40   Johnson v. Edwards, 467 N.W.2d 333, 335 (Minn. Ct. App. 1991).

41   *E.g.,* N.J. STAT. ANN. § 15A:5-8.b ("If the requirements of this section have not been complied with, the meeting shall, on the demand of any member in person or by proxy, be adjourned . . . ."); *see also* CANNON, *supra* note 1, at 90 (stating a member can raise a point of order if a quorum is not present and the chair must then rule).

42   DEMETER, *supra* note 2, at 203 citing nine specific legal cases on p. 342.

43   *E.g.,* CAL. CORP. CODE § 5512(c); 15 PA. STAT. ANN. § 5756(a)(2).

44   ROBERT'S RULES, *supra* note 4, at 347. But see *Corvelli v. Fonseca*, 732 A.2d 1147 (N.J. Super. Ct. Law Div. 1999), where the failure of a council person to attend even cancelled meetings because of a lack of a quorum was used in determining whether his absences constituted cause for declaring his office vacant. *Id.* at 1151.

45   DEMETER, *supra* note 2, at 150, cites four permissible motions when there is no quorum: (1) "fix another day at which to convene . . . (2) . . . adjourn, (3) . . . recess . . . (4) adopt any motion . . . to procure a quorum . . . ."

46   ROBERT'S RULES, *supra* note 4, at 347.

47   DEMETER, *supra* note 2, at 150.

48   Lewis v. Town of Nederland, 934 P.2d 848, 850 (Colo. App. 1996) (appointing a new trustee in an emergency meeting due to inabilities to achieve a quorum).

49   Lensa Corp. v. Poinciana Gardens Ass'n, 765 So. 2d 296, 297-98 (Fla. Dist. Ct. App. 2000).

      In a Minnesota case, less than a quorum could act to add new board members even after board members left a meeting in protest. Johnson v. Edwards, 467 N.W.2d 333, 335 (Minn. Ct. App. 1991). A request for an injunction by the departing board members was denied. *Id.* at 336.

50   Barker v. Lake Camelot Property Owner's Ass'n, No. 2007AP2007, 2008 WL 878525, at *4 (Wis. Ct. App. April 3, 2008). Moreover, the plaintiff did not waive this quorum requirement. *Id.*

51   Siteman v. City of Allentown, 695 A.2d 888, 891, (Pa. Commw. Ct. 1997).

52   *E.g.*, N.J. STAT. ANN. § 15A:3-1.a(11) ("[The corporation may] make and alter bylaws for the administration and regulation of the affairs of the corporation."); CAL. CORP. CODE § 5132(c) (5) ("Any . . . provision . . . for the conduct of the affairs of the corporation . . . .").

53   15 PA. STAT. ANN. § 5709. This is a rather unusual grant of authority to the president and includes "the authority to establish rules for the conduct of the meeting." *Id.*

54   *See, e.g.*, Cabrol v. Town of Youngsville, 106 F.3d 101, 106 (5th Cir. 1997); Cleary v. News Corp., 30 F.3d 1255, 1257-58 (9th Cir. 1994).

55   DEMETER, *supra* note 2, at 178.

56   *See, e.g.*, Glad Tidings Assembly of God v. Neb. Dist. Council of the Assemblies of God, Inc., 734 N.W.2d 731, 736-37 (Neb. 2007).

57   It has been noted that a lack of knowledge of rules of procedure by the presiding officer was not relevant regarding ejection of a member from a meeting. Mannix v. Commonwealth, 522 S.E.2d 885, 888 (Va. Ct. App. 2000).

58   Cahill v. Bertuzzi, No. 13-09-00183-CV, 2010 WL 2163136, at *7 (Tex. Ct. App. May 27, 2010). The court would only intervene in the affairs of a political party if there was an infringement of a constitutional or statutory right. Cochran v. Supinski, 794 A.2d 1239, 1248 (Del. Ch. 2001) ("When an unelected branch of government is called upon to pass upon a matter affecting the internal workings of a political party and no constitutional or statutory standards exist to give the court firm guidance, special caution is in order."); Cullen v. Auclair, 714 A.2d 1187, 1189 (R.I. 1998) ("Only where the challenged action of a political party infringes on a specific constitutional or statutory right, usually the right to vote or hold public office, will the courts intervene." (quoting Lee v. Nielsen, 388 A.2d 1176, 1179 (R.I. 1978))).

59   *In re* Dupont, 142 S.W.3d 528 (Tex Ct. App. 2004)

60   Reform Party of U. S. v. Gargan, 89 F. Supp. 2d 751, 757-58 (W.D. Va. 2000); *see also* 59 AM. JUR. 2D *Parliamentary Law* § 5 (2013). Courts will not interfere with a decision of unit owners even if <u>RONR</u> was not strictly followed at meetings. *See, e.g.*, Bella Vista Condo. Ass'n v. Byars, No. CV03180606, 2005 WL 3292533, at *3 (Conn. Super. Ct Nov. 8, 2005).

[61] Levesque v. Killingly Planning & Zoning Comm., No. CV04400496, 2006 WL 2949123, at *1 (Conn. Super. Ct. Sept. 29, 2006). The court mentions at the outset that "the Plaintiff effectively abandoned his argument that the failure to follow Roberts Rules of Order was itself a defect." *Id.* Instead, "[t]he Plaintiff argued only that the chairman's decision not to follow the rules was evidence of her conflict of interest." *Id.* However, the plaintiff failed to provide evidence that the commission regularly followed Robert's Rules and the thus the court found "no significance to the failure to follow the Rules." *Id.*

[62] State *ex rel.* Savarese v. Buckeye Local Sch. Dist. Bd. of Edn., 660 N.E.2d 463, 466-67 (Ohio 1996), quoting from the Handbook of Ohio School Law (1995),
It has been held that only a member of a Board of Commissioners may object to the board's failure to follow parliamentary procedure even when RONR is referenced in the bylaws. Sewell v. Huey, 779 So. 2d 1003, 1007-08 (La. Ct. App. 2001).

[63] Lewis v. Town of Nederland, 934 P.2d 848, 851 (Colo. App. 1996).

[64] Cabrol v. Town of Youngsville, 106 F.3d 101, 106 (5th Cir. 1997).

[65] *E.g.,* Consol. Waste Sys., LLC v. Solid Waste Region of the Metro. Gov., Nos. M2002-00560-COA-R3-CV, M2001-01662-COA-R3-CV, 2003 WL 21957137, at *5 (Tenn. Ct. App. 2003).

[66] State *ex rel.* Miller v. DeCoster, 608 N.W.2d 785, 792-93 (Iowa 2000).

[67] *Compare* Old Carrollton Neighborhood Ass'n v. City of New Orleans, 859 So. 2d 713, 719-20 (La. Ct. App. 2003) (finding a zoning board must follow its own rules caused by a reduced quorum), *with* State *ex rel.* Conway v. Villa, 847 S.W.2d 881, 884 (Mo. Ct. App. 1993) (stating that the trial court held that "alleged procedural irregularities and rules violations . . . cannot invalidate a budget already deemed approved").

[68] Bd. of Dirs. of the Alpaca Owners & Breeders Ass'n v. Clang, 80 P.3d 945, 947-48 (Colo. App. 2003).

[69] Glover v. Overstreet, 984 S.W.2d 406, 409 (Ark. 1999). "[L]ongstanding custom" of a church was used "regarding the qualifications for voting members." Washington v. James, 962 So. 2d 1154, 1160 (La. Ct. App. 2007).

[70] DEMETER, *supra* note 2, at 243, disagrees with this writer contending that "[c]ustom has the force of law" and can only be "stopped by action of the body." Moreover, to discontinue a custom requires a two-thirds vote without notice or a majority vote with notice. *Id.*

[71] DEMETER, *supra* note 2, at 14, uses the term "Order of Business."

[72] RIDDICK & BUTCHER, *supra* note 14, at 8, opposes inclusion of the meeting agenda in the bylaws.

[73] *Id.* at 7.

[74] 15 PA. STAT. ANN. § 5709(b) ("Except as otherwise provided in the bylaws, the presiding officer shall determine the order of business . . . of the meeting.").

[75] RIDDICK & BUTCHER, *supra* note 14, at 7.

[76] See *Piscottano v. Town of Somers*, 396 F. Supp. 2d 187 (D. Conn. 2005), for a case involving a disagreement as to the authority of the chair to refuse to amend an agenda during a board of selectmen meeting.

[77] ROBERT'S RULES, *supra* note 4, at 353. The use of the term "old business" is considered archaic and misleading and must be avoided.

[78] City of King City v. Cmty. Bank, 32 Cal. Rptr. 3d 384, 391 (Ct. App. 2005).

[79] Underwood v. Ala. State Univ., 51 So. 3d 1010, 1015-16 (Ala. 2010).
    In Shields v. Charter Tp. of Comstock, 617 F. Supp. 2d 606 (W.D. Mich. 2009), a vote by a township board to change its agenda during a meeting was approved. *Id.* at 610. "A vote on whether to modify a particular agenda or to adjourn a particular meeting is no more a policy decision of the Board than is a decision on whether to have turkey or chicken for dinner on a particular night." *Id.* at 617.

[80] Holbrook v. City of Santa Monica, 51 Cal. Rptr. 3d 181, 184-86 (Ct. App. 2006) (denied based on standing).

[81] In an Indiana case, only a majority vote was required. Hughes v. City of Gary, 741 N.E.2d 1168, 1171 (Ind. 2001). A city ordinance was unsuccessfully cited in an effort to establish a "special order of business at a time certain," but the court held that there was only a vote to defer action to another meeting. *Id.*

[82] *E.g.*, 15 PA. STAT. ANN. § 5508(a), N.Y. NOT-FOR-PROFIT CORP. LAW § 621(a); N.J. STAT. ANN. § 15A:5-24.a. In California, the minutes must be kept in writing or in a form capable of being converted into writing. CAL. CORP. CODE § 6320(b).

[83] *City of King City*, 32 Cal. Rptr. 3d at 391.

[84] *See, e.g.*, STURGIS, *supra* note 27, at 198; CANNON, *supra* note 1, at 135-36.

[85] Mueller v. Zimmer, 124 P.3d 340. 361-62 (Wyo. 2005).

[86] Cmty. Collaborative of Bridgeport, Inc. v. Ganim, 698 A.2d 245, 255 (Conn. 1997). In an Ohio case, minutes were critical to show what took place at a meeting and in evaluating the merits of a case. *See* Am. Ass'n of Univ. Professors Med. Coll. of Ohio Chapter v. Med. Coll. of Ohio, 2007-Ohio-5153, *available at* http://www.sconet.state.oh.us/rod/docs/pdf/13/2007/2007-ohio-5153.pdf.
    In another case, minutes from historical town meetings were heavily utilized by a court in deciding litigation involving a town government. Zaskey v. Town of Whately, 813 N.E.2d 860 (Mass. Ct. App. 2004); *see also* Pamintuan v. Nanticoke Memorial Hosp., 192 F.3d 378 (3d Cir. 1999) (relying heavily on minutes from hospital department's monthly meeting minutes in upholding suspension of physician).

[87] His Way, Inc. v. McMillin, 909 So. 2d 738, 746-47, (Miss. App. 2005).

[88] *Mueller*, 124 P.3d at 340. Irrelevant minutes are inadmissible as evidence. *See, e.g.*, Martha Graham Sch. v. Martha Graham Ctr., 455 F.3d 125 (2nd Cir. 2006).

[89] For a discussion on the complications tape and similar recording can have, see Harry S. Rosenthal, *Should Meetings Be Tape Recorded?*, NAT'L PARLIAMENTARIAN, Vol. 68, Third Quarter 2007.

[90] ROBERT'S RULES, *supra* note 4, at 468.

[91] RIDDICK & BUTCHER, *supra* note 14, at 113; *see also* CAL. CORP. CODE § 6320(b) ("[M]inutes and other books and records shall be kept either in written form or in any form capable of being converted into clearly legible paper . . . .").

[92] Lake Forest Master Cmty. Ass'n v. Orlando Lake Forest Joint Venture, 10 So. 3d 1187, 1192 (Fla. Dist. Ct. App. 2009); Zaskey v. Town of Whately, 813 N.E.2d 860, 866 (Mass. Ct. App. 2004). Extrinsic evidence may be used to supplement and clarify minutes and to ascertain what a local government did at a meeting. City of King City v. Cmty. Bank, 32 Cal. Rptr. 3d 384, 391 (Ct. App. 2005).

[93] Harry S. Rosenthal, *Seize the Minutes*, NAT'L PARLIAMENTARIAN, Vol. 70, Third Quarter 2009.

[94] For a discussion on the types of information that can be included in the minutes, see *id*.

[95] Lewis v. Bedford Cnty. Bd. of Zoning, 174 S.W.3d 241, 244 (Tenn. Ct. App. 2004).

[96] *See, e.g.*, Baldwin Cnty. Electric Membership Corp. v. Catrett, 942 So. 2d 337, 342 (Ala. 2006). Under Mississippi law, city meeting minutes can be approved up to 30 days from after a meeting is reconvened. *See* Bailey v. City of Starkville, 807 So. 2d 465, 466 (Miss. Ct. App. 2001) (citing MISS. CODE ANN. § 21-15-33 (2000)). A 10-day period to appeal a city council meeting begins to run from the adjournment of the meeting, not when the meeting minutes are approved. *See, e.g.*, Rankin Grp., Inc. v. City of Richland, 8 So. 3d 259, 260-61 (Miss. Ct. App. 2009) (citing MISS. CODE ANN. § 11-51-75).
See DEMETER, *supra* note 2, at 21-25, for an excellent discussion on meeting minutes.

[97] Chateau DeVille Condo. Ass'n v. Mikhail, 583 So. 2d 358, 360 (Fla. Dist. Ct. App. 1991).

[98] *See generally* Roberts v. Madison Cnty. Realtors Ass'n, 465 S.E.2d 328 (N.C. Ct. App. 1996), *rev'd on other grounds* 474 S.E.2d 783 (N.C. 1996).

[99] STANDARD CODE, *supra* note 11, at 227.

[100] Scarnati v. Ohio State Univ., 2003-Ohio-7122, at ¶ 27.

[101] DEMETER, *supra* note 2, at 21.

[102] Dzwonar v. McDevitt, 828 A.2d 893, 903 (N.J. 2003).

[103] ROBERT'S RULES, *supra* note 4, at 96. In a Wyoming case, the board of county commissioners had to take minutes of its executive session staff meeting with such minutes taken by the county clerk. Fontaine v. Board of Cnty. Comm'rs, 4 P.3d 890 (Wyo. 2000).

[104] *E.g.*, N.Y. NOT-FOR-PROFIT CORP. LAW § 621(a); N.J. STAT. ANN. § 15A:5-22; 15 PA. STAT. ANN. § 5508(a); CAL. CORP. CODE § 6320.

[105] ROBERT'S RULES, *supra* note 4, at 458.

[106] DEMETER, *supra* note 2, at 23; ROBERT'S RULES, *supra* note 4, at 460; *see also* N.Y. NOT-FOR-PROFIT CORP. LAW § 621(b) ("during usual business hours"). A church member had a right of inspection although no longer a member of the board of deacons. Smith v. Calvary Baptist Church, 826 N.Y.S.2d 431, 432 (App. Div. 2006) (citing N.Y. NOT-FOR-PROFIT CORP. LAW § 621) (holding petitioner had right to compel inspection but petition was overbroad). A ten

day notice of requirement to inspect a nonprofit's records was upheld. Mulligan v. Panther Valley Property Owners Ass'n, 756 A.2d 1186, 1194 (N.J. Super. Ct. App. Div. 2001) (citing N.J. Stat. Ann. § 15A:5-24c).

[107] Leary v. Foley, 884 So. 2d 655, 658 (La. Ct. App. 2004); *see also* N.Y. Not-for-Profit Corp. Law § 621(b) (allowing any person who has been a member for the preceding six months may see the records).

Membership must first be established before records have to be made available. *See generally* Ferrill v. Nahra, 795 A.2d 1208 (Vt. 2002).

[108] Nero v. Cont'l Country Club R.O., Inc. 979 So. 2d 263, 269 (Fla. Dist. Ct. App. 2007).

[109] Dole v. Local 427, 760 F. Supp. 423, 429 (D.N.J. 1991).

[110] *E.g.,* N.Y. Not-for-Profit Corp. Law § 621(c); 15 Pa. Stat. Ann. § 5508(b). Gaining control of management is a proper purpose to obtain access to corporate records. *See* Kalanges v. Champlain Valley Exposition, Inc., 632 A.2d 357, 359-60 (Vt. 1993).

[111] Schein v. N. Rio Arriba Elec. Coop., Inc., 1997-NMSC-11, ¶ 11, 122 N.M. 800, 932 P.2d 490.

[112] A & A Properties N.Y. Ltd. v. Soundings Condo., 675 N.Y.S.2d 853, 854 (Sup. Ct. 1998).

[113] *Nero,* 979 So. 2d at 269.

[114] State *ex rel.* v. Ohio State Univ. Bd. of Trustees, 108 Ohio St. 3d 288, 2006-Ohio-903, 843 N.E.2d 174, at ¶ 28-33.

[115] Nw. Ga. Health Sys., Inc. v. Times-Journal, Inc., 461 S.E.2d 297, 299-300 (Ga. Ct. App. 1995).

[116] Jefferson v. Franklin, 692 So. 2d 602, 604 (La. Ct. App. 1997).

[117] Lawless v. Del. River Port Auth., No. 11-7306, 2013 WL 180347, at *2-4 (E.D. Pa. Jan. 16, 2013).

[118] For a discussion, see In re *Living Centers of Texx, Inc.,* 175 S.W. 3d 253 (Tex. 2005).

[119] Burton v. Univ. of Iowa Hosps. & Clinics, 566 N.W.2d 182, 187-88 (Iowa 1997).

[120] Chantiles v. Lake Forest II Master Homeowners Ass'n, 45 Cal. Rptr. 2d 1, 7-8 (Ct. App. 1995).

[121] Neumann v. Vill. of Winnipesaukee Timeshare Owners' Ass'n, 784 A.2d 699 (N.H. 2001).

CHAPTER 3

Motions
(General Discussion)

§ 15 MAIN MOTIONS

A main motion introduces a new substantive matter before the assembly.[1] A member may only offer a motion after he or she is formally recognized by the chair and thus invited to speak. Only one main motion can be on the floor at one time.[2] Only a member of the assembly can offer a motion.[3] A resolution is necessary to make every main motion on the floor. It must be processed to some type of resolution and recorded in the minutes; a resolution cannot be ignored.[4] There are also incidental main motions, similar in nature to secondary motions, that are procedural in nature that may or may not relate to specific substantive business.[5]

Once the assembly votes on a main motion the assembly cannot vote on a main motion on the same subject at the same meeting.[6] Sometimes a judgment will need to be made on whether a new motion is sufficiently different from a prior motion to be allowable. If a main motion is sufficiently modified, the motion may again come up for a vote at the same meeting.[7] However, a main motion can be amended, and that amendment can then be amended.[8] Only two amendments to a main motion may be pending at one time.

The most recent edition of the <u>Standard Code of Parliamentary Procedure</u> has introduced the Main Motion to Adopt In-Lieu-Of. Its intent, according to the text is "to improve significantly the efficiency of conducting business in large conventions by removing the need to process all main motions on the same subject."[9]

A main motion requires a second, is debatable, and amendable, and the person proposing a main motion cannot interrupt another speaker to make the motion; it also requires a majority vote to pass.[10] A main motion can be withdrawn or changed by the maker before the chair has fully stated the motion.[11] After the chair fully states (puts) the motion, the motion is "owned" by the assembly. A withdrawal or change by the maker once the chair has fully stated a main motion must be approved by the assembly. A member of the assembly may suggest a "friendly" amendment to the maker before the chair states the motion, and the maker can then accept or reject the proposed amendment.

§ 16 BYLAW AMENDMENTS

State statutes set forth the authority of members and boards of directors to amend an organization's bylaws. The bylaws should include details and procedures on how an organization can amend its bylaws.[12] Generally, the bylaws may be amended with the approval of the membership.[13] Some authority provides that the membership can override the board regarding bylaw amendments.[14] This will depend on state law and provisions in the articles of incorporation and bylaws.

In some organizations only the board can amend the bylaws. This is the case, of course, with non-membership organizations. First giving notice of the proposed bylaw amendments to the membership (when only the board has the authority for changes) so that the members can then offer their comments to the board is a good practice but usually not mandatory.

State statutes provide that prior notice must be given to the membership[15] before they vote. Similarly, a board member proposing a bylaws amendment should give prior notice of the proposed bylaw amendment to the other board members before the board votes to amend the bylaws. Prior notice of the proposed amendment must be provided in the manner authorized in the bylaws.[16] According to one parliamentary reference, if the bylaws do not cover the subject of notice, notice by a member at the prior meeting is sufficient.[17]

Under the California statute a bylaws amendment "requires approval by the members of a class if that action would materially and adversely affect the right of that class as to voting or transfer in a manner different than that action affects another class."[18]

Rules vary regarding prior notice and what is permissible at the time the bylaw amendment being considered is on the floor. Some organizations only allow a vote on the precise proposed amendment as set forth in the prior notice. Others allow for amendments to the amendments to the second degree on the floor if the proposed amendments to the original amendments are germane and within the scope of the notice.[19] Most if not all parliamentary references allow for such floor amendments to the originally proposed amendments if there is no organizational or other rule to the contrary. This is an area with much common misunderstanding and anxiety since a proposed bylaw amendment can be significantly amended again on the floor at a meeting - unless the bylaws, the organization's rules or a statute preclude this practice.

Bylaws amendments are presented as main motions,[20] take a second, and are debatable. Notice and a two-thirds vote are required for passage.[21] Some authorities allow for amendment by a majority vote of those present[22] while others require a vote of the majority of the entire membership if the bylaws are silent.[23] A quorum must be present.[24] The bylaws should be explicit on what type of vote is needed for amendment and how that vote is calculated.

When amendments to the original amendments are proposed on the floor such changes only require a majority vote on those later amendments even if the makers of such motions have not given prior notice of their intention to propose the floor amendments.[25] After all of the additional floor amendments to the original amendments are thus voted on, the entire document is voted on en mass with the appropriate percentage of approval (often two-thirds) then required. This then is a two-step process. But a court in Massachusetts found the two-step process unnecessary and ruled that one vote could be taken for both of the amendments to the amendment and the final amended document.[26] In this writer's opinion, at times an organization can dispense with the two-step process when a clear consensus on the outcome is reached with one vote and no harm results.

When there is a substantial or entire rewrite of the bylaws, it is called a revision. The preparers of proposed bylaws changes should title the new bylaws document as either amendments or a full revision before submitting the document for approval. There is disagreement among parliamentary references about whether adoption of a revision takes a two-thirds vote or only a majority vote.[27] Moreover the approval process for bylaw amendments versus a revision may differ. A revision is similar to adopting a new set of bylaws.

The bylaws should specify who is authorized to propose bylaw amendments. If the bylaws do not cover the subject, any member can propose a bylaw change by giving notice at the prior meeting.[28] As noted above, in some organizations the power to amend the bylaws rests with members, the directors, or both.[29] A bylaws committee may also have a role to play - even if preliminary. Normally a bylaws committee can either recommend and/or draft bylaws amendments but should not have final authority for approval.

The legality of certain proposed bylaws amendments has been contested. In general, certain pre-existing contract rights - especially those related to property - cannot be subsequently undermined by a bylaws amendment. In a sample of legal cases the following has been noted. In a North Dakota case, amendments cannot be unfair or disproportionately impact a minority of members.[30] A proposed bylaws amendment cannot conflict with a condominium declaration.[31] In a California case, the creation of a new class of members which materially and adversely affects the rights of a minority must be approved by that minority class of membership.[32] A Florida court mentioned: "It is firmly established that a [nonprofit] corporation is prohibited from amending its bylaws so as to impair a member's contractual right."[33] However, a Tennessee appellate court upheld the right of a townhouse association to amend its bylaws to prohibit a unit owner from leasing her unit to a third party.[34]

§ 17 PRIVILEGED MOTIONS

Privileged motions have no direct connection to a pending motion on the floor or its disposition.[35] They are considered urgent, have the highest rank, and require immediate attention.[36]

RONR lists five privileged motions, beginning with the highest in order of precedence, among themselves:

(1) Fix the Time to Which to Adjourn;
(2) Adjourn;
(3) Recess;
(4) Raise a Question of Privilege; and
(5) Call for the Orders of the Day.[37]

This class of motions is called "privileged questions" and not "questions of privilege."[38] They may be offered at any time, interrupt a speaker if urgent[39] and are not debatable.[40] Under Riddick, when no other business is pending, the privileged motions to adjourn, adjourn to a time certain, or to recess are a main motion.[41] As main motions they are ranked and debatable.[42]

Demeter lists three functions of privileged motions: "observance of orderly procedure; protection of the organization and the well being of the members; and perpetuation of the existence of the organization."[43]

§ 18 SUBSIDIARY MOTIONS

"Subsidiary motions "apply to the main motion and help change the main motion, dispose of the motion, and help control the debate on the motion."[44] They are usually applied to any main motions but some can be applied only to certain motions.[45] Such motions can only be used when a main motion is pending[46] and should be voted upon prior to the main motion.[47]

Demeter[48] lists seven subsidiary motions, beginning with the highest in order of precedence, among themselves:

1. Lay on the table
2. Previous question
3. Limit or extend debate
4. Postpone to a definite time
5. Refer to a committee
6. Amend the main motion
7. Postpone indefinitely[49]

Subsidiary motions require a second, and a majority vote except for motions on a previous question, and limiting or extending debate[50] which require a two-thirds vote for adoption. A speaker cannot be interrupted in order to allow for the making of subsidiary motions.[51] More than one subsidiary motion can be pending at the same time "provided they have been proposed in the order of their rank.[52] Some subsidiary motions can be applied to another subsidiary motion.[53]

At a special meeting, a privileged, subsidiary, incidental or other motions may be brought in connection with the main motion which is the subject of the meeting.[54]

§ 19 INCIDENTAL MOTIONS

Incidental motions are procedural motions that affect the main motion on the floor. "Incidental motions are motions that deal with how the assembly conducts its business more than with the substance of the business itself."[55] When properly made an incidental motion must be disposed of first.[56] When more than one incidental motion is made, they are disposed of "as each one is raised."[57]

At least two parliamentary references use the term "procedural motions" instead of incidental motions.[58] Some of these motions, such as point of order and calling a member to order, are handled by the chair.[59] They "have no order of precedence."[60]

By their nature they may interrupt business or another speaker.[61] These motions whether termed incidental in some references or included under another category, will be further discussed elsewhere in this text.

§ 20 RESTORATIVE MOTIONS

Restorative motions are those that bring back business to the assembly. They include the motions to reconsider, rescind, and to amend something previously adopted.[62] An example of the latter is a motion to amend previously approved minutes. At one time they were sometimes called unclassified motions.

A motion may be offered by a member which fits the particular situation but is not easily classified. The presiding officer should determine the proper characteristics of the motion and which rules apply.[63]

1   *See, e.g.,* SARAH CORBIN ROBERT, HENRY M. ROBERT III, WILLIAM J. EVANS, DANIEL H. HONEMANN & THOMAS J. BALCH, ROBERT'S RULES OF ORDER NEWLY REVISED 110, 113 (11th ed. 2011) [hereinafter ROBERT'S RULES] (listing five characteristics of a main motion); HUGH CANNON, CANNON'S CONCISE GUIDE TO RULES OF ORDER 5 (2001) (noting that a motion "puts a matter or item of business before the assembly for its deliberation and decision").

2   ROBERT'S RULES, *supra* note 1, at 100; FLOYD M. RIDDICK & MIRIAM H. BUTCHER, RIDDICK'S RULES OF PROCEDURE: A MODERN GUIDE TO FASTER AND MORE EFFICIENT MEETINGS 104 (1985); ALICE STURGIS, THE STANDARD CODE OF PARLIAMENTARY PROCEDURE 33 (4th ed., rev. 2001).

3   GEORGE DEMETER, DEMETER'S MANUAL OF PARLIAMENTARY LAW AND PROCEDURE 51 (2001).

4   AMERICAN INSTITUTE OF PARLIAMENTARIANS, STANDARD CODE OF PARLIAMENTARY PROCEDURE 37 (2012) [hereinafter STANDARD CODE].

5   ROBERT'S RULES, *supra* note 1, at 101.

6   *Id.* at 110, 113 (listing five main motions that are not permitted).

7   Gumtow-Farrior v. Crook Cnty., LUBA No. 2003-105, at *3-4 (Or. Land Use Bd. of Appeals Nov. 19, 2003), http://www.oregon.gov/LUBA/docs/opinions/2003/11-03/03105.pdf.

8   A town had the authority to amend with the same subject matter, a main motion, and have it voted on at a second scheduled meeting. Grant v. Town of Barrington, 943 A.2d 829, 832-33 (N.H., 2008). For other cases in which a motion was amended, see *Nasierowski Brothers Investment Co. v. City of Sterling Heights*, 949 F.2d 890, 892, (6th Cir. 1991), and *Lang v. Oregon-Idaho Annual Conference of the United Methodist Church*, 21 P.3d 1116, 1119 (Or. Ct. App. 2001).

9   STANDARD CODE, *supra* note 4.

> 1. If adopted, a main motion introduced not only enacts the motion itself, but also defeats the other main motion or motions named.
> 2. If the main motion is defeated, any of the other in-lieu-of motions named may be introduced by a member for consideration and vote by the assembly.

10 STANDARD CODE, *supra* note 4, at 38. For detailed characteristics of a main motion, see ROBERT'S RULES, *supra* note 1, at 102-104. For example, it takes no precedence over other motions, must be seconded, is debatable, is amendable, and usually [but not always] requires a majority vote.

11 DEMETER, *supra* note 3, at 56.

12 STANDARD CODE, *supra* note 4, at 240-41; *see also* Smith v. Dugualla Cmty., Inc., No. 51594-2-I, 2003 WL 22701575, at *2 (Wash. Ct. App. Nov. 17, 2003) (citing WASH. REV. CODE ANN. § 64.38.030).

13 *See, e.g.,* 15 PA. STAT. ANN. § 5504(a) (West 2013); N.Y. NOT-FOR-PROFIT CORP. LAW § 602(c) (McKinney 2013); N.J. STAT. ANN. § 15A:2-10(a) (West 2013 & Supp. 2014); CAL. CORP. CODE § 5150 (West 2013 & Supp. 2014).

14 *See, e.g.,* Rogers v. Hill, 289 U.S. 582, 589 (1933).

15   *See, e.g.,* 15 Pa. Stat. Ann. § 5504(a); N.Y. Not-for-Profit Corp. Law § 602(d)(2)(e) (pertaining to election of directors); Cal. Corp. Code § 5150(d)(3).

16   Demeter, *supra* note 3, at 187.

17   *Id.* Demeter implies that the notice is given at the immediately prior meeting in which the bylaw amendment is proposed. *Id.* at 188-89. Riddick & Butcher, *supra* note 2, at 36, does not specify that notice must be given at the immediately preceding meeting.

18   Cal. Corp. Code § 5150(b).

19   Robert's Rules, *supra* note 1, at 307; Riddick & Butcher, *supra* note 2, at 37.

20   Robert's Rules, *supra* note 1, at 592; Demeter, *supra* note 3, at 189. RONR further describes the motion as a motion to amend something previously adopted. Robert's Rules, *supra* note 1, at 592.

21   Robert's Rules, *supra* note 1, at 592; Riddick & Butcher, *supra* note 2, at 36-37; *see, e.g.,* Bae v. Korean Am. Fed'n of Los Angeles, No. B186395, 2007 WL 1290255, at *2 (Cal. Ct. App. May 3, 2007). Sturgis, *supra* note 2, at 208, notes that some organizations only require a majority vote, but a two-thirds vote is more common. Or, with prior notice, a majority vote of the entire membership. *Id.*

22   Riddick & Butcher, *supra* note 2, at 37; Robert's Rules, *supra* note 1, at 594-95; *see also* Smith v. Dugualla Cmty., Inc., No. 51594-2-I, 2003 WL 22701575, at *2 (Wash. Ct. App. Nov. 17, 2003) (allowing for bylaw amendments by a "simple majority of members present at a meeting in person or by proxy").

23   Robert's Rules, *supra* note 1, at 592; Sturgis, *supra* note 2, at 208. As noted above Sturgis states a two-thirds vote or, with prior notice, a majority of the entire membership. *Id.*

24   Barker v. Lake Camelot Prop. Owner's Ass'n, 2008 WI App 83, ¶. 15-17.

25   Robert's Rules, *supra* note 1, at 594-95; *see also* Riddick & Butcher, *supra* note 2, at 37 which notes that majority votes are taken to dispose of amendments to the proposed amendments, followed by a vote of the new amendment as amended - usually a two-thirds vote under most organization's bylaws.

26   Wolf v. Town of Mansfield, 851 N.E.2d 1115, 1118 (Mass. App. Ct. 2006).

27   Standard Code, *supra* note 4, at 244-45 (same vote as to amend); Riddick & Butcher, *supra* note 2, at 38 (two-thirds vote unless otherwise provided for); Demeter, *supra* note 3, at 183 (two-thirds vote).

28   Demeter, *supra* note 3, at 187.

29   *See supra* notes 11-13 and accompanying text. For a contest over whether the directors or registered members can vote to amend the bylaws, see *Bae v. Korean American Federation of Los Angeles,* No. B186395, 2007 WL 1290255 (Cal. Ct. App. May 3, 2007).

30   Buckingham v. Weston Vill. Homeowners Ass'n, 571 N.W.2d 842, 845 (N.D. 1997).

31   Kiekel v. Four Colonies Homes Ass'n, 162 P.3d 57, 61-62 (Kan. Ct. App. 2007).

32   Lake Arrowhead Chalets Timeshare Owners Ass'n v. Lake Arrowhead Chalets Owners Ass'n, 59 Cal. Rptr. 2d 875, 877-78 (Ct. App. 1996).

33   Feldkamp v. Long Bay Partners, 773 F. Supp. 2d 1273, 1283 (M.D. Fla. 2011) (citing Bhd.'s Relief & Comp. Fund v. Cagnina, 155 So. 2d 820 (Fla. Dist. Ct. App. 1963)).

34   Pres. at Forrest Crossing Townhome Ass'n v. DeVaughn, No. M2011-02755-COA-R3-CV, 2013 WL 396000, at *8 (Tenn. Ct. App. Jan 30, 2013), *appeal denied*, (Tenn. 2013).

35   DEMETER, *supra* note 3, at 104.

36   See STANDARD CODE, *supra* note 4, at 73-76, for an excellent summary of privileged motions. For a case in which there was a challenge on how the chair handled a motion to adjourn, see *Gordon Properties. LLC. v. First Owners' Association of Forty Six Hundred Condominium, Inc.*, 435 B.R. 326 (Bankr. E.D. Va. 2010).

37   ROBERT'S RULES, *supra* note 1, at 67-68. DEMETER, *supra* note 3, at 102, uses the title "Fix a day to which to adjourn." STURGIS, *supra* note 2, at 17, only recognizes the privileged motions to adjourn, recess, and a question of privilege.

38   ROBERT'S RULES, *supra* note 1, at 67.

39   RIDDICK & BUTCHER, *supra* note 2, at 150 ("Privileged motions may be submitted at any time and may interrupt the pending business - but not the speaker unless the matter is urgent.").

40   DEMETER, *supra* note 3, at 103

41   RIDDICK & BUTCHER, *supra* note 2, at 151. One court has noted that for a chair to call a privileged motion to recess a member must first make the motion followed by an affirmative majority vote. Lecht v. Stewart, 453 A.2d 1079 (R.I. 1984).

42   DEMETER, *supra* note 3, at 103.

43   *Id.*

44   STANDARD CODE, *supra* note 4, at 50.

45   *Id.*; ROBERT'S RULES, *supra* note 1, at 64.

46   DEMETER, *supra* note 3, at 62.

47   *Id.*

48   DEMETER, *supra* note 3, at 62.

49   See STANDARD CODE, *supra* note 4, at 50-82 for an excellent discussion of the most frequently used subsidiary motions including amend, refer to committee, postpone to a certain time, limit or extend debate, close debate, and table. For a similar listing, see ROBERT'S RULES, *supra* note 1, at 63-64.

50   DEMETER, *supra* note 3, at 63.

51   ROBERT'S RULES, *supra* note 1, at 65.

52   DEMETER, *supra* note 3, at 64.

53   ROBERT'S RULES, *supra* note 1, at 65.

54   *Id.* at 93.

55   STANDARD CODE, *supra* note 4, at 83.

56   DEMETER, *supra* note 3, at 121.

57   *Id.*

58   RIDDICK & BUTCHER, *supra* note 2, at 119-20. Cannon also does not use the term, but RONR does so prominently. Riddick's list of such motions overlaps with the list used by RONR.

59   RIDDICK & BUTCHER, *supra* note 2, at 120.

60   STANDARD CODE, *supra* note 4, at 12.

61   *Id.*

62   ROBERT'S RULES, *supra* note 1, at 24, refers to these as "motions that bring a question again before the assembly" in the footnote. According to RONR the motion to amend something previously adopted must be seconded, is debatable and amendable, and requires a majority with notice or two-thirds without notice.

63   STANDARD CODE, *supra* note 4, at 13.

CHAPTER **4**

Privileged and Subsidiary Motions Listed in Descending Order of Priority

§ 21 MOTION TO ADJOURN OR FIX THE TIME TO ADJOURN

A motion to adjourn ends a meeting. State nonprofit statutes recognize adjournments of board meetings[1] and meetings of members.[2] Any member can move to adjourn as a privileged motion. It requires a second, is not debatable, is not amendable, requires a majority vote, and cannot interrupt a speaker.[3] A motion to adjourn can be either a main motion or privileged motion depending upon the circumstances.[4]

As stated in RONR, "*privileged motions* do not relate to the pending business, but have to do with special matters of immediate and overriding importance which, without debate, should be allowed to interrupt the consideration of anything else."[5]

The presence of a quorum is not required for a motion to fix the time to which to adjourn and an adjournment motion itself.[6] When the chair notices a lack of a quorum he cannot take any vote except for a motion to adjourn[7] and some others.[8] The president can, at times, use general consent to adjourn especially when the business of the meeting has ended.[9] A proxy grants the right for a vote for adjournment even though the grantor of a proxy is not present and the proxy is included for purposes of calculating a majority vote to adjourn.[10]

Questions arise as to when a motion to adjourn has properly been called. The motion is out of order when a matter is being voted on,[11] for purposes of delay,[12] or after a vote is taken to go into committee of the whole.[13] In a Texas case, a motion to adjourn a homeowner's association meeting was deemed justified in order to evaluate who was entitled to vote.[14] In a New York case, there was insufficient reason given to adjourn a governmental meeting in order to go into executive session.[15]

To illustrate how the rules concerning adjournment operated, the rules of a local labor union provide, "A motion to adjourn shall always be in order except: (1) when a member has the floor; (2) when members are voting; (3) when a motion is pending."[16]

In addition, what business can be taken up at the next meeting following an adjournment can depend on whether the adjournment at the current meeting specifies that it is an adjournment to a certain time or as an adjournment *sine die*.[17] The meeting that takes place after an adjournment *sine die* is a brand new meeting. In a Virginia case, a motion to adjourn *sine die* was significant at the annual meeting of a property owners association when there was no quorum since it prevented the election of new members to the board.[18]

The motion to fix the time to which to adjourn has no affect on when the present meeting ends. The purpose of such a motion is to establish when another meeting will be held to continue the business of the current session.[19] This motion must be seconded, is not debatable, is amendable, requires a majority vote, and cannot interrupt another speaker.[20]

In a Florida case, a community association was able to reconvene a membership meeting after an adjournment by announcing the date, time, and place of the next meeting at the original meeting.[21] This case illustrates a significant principle about whether an adjourned meeting can simply be scheduled at the prior meeting. As mentioned elsewhere, in this writer's opinion it is good practice to provide a fresh notice to all members - whether required or not.

§ 22 MOTION TO RECESS

There can be a recess during a meeting for a short period of time.[22] Recesses are used for various purposes.[23] A recess creates an intermission and business resumes where it was left off.[24] A recess is not in order while a vote is being taken by an assembly.[25] A scheduled recess can be postponed by a two-thirds vote.[26]

Cases have shown that recesses can be cal ed for a number of valid reasons such as when a quorum is not present.[27] A claim was made in a New York case that the state's open meeting law was violated during a recess.[28]

A recess is a privileged motion when made while another motion is pending. It is a main motion when it is offered while no other business is pending. It must be seconded, is not debatable, is amendable, cannot interrupt another speaker, and cannot be reconsidered.[29] This motion is out of order when another person has the floor.

§ 23 QUESTION OF PRIVILEGE

Any member at a meeting may raise a question of privilege either collectively for the attendees or for himself. The request is independent of the business on the floor but pertains to ancillary aspects of the meeting. For example, the meeting room may be too cold or members may be unable to hear a speaker due to background noise.[30]

Cannon distinguishes between procedural versus non-procedural personal privilege.[31] The latter pertains to more general, somewhat innocuous topics such as recognizing or giving thanks to others.

Cannon further notes that although well-intentioned, non-procedural questions of privilege can pose a risk to the success of a meeting.[32]

A question of privilege can be raised by any individual, does not take a second, and can interrupt a speaker. The request can also be made as a main motion, can interrupt a speaker if warranted, requires a second, is debatable, not amendable, takes a majority vote, and can be reconsidered.[33] The chair's ruling on a question of privilege can be appealed.

Although the term raising a question of privilege is rarely found in case law, illustrations of its de facto use can be seen. For example, the size of a meeting hall was challenged[34] as was the late hour of a meeting[35] - without specifically using the term a question of privilege.

§ 24 MOTION TO POSTPONE TEMPORARILY (TABLE)

The motion to table, also called a motion to lay on the table, delays consideration of a main motion then on the floor until later in the same meeting or until the next new session.[36]

The motion can be used because of an intervening urgency during a meeting. The main motion that was postponed can be retrieved by a motion to take from the table[37] "at either (1) the *same* session, or (2) the *next new* session, provided no other business is before the body when it is proposed."[38] During that intervening time, the postponed motion cannot be considered during the current meeting or convention "until a certain time, event, date, meeting, or position on the agenda."[39] If the main motion is not brought up again by taking it from the table, the main motion dies. Thereafter the motion on the floor that was postponed can be offered as a new motion.[40]

This motion must be seconded, is not debatable, is not amendable, cannot interrupt another speaker, and requires a majority vote.[41]

There are differences of opinion and some confusion about terms and usages for table, temporarily postpone, indefinitely postpone, and the like. Some references tend to merge them together while other parliamentary references define each term differently.[42] Courts have also blurred the lines when referring to these motions.[43]

The term "table" has taken on a life of its own.[44] Technically the term simply means a delay in considering a main motion to later in the same meeting or a meeting in the next session when there is a good reason to do so. However, "table" has come to mean in popular parlance any delay, put off of, or postponement of a matter - especially indefinitely. The recent edition of the Standard Code of Parliamentary Procedure now recognizes and includes a Motion To Table (Dispose without Direct Vote).[45]

§ 25 MOTION TO CLOSE DEBATE

A motion to close debate, also called a motion to move the previous question, ends debate on the floor and other motions attached to it. It requires an immediate vote on the motion.[46] Attached motions are other motions that have been appended during debate.

The member making the motion must first be recognized by the presiding officer and cannot simply call out the request. The motion requires a second, is not debatable, and takes a two-thirds vote[47] (because it cuts off the rights of others). The motion is not amendable and may not interrupt another speaker.[48] In a Massachusetts case, the court decided that a motion to close debate took priority over a motion to limit debate.[49]

One parliamentary reference notes that the maker of the main motion should not move to close debate on his own motion until at least one other member has spoken.[50] Similarly, a member should not attempt to close debate on his own underlying motion immediately after making it.[51] There is disagreement on allowing the quick use of this motion before some or all others have spoken in debate. While technically correct, in this writer's opinion, a premature cutting off of debate deprives the assembly of an opportunity to consider the issues fully. For example, some presiding officers make an informal list of those who wish to speak to an issue. In this writer's opinion, depriving members of this opportunity to speak is often detrimental to the full airing of a matter and seen by some as unfair.

§ 26 MOTION TO LIMIT OR EXTEND DEBATE

In their standing rules many organizations limit a speaker to 2, 5, or 10 minutes. They may also impose a specific limit on how long a subject may be debated. A motion to limit or extend debate reduces or increases the period of time to debate a pending motion. When so used, it is a subsidiary motion that affects how a motion already on the floor is handled. Or, when offered by itself when no other motion is on the floor, it is an incidental main motion.

This motion can be used to reduce the number or length of speeches permitted or specify the time when debate will end.[52] This motion should not be confused with a motion to call the question.[53] Its effect is to suspend the rules regarding debate.[54] This motion requires a second, is amendable, non-debatable, and requires a two-thirds vote.[55] The latter is required because it affects a basic member right. Sometimes a presiding officer will use the device of unanimous consent to limit or extend debate - without seeking a formal vote - because the circumstances in a meeting warrant such action.

§ 27 MOTION TO POSTPONE (A MOTION) TO A DEFINITE TIME

A motion to postpone to a definite time is applied to a motion already on the floor.[56] The effect of the motion is to delay consideration of the pending motion until later on in the same meeting or until a later meeting. In a Wyoming case a county board of commissioners was able to postpone a motion at a meeting for one week and vote to reconsider a prior tied vote since it was deemed merely a recess.[57]

If the motion is postponed to a later meeting, it cannot be offered in such a manner that the main motion then becomes moot.[58] The motion should be distinguished from a motion to postpone indefinitely although one parliamentary reference argues that these two motions should be combined.[59] As will be noted in Section 31, the motion to postpone indefinitely is another way to "kill" a motion.

This motion may be used to delay consideration of a motion on the floor until after a specific event or another subject is considered. A question cannot be postponed for more than a quarterly period.[60] It cannot be used to delay a motion from one annual meeting to another or from one convention to another.[61]

This motion requires a second and allows for limited debate.[62] Additionally, the motion cannot interrupt a speaker and requires a majority vote.[63]

§ 28 MOTION TO REFER (TO COMMITTEE)

State statutes allow for a nonprofit organization to create committees.[64] A motion to refer a matter allows an assembly to send an item of business on the floor to a committee[65] for further study or follow-up action. Parliamentary references recognize this motion and it is a highly useful device. For example, it can be a safety valve to postpone or avoid a confrontation of factions over a heated issue.

During the time the matter being studied is with a committee, the subject cannot be acted upon by the assigning body. However, a committee can be discharged by a two-thirds vote before it completes its assignment. At that point the assigning body can act on the subject. Additional instructions may be given by the assigning authority at any time before the committee gives its report.[66]

There are two basic components to the motion: to whom the motion is referred and instructions for the recipient.[67] The matter should be referred to a standing committee if the subject falls under that committee's aegis. A special committee could be formed if a standing committee does not exist for the subject. The committee members can be named when the committee is created or a later point - subject to appropriate approval.[68] If the body must approve the committee members, this can be ratified at the next meeting.[69] If no committee chairman is specified, the first named committee member is the chair.

Case law, for example, has illustrated the following committee referrals. In a New York case a sub-committee was formed to consider and recommend discipline of a parent member of a school leadership team.[70] A court in South Carolina decided that an ordinance introduced by title only at first reading could then be referred to a committee to develop a text.[71] A liquor control board in a Georgia case was able to hold a hearing concerning a violation or refer it to a committee for a hearing and a recommendation.[72] However, it has been held by a Louisiana court that while a college president nominating committee is still evaluating candidates for a vacancy, the trustees can make a selection from other candidates.[73]

This motion may be a secondary motion attached to a motion already on the floor or it may be offered as a main motion by itself. This motion must be seconded, cannot interrupt another speaker, is debatable and amendable, requires a majority vote, and can be reconsidered.[74] A special committee can be dissolved by a two-thirds vote of the assigning assembly even before the committee's work is finished. When a special committee provides its final report to the assembly, the committee automatically dissolves. However, even when a committee is automatically dissolved, a formal motion to dissolve a special committee may be presented.

§ 29 MOTION TO AMEND A MOTION (NOT THE BYLAWS)

This Section discusses a motion to amend a motion already on the floor. Excluded here is the procedure to amend the bylaws which is discussed in Section 16.[75] It is essential that meeting attendees understand the availability and use of a motion to amend. Instead of rejecting a flawed motion on the floor, participants are quite able to simply propose a change to that same motion. An improvement of a pending motion benefits the organization.

A motion on the floor can be proposed for change through a motion to amend.[76] A motion to amend changes the wording of part or all of a main motion.[77] The Standard Code of Parliamentary Procedure lists four ways to amend: by addition (insertion); by deletion (striking out); by striking out and inserting, and, by substitution.[78] Proposed amendments must be seconded, cannot interrupt another speaker, are debatable and amendable, and, as noted below, require a majority vote.[79]

A motion on the floor can only be subject to amendment twice at any one point in time.[80] The first pending amendment is said to be a primary amendment and the subsequent attached pending amendment is said to be secondary.[81] A third amendment at the same time is not permitted. However, when one pending amendment is disposed of another can take its place.

The last proposed amendment is voted on first. If that is approved by a majority vote,[82] the motion with the approved amendment then becomes the pending motion. If the proposed amendment is defeated, the immediately preceding motion is on the floor.[83] Confusion sometimes results and the assembly mistakenly believes that a vote in favor of the amendment is a final vote on the motion.[84] If the assembly obviously accepts a motion as amended as its final approval of the matter, there may be no resulting harm in bypassing a step.

The proposed amendment must be germane to the subject.[85] In addition to the lack of a proposed amendment not being germane, RONR lists six other reasons when a proposed amendment is improper.[86] A member can move to amend his own proposed motion.[87] Proposed amendments that are absurd are disallowed.[88]

A noncontroversial amendment proposed to merely improve a motion is called a friendly amendment. The maker of the pending motion is free to accept or reject the suggested friendly amendment. If the initial motion has not yet been submitted to the assembly by the presiding officer, the maker can accept the friendly motion - not needing the consent of the assembly. If rejected by the maker, or if another member objects when the motion is already on the floor, the assembly must then, by majority vote[89] decide on whether to accept the friendly amendment. The proper use of unanimous consent by the chair of the meeting in handling friendly amendments can help move meetings along.

Motions that have already been adopted in prior sessions can also be amended by a two-thirds vote or a majority vote upon prior notice.[90]

§ 30 MOTION TO POSTPONE INDEFINITELY

A motion to postpone indefinitely has the effect of suppressing or killing a pending main motion for the rest of that meeting or session.[91] At least two parliamentary references recognize this type of motion and note its strategic use under certain circumstances[92] while others disfavor its use.[93]

This motion has been mentioned in some court opinions. For example, in a Rhode Island case a town council hearing for the termination of municipal employment was "tabled indefinitely" since no further action was scheduled for the hearing.[94] Tabled indefinitely was construed to mean not continued to a date certain.[95]

A second is required, is not amendable, cannot interrupt another speaker, and requires a majority vote.[96] The motion to postpone indefinitely is thought to give a tactical advantage to those opposed to the underlying motion because it allows for a new round of debate about the merits of the underlying motion. It is also thought to provide an opportunity to indirectly test the original motion.

---

1   CAL. CORP. CODE § 5211(a)(4) (West 2013 & Supp. 2014) ("A majority of the directors present, whether or not a quorum is present, may adjourn any meeting to another time and place.").

2   N.Y. NOT-FOR-PROFIT CORP. LAW § 605(b) (McKinney 2013); 15 PA. STAT. ANN. § 5755(C) (West 2013); N.J. STAT. ANN. § 15A:5-4.b (West 2013 & Supp. 2014).

3   SARAH CORBIN ROBERT, HENRY M. ROBERT III, WILLIAM J. EVANS, DANIEL H. HONEMANN & THOMAS J. BALCH, ROBERT'S RULES OF ORDER NEWLY REVISED 236 (11th ed. 2011) [hereinafter ROBERT'S RULES].

4   See id. at 233-36, for a fuller description of this as a main or a privileged motion.

5   Id. at 66.

6   Id. at 347.

7   Siteman v. City of Allentown, 695 A.2d 888, 890 (Pa. Commw. Ct. 1997) (citing ROBERT'S RULES OF ORDER § 39 (1981)).

8   As noted elsewhere in this text, according to <u>RONR,</u> the motions permitted when there is a lack of a quorum are fix the time to adjourn, adjourn, recess, or take measures to obtain a quorum. ROBERT'S RULES, supra note 3, at 347.

9   FLOYD M. RIDDICK & MIRIAM H. BUTCHER, RIDDICK'S RULES OF PROCEDURE: A MODERN GUIDE TO FASTER AND MORE EFFICIENT MEETINGS 4 (1985). HUGH CANNON, CANNON'S CONCISE GUIDE TO RULES OF ORDER 8 (2001), gives the presiding officer the opportunity to declare a meeting adjourned when the assembly has completed the agenda.
    A presiding officer at a union meeting had the authority to adjourn a meeting because a member did not face the chair during his remarks. George v. Local Union No. 639, 825 F. Supp. 328, 330-31 (D.D.C 1993).

10 Neumann v. Vil. of Winnipesaukee Timeshare Owners' Ass'n, 784 A.2d 699, 702-03 (N.H. 2001).

11 GEORGE DEMETER, DEMETER'S MANUAL OF PARLIAMENTARY LAW AND PROCEDURE 117 (2001).

12 Id.

13 Id.

14 Nelson v. Big Woods Springs Improvement Ass'n, 322 S.W.3d 678, 682-83 (Tex. App. 2010) (noting the characteristics of a motion to adjourn and stating it "takes precedence

over all other motions, is not debatable, and will carry by a majority vote" (citing HENRY M. ROBERT ET. AL., ROBERT'S RULES OF ORDER, NEWLY REVISED (10th ed. 2000))); *see also* Shields v. Charter Twp., 617 F. Supp. 2d 606, 613-14 (W.D. Mich. 2009) (upholding a motion to adjourn when a board member was speaking during a township board meeting); Sovich v. Shaughnessy, 705 A.2d 942, 945-46 (Pa. Commw. Ct. 1998) (finding that city council properly adjourned a meeting when there was insufficient seating for members of the public to attend and rescheduled a new meeting for this reason).

[15]   Zehner v. Bd. of Educ., 2010-4926, 2010 WL 3895339, at *3 (N.Y. Sup. Ct. Oct. 1, 2010).

[16]   George v. Local Union No. 639, 825 F. Supp. 328, 331 (D.D.C. 1993).

[17]   RIDDICK & BUTCHER, *supra* note 9, at 4-5.

   Sine die means that no further meetings are scheduled and the current session(s) are final.

[18]   Gordon Props., LLC v. First Owners' Ass'n, 435 B.R. 326, 342-43 (Bankr. E.D. Va. 2010).

[19]   ROBERT'S RULES, *supra* note 3, at 242.

[20]   AMERICAN INSTITUTE OF PARLIAMENTARIANS, STANDARD CODE OF PARLIAMENTARY PROCEDURE (2012) [hereinafter STANDARD CODE], does not recognize the motion to fix the time to which to adjourn per se, but addresses it in other ways.

[21]   Lake Forest Master Cmty. Ass'n v. Orlando Lake Forest Joint Venture, 10 So. 3d 1187, 1192 (Fla. Dist. Ct. App. 2009).

[22]   *E.g.,* CANNON, *supra* note 9, at 99, 136.

[23]   *See, e.g.,* Underwood v. Ala. State Univ., 51 So. 3d 1010, 1011 (Ala. 2010) ("Board agreed to 'recess the meeting until a future date to reconvene at the call of the Chair.'")

[24]   RIDDICK & BUTCHER, *supra* note 9, at 164. For example, in a Mississippi case, a meeting called pursuant to a motion to recess the prior meeting properly took up action from the end of the prior meeting. Bailey v. City of Starkville, 807 So. 2d 465, 466 (Miss. Ct. App. 2001).
   In a Wyoming case, a commissioners' board "continued" their meeting to a future day although the arguable effect was a recess. Hirschfield v. Bd. of Cnty. Comm'rs, 944 P.2d 1139, 1144-45 (Wyo. 1997).

[25]   CANNON, *supra* note 9, at 136.

[26]   ROBERT'S RULES, *supra* note 3, at 232.

[27]   Israel v. Matthews, 568 N.Y.S.2d 817, (App. Div. 1991) (citing ROBERT'S RULES OF ORDER, NEWLY REVISED 295); *see also* DEMETER, *supra* note 11, at 150.
   In a Massachusetts school committee meeting, the acting chairperson called a recess to have a member removed following a heated debate. Vacca v. Barletta, 933 F.2d 31 (Mass. Ct. App. 1991). In another case, the chair of a meeting of a town board of selectmen used a number of self-called recesses during a controversial meeting. Piscottano v. Town of Somers, 396 F. Supp. 2d 187, 194-95 (D. Conn. 2005).

[28]   Cablevision Sys. Long Island Corp. v. Village Massapequa Park, 16555/05, 2006 WL 3703887, at *3 (N.Y. Sup. Ct. Jan. 23, 2006).

29   ROBERT'S RULES, *supra* note 3. at 231.

30   DEMETER, *supra* note 11, at 106, further breaks down the subject of such a request to "the members' Safety, Health, or Integrity or protection of their Property (catchword: S-H-I-P)." In one case, an employee was entitled to protection from an unruly attendee while attending a meeting. Torres v. Ind. Family & Soc. Serv. Admin., 905 N.E.2d 24 (Ind. Ct. App. 2009).

31   CANNON, *supra* note 9, at 44-46.

32   *Id.* at 45.

33   *E.g.*, ROBERT'S RULES, *supra* note 3. at 225-27. Procedures vary depending on whether the question is raised as an individual matter or by motion.

34   *See* Garlock v. Wake Cnty. Bd. of Educ., 712 S.E.2d 158, 176 (N.C. Ct. App. 2011) (framing the privilege issue arising from public access as an alleged violation of the state open meetings law). The court in *Garlock* also held that a meeting of county education directors could not require tickets for public attendees unless there was advance notice. *Id.* at 175-76.

35   Foxfield Subdivision v. Vill. of Campton Hills, 920 N.E.2d 1102, 1111 (Ill. App. Ct. 2009). A challenge to a council meeting using an adjoining room to accommodate an overflow crowd was denied wherein the overflow crowd could still hear the meeting and come into the hearing room to speak at the podium. Sovich v. Shaughnessy, 705 A.2d 942, 946 (Pa. Commw. Ct. 1998)

36   DEMETER, *supra* note 11, at 98.

37   *Id.* at 99.

38   *Id.*

39   STANDARD CODE, *supra* note 20, at 64.

40   *Id.* at 69.

41   ROBERT'S RULES, *supra* note 3. at 211-12. Compare the STANDARD CODE, in which tabling a motion requires a two-thirds vote. at 71.

42   For example, Riddick proposes the adoption of "only one motion to postpone and to place it on the ladder of precedence now given to the motion to postpone to a time certain." RIDDICK & BUTCHER, *supra* note 9, at 143. Cannon states that "table" is "[a] motion to postpone that is not recommended in this book because it postpones and in practice often kills the pending motion without debate and vote by a simple majority. CANNON, *supra* note 9, at 168. RONR defines lay on the table to "enable[] the assembly to lay the pending question aside temporarily when something else of immediate urgency has arisen or when something else needs to be addressed before consideration of the pending question." ROBERT'S RULES, *supra* note 3, at 209.

43   *See* Glover v. Overstreet, 984 S.W.2d 406, 407 (Ark. 1999) (using the term "tabling" a motion instead of "postponing" an item of business until another meeting); *see also* Cabrol v. Town of Youngsville, 106 F.3d 101, 104 (1997) (using the term "table" instead of "postpone" at a town council meeting); Shands v. City of Kennett, 789 F. Supp. 989, 992 (E.D. Mo. 1992) (same).

44   Other opinions have used the term "table" inexactly. *See, e.g.,* Monge v. City Pekin, 614 N.E.2d 482, 483 (Ill. App. Ct. 1993) (motion to table ordinances indefinitely); Boris v. Garbo Lobster Co., 750 A.2d 1152, 1154 (Conn. App. Ct. 2000).

45   STANDARD CODE, *supra* note 20, at 70-72. This motion ends all further action on a main motion, is not debatable and requires a two-thirds vote.

46   All five of the parliamentary references cited in this text recognize the motion to close debate. ROBERT'S RULES, *supra* note 3, at 44, 386-87; CANNON, *supra* note 9, at 96; DEMETER, *supra* note 11, at 90-92; RIDDICK & BUTCHER, *supra* note 9, at 44-45; ALICE STURGIS, THE STANDARD CODE OF PARLIAMENTARY PROCEDURE 65-68 (4th ed., rev. 2001).

      For examples of a question being called at a town meeting, see *Wolf v. Town of Mansfield,* 851 N.E.2d 1115, 1117 (Mass. App. Ct. 2006) and In re *Dupont,* 142 S.W.3d 528, 529 (Tex. App. 2004). In a Wisconsin case, the minutes of a committee meeting showed that a question was "called" which "suggested" a committee vote on the matter. Tomorrow-Madison v. Regents of the Univ. of Wis. Sys., 698 F. Supp. 2d 1058, 1071 (W.D. Wis. 2010).

47   ROBERT'S RULES, *supra* note 3, at 199-200. In one case, a claim was made that a four-to-three vote, with one abstention, called a question at a commission meeting, despite the requirement of a two-thirds vote. Munhall v. Inland Wetlands Comm'n, 602 A.2d 566, 567 n.2 (Conn. 1992) (the court did not rule on this claim). In another case, a motion was made and seconded to call the question at a town meeting which passed with a vote of 45 in favor and 20 against. Savalle v. Hilzinger, 1 A.3d 1098, 1099-1100 (Conn. App. Ct. 2010) (decided on other grounds).

48   ROBERT'S RULES, *supra* note 3, at 199-200.

49   MacKeen v. Town of Canton, 399 N.E.2d 22, 25 (Mass. 1980).

50   RIDDICK & BUTCHER, *supra* note 9, at 45.

51   *See, e.g.,* DEMETER, *supra* note 11, at 95-96. But if no one rises to speak, the original moving party can move the previous question. *Id.*

52   ROBERT'S RULES, *supra* note 3, at 191.

53   *Id.* Riddick notes other variations of this motion such as allowing two more speakers, one from each side of an issue. RIDDICK & BUTCHER, *supra* note 9, at 103

54   For instance, in one case a motion to "suspend the rules and extend the time for debate" is mentioned to delegates at a national convention. Marshall v. Am. Fed'n of Gov't Emps., 996 F. Supp. 1319, 1330 (W.D. Okla. 1997).

55   ROBERT'S RULES, *supra* note 3, at 193.

56   *Id.* at 179; RIDDICK & BUTCHER, *supra* note 9, at 143.

57   Hirschfield v. Bd. of Cnty. Comm'rs, 944 P.2d 1139, 1144-45 (Wyo. 1997). For an example where a zoning board's decision to postpone consideration of an application until the board's next meeting was without controversy, see *Silver v. Franklin Township Board of Zoning Appeals,* 966 F.2d 1031, 1033 (6th Cir. 1992).

58   *E.g.,* ROBERT'S RULES, *supra* note 3, at 184.

[59]   *See, e.g.,* RIDDICK & BUTCHER, *supra* note 9, at 143.

[60]   *E.g.,* ROBERT'S RULES, *supra* note 3, at 183.

[61]   STANDARD CODE, *supra* note 20, at 63.

[62]   In one instance, two motions to postpone failed for lack of a second at a city council meeting. Kristufek v. City of Breezy Point, No. A06-1220, 2007 WL 1674557, at *1 (Minn. Ct. App. June 12, 2007).

[63]   ROBERT'S RULES, *supra* note 3, at 182.

[64]   *E.g.,* CAL. CORP. CODE § 5151(c)(4) (allowing bylaw provisions for "[t]he appointment and authority of committees"); 15 PA. STAT. ANN. § 5731(a)(1) (authorizing the board by resolution to establish one or more committees); N.Y. NOT-FOR-PROFIT CORP. LAW § 712 (authorizing creation of committees by the board through resolution, certificate of incorporation or the bylaws). Committees can be created by the assembly including the board. *See, e.g.,* ROBERT'S RULES, *supra* note 3, at 492; STURGIS, *supra* note 46, at 179.

[65]   RIDDICK & BUTCHER, *supra* note 9, at 46-47. Riddick distinguishes the use of the terms commit, recommit, and refer but all with the same goal - delay consideration of a matter until it is studied and brought back. *Id.; see also* DEMETER, *supra* note 11, at 82 (asserting that commit and refer mean the same thing).

[66]   STANDARD CODE, *supra* note 20, at 13.

[67]   CANNON, *supra* note 9, at 106. For example, a question about ownership of an invention or a patent was referred to an ad-hoc university committee. Luft v. Clark, No. 08-19771, 2010 WL 2486138, at *2 (N.Y. Sup. Ct. June 3, 2010). In another case, a motion to refer was made from a city zoning board to a planning commission due to certain noted ongoing confusion. Old Tuckaway Asscs. Ltd. P'ship v. City of Greenfield Bd. of Appeals, 509 N.W.2d 323, 327 n.3 (Wis. Ct. App. 1993).

[68]   DEMETER, *supra* note 11, at 83.

[69]   *Id.*

[70]   Meer v. Klein, No. 108315-08, 2008 WL 5108134 (N.Y. Sup. Nov. 24, 2008).

[71]   McSherry v. Spartanburg Cnty. Council, 641 S.E.2d 431, 433-34 (S.C. 2007) (following council procedure).

[72]   2025 Emery Highway, L.L.C. v. Bibb Cnty., Ga., 377 F. Supp. 2d 1310, 1323-24 (M.D. Ga. 2005).

[73]   Townsend v. Trs. of La. Coll., 2005-283, p. 2-3 (La. App. 3 Cir. 4/12/06); 928 So. 2d 715, 718-20 (relying on the wording of a bylaw provision).

[74]   ROBERT'S RULES, *supra* note 3, at Table of Rules 12-13. The motion to commit can be reconsidered if the committee has not begun consideration.

[75]   *See supra* Chapter 3, § 16.

[76] *See, e.g.*, 15 PA. STAT. ANN. § 5706 (allowing for "clarifying or other amendments as do not enlarge its original purpose" at a meeting after a written notice with a proposed resolution is sent out).

[77] For an illustration of a motion to amend a main motion in executive session which was successfully challenged, see *Nasierowski Brothers Investment Co. v. City of Sterling Heights*, 949 F.2d 890 (6th Cir. 1991). For an example of amendments being recognized during the course of consideration of a zoning application, see *Carroll v. Town of Rockport*, 2003 ME 135, ¶ 20, 837 A.2d 148, 154.

[78] STURGIS, *supra* note 46, at 47-48. Demeter adds another way to amend, "By adding words to the end of the motion." DEMETER, *supra* note 11, at 76. For an example of the confusion that can result when a substitute motion is introduced and there is a discrepancy between the original motion and the subsequent motion, see *Residents of Highland Road, LLC v. Parish of East Baton Rouge*, 2008-2542 (La. App. 1 Cir. 7/22/09).

[79] *E.g.*, DEMETER, *supra* note 11, at 68; ROBERT'S RULES, *supra* note 3, at 133.

[80] STURGIS, *supra* note 46, at 50. These are sometimes called first and second ranks.

[81] *Id.* at 50.

[82] *See* Delcarpio v. St. Tammany Parish Sch. Bd., 865 F. Supp. 350, 354 (E.D. La. 1994) (demonstrating failure of a motion to amend by substitution with a tie vote).

[83] *See, e.g.*, Emmett McLoughlin Realty v. Pima Cnty., 132 P.3d 290, 296 (Ariz. Ct. App. 2006).

[84] *See, e.g.*, Lewis v. Cleveland Mun. Airport Auth., 289 S.W.3d 808, 824 (Tenn. Ct. App. 2008) (stating that because a motion to amend by a substitute motion was passed by a majority vote "there was no need to take a vote on the original motion").

[85] *E.g.*, RIDDICK & BUTCHER, *supra* note 9, at 12; ROBERT'S RULES, *supra* note 3, at 136.

[86] ROBERT'S RULES, *supra* note 3, at 138-39:

1. Not germane to the question to be amended;
2. Makes the adoption of the amended question equivalent to a rejection of the original motion;
3. Would cause the question as amended out of order;
4. Proposes to change one of the forms of amendment ... into another form;
5. Would have the effect of converting one parliamentary motion into another; and
6. Strikes out the word *"Resolved"* or other enacting words.

[87] DEMETER, *supra* note 11, at 70.

[88] *Id.* at 72.

[89] See CANNON, *supra* note 9, at 86, 104 and 124, for a discussion on how a friendly amendment is processed.

[90] DEMETER, *supra* note 11, at 72. Under Demeter only a majority vote is needed to amend motions previously adopted at the present session. *Id.* at 72.

[91]   *See, e.g.*, ROBERT'S RULES, *supra* note 3, at 127-28; *see also* Monge v. City Pekin, 614 N.E.2d 482, 483 (Ill. App. Ct. 1993) (using the term "motion to table . . . ordinances indefinitely" instead of the more technically correct motion to postpone indefinitely); Payne v. Shelby Cnty. Comm'n, 12 So. 3d 71, 75 n.4 (Ala. Civ. App. 2008) (using the term "tabled indefinitely").

[92]   DEMETER, *supra* note 11, at 66-67. ROBERT'S RULES, *supra* note 3, at 126-28.

[93]   RIDDICK & BUTCHER, *supra* note 9, at 143 (suggesting a laddering of motions to postpone); CANNON, *supra* note 9, at 105 ("The Chair should not take a motion to postpone indefinitely, for this motion does no more than negate the main motion . . . ."). Standard Code does not recognize the motion to postpone indefinitely but does recognize a motion to table which can serve a similar purpose. STANDARD CODE, *supra* note 20, at 70-72.

[94]   Clayton v. Town of West Warwick, 898 F. Supp. 62, 67 (D.R.I. 1995); *see also* R & K Bldg. Corp. v. City of Woonsocket Zoning Bd. of Review, No. 04-803, 2005 WL 375083, at *2 (R.I. Super. Ct. Feb. 11, 2005) (planning board "tabled indefinitely" an application for a subdivision); Raab v. Bouchard, No. PC 04-6776, 2005 WL 1364958, at *2 (R.I. Super. Ct. June 8, 2005) (application for the transfer of a liquor license was "tabled indefinitely" by a city council)

[95]   Genereux v. Bruce, C.A. No. PC 09-7295, at *17 (R.I. Super. Ct. Apr. 4, 2011), *available at* http://www.courts.ri.gov/Courts/SuperiorCourt/DecisionsOrders/09-7295.pdf; *see also* Vil. of Johnson City v. Johnson City Firefighters Ass'n, 2010 WL 390931, at *3 (N.Y. Sup. Ct. Jan. 21, 2010) (village board "tabled indefinitely" a proposed board resolution). One court noted the comment of an employee of a county department that "tabling an action was a more severe measure than merely continuing it." *Payne*, 12 So. 3d at 75 n.4.

[96]   ROBERT'S RULES, *supra* note 3, at 127.

CHAPTER 5

Incidental Motions
(No Order of Precedence)

§ 31 APPEAL

When a member disagrees with a decision or ruling of the presiding officer, he or she may appeal this decision to the full assembly.[1] The <u>Standard Code of Parliamentary Procedure</u> has an excellent list of rules and characteristics for a motion to appeal a chair's ruling.[2]

There is often a lack of understanding on the availability and purpose of an appeal. A presiding officer leads a meeting, but the meeting is "owned" by the assembly. The appeal of a presiding officer's decision should not be aimed at the presiding officer personally, and he or she should not take offense at an appeal.[3]

After an appeal is taken, the presiding officer speaks first in support of his or her ruling. Next each member present has the right to speak to the appeal. Lastly the presiding officer can speak a second time. A vote is then taken to support or overrule the chair's decision. A tie vote supports the chair's ruling.[4]

In a California case, a court honored two appeals from a ruling of the chair and found that two motions were out of order.[5] In a New

York case, a refusal to allow an appeal of the decision of a supervisor of a town board was upheld when the town was without a formal procedure for allowing the appeal and such denial was within the existing informal rules and procedures.[6]

§ 32 DIVISION OF THE QUESTION

Some motions on the floor can include two or more parts, each of which can logically stand on its own. The assembly can divide each of the parts and vote on them separately.[7] This includes amendments to the same motion.[8]

There is a split among parliamentary references about whether a single member can make this request (i.e., divide the motion and the assembly then acts on each part of the divided motion separately) or if a proposed division must first be approved by the assembly.[9]

The request if made by a single person is made to the presiding officer. He or she then decides if the motion is divisible.[10] The Standard Code of Parliamentary Procedure says that if the chair rejects the request, the decision of the chair can be appealed.[11] Riddick also notes that a negative decision of the chair that a question is divisible is appealable to the assembly.[12]

If division of the question is offered as a motion, it must be seconded, is not debatable, is amendable, requires a majority vote, and cannot be reconsidered.[13] Parliamentary references disagree about whether the request can interrupt a speaker.[14] The request is preferably made immediately but "may be proposed at any time before the vote has begun."[15]

§ 33 MOTION TO WITHDRAW

The maker of a motion may make a request to have it withdrawn. If this is sought before the presiding officer has presented the original motion to the assembly, the member has the right to withdraw the motion.[16] The approval of the seconder (if it has been seconded at that point) is not needed.[17]

If the presiding officer has already presented the motion to the assembly the assembly must unanimously consent to the withdrawal.[18] If there is even one objection to the withdrawal, the requested withdrawal must be voted upon.

Another option is for a motion to withdraw the underlying motion. The motion can be suggested by the presiding officer or any member can move to grant permission. If the request is made by the original maker of the motion, a second is required. If the request is made by someone other than the original motion maker, a second is not needed.[19]

The motion to withdraw can be made anytime up to the final vote - even after the original motion has been amended.[20] All other motions adhering to the original main motion are also withdrawn if the original motion is withdrawn.[21]

A withdrawn motion can be brought back again for action at the same meeting. Withdrawn motions are usually excluded from the minutes if they have been withdrawn prior to being stated by the presiding officer.[22] However, under RONR there may be occasions when the withdrawn motion should be included in the minutes.[23]

The motion to withdraw is not debatable, not amendable, and takes a majority vote. There is some parliamentary reference that the request can interrupt a speaker if "immediate attention" is needed.[24] Under RONR, "[a] motion to grant the request of another member does not require a second."[25]

§ 34 OBJECTION TO CONSIDERATION

Parliamentary references consider this perhaps the most controversial motion. Under this motion a member may quickly object to the assembly from even considering the objected to motion. A motion objecting to consideration can only be made immediately after the main motion is offered. Some of the reasons for objection may include a claim that the subject motion is too sensitive, discriminatory, defamatory, in poor taste, or damaging to the organization.

The motion to object to consideration can interrupt a speaker, does not require a second, is not debatable, not amendable, and requires a two-thirds vote against consideration.[26] RONR expresses no concerns about the use of this motion. Cannon includes it in its list of motions without further comment in the text.[27] Sturgis states that "this motion is not used, since there are simpler ways to prevent discussion of a question."[28]

Riddick comments that a majority of members can raise objection to considering a motion after discussion has begun; and that the entire membership can then make the decision about objecting to consideration after they have determined the best use of their time after hearing what it is about.[29] Demeter delineates all of the motions to which the motion to object to consideration does not apply.[30]

This motion is rarely used. It arguably deprives the maker of the main motion and the assembly of the opportunity to even learn about a proposal. However, adopting this motion could conceivably help an organization publicly avoid discussing a dubious situation.

§ 35 PARLIAMENTARY INQUIRY (REQUEST FOR INFORMATION)

A parliamentary inquiry has been defined as "a request for the chair's opinion on a matter of parliamentary procedure as it relates to the business at hand - not involving a ruling."[31]

As a general principle, members are allowed to request procedural and substantive information regarding a motion from the presiding officer.[32] Answering such inquiries is one of the duties of a presiding officer.[33] Parliamentary references disagree on whether a parliamentary inquiry differs from a request for information.[34] Having information helps a voter and, if not abused, this request should be favorably received. A parliamentary inquiry seeks information about meeting procedure. A "question of information is used when it is desired to ask a question on the merits or 'contents' of the motion itself."[35]

A second to a parliamentary inquiry is not required and it is not debatable. There is disagreement on whether or not a parliamentary inquiry can interrupt a speaker.[36] There is no appeal from a chair's answer to a parliamentary inquiry since only an opinion is given, not a ruling. "[C]ourts will not disturb the ruling on a parliamentary question made by a deliberative body."[37]

§ 36 POINT OF ORDER

By raising a point of order, any member can point out a violation of the rules, an error of some kind, an omission or other mistake regarding the procedure.[38] In addition, the presiding officer himself should point out an error when necessary.[39] When a point of order is raised by a member, the chair must rule whether the point is well taken or deny the point of order.[40] If the point is well taken, the appropriate correction should be made.

The device of raising a point of order is worthwhile in keeping a meeting on track so long as it is not abused or overused.

A point of order must be raised promptly at the time of the alleged breach[41] and it can interrupt a speaker. However, some procedural errors are deemed to be continuing and questions about them can be raised at any time after the breach.[42] For example, a breach of the bylaws or an ordinance is deemed to be ongoing and subject to a later point of order.

Any member can appeal an adverse decision of the chair on a point of order.[43] The chair may initially decide to let the assembly decide a point of order. There is no appeal from a decision of the assembly.[44] In a California case, appeals from point of order rulings were upheld when successfully appealed at a meeting.[45]

Points of order have been raised at labor union meetings with different results.[46] At least two parliamentary references recommend that a record of points of order and their rulings be kept by an organization.[47] In this writer's opinion, this practice is usually not practical and its value as a binding precedent is problematical.

A sample of court cases mentioned the following. A use of a point of order was raised as a hypothetical in a Georgia opinion regarding a county commission meeting.[48] Unruly citizens at council meetings have been ruled out of order. A citizen's attempt to raise a point of order in an Indiana case was denied at a meeting because it was not time for public comment.[49] A point of order was raised at a council meeting whether a council member should recuse himself due to an alleged conflict of interest.[50] The use of a point of order in California was mentioned regarding the presence of quorum during a legislative vote.[51]

§ 37 MOTION TO SUSPEND THE RULES

Adoption of a motion to suspend the rules temporarily bypasses an existing procedural rule. It is often used in conjunction with a substantive main motion so that other business can be addressed and taken up out of order.

Thus a suspension of a rule can be and often is attached to a substantive motion on the floor. It can also be proposed as an incidental main motion. It is used "temporarily until the business for which the suspension was requested has been considered."[52] The motion must be seconded, is not debatable, is not amendable, and cannot interrupt another speaker.[53] A two-thirds vote is required.[54]

There are circumstances in which a suspension of the rules is improper. Bylaws cannot be suspended except for those procedures in which the bylaws themselves specifically allow for suspension.[55] Fundamental parliamentary principles and individual rights can never be suspended.[56] For example, the principle that only one question at a time can be considered or that a member has a right to vote cannot be suspended.[57] Rules protecting absentees such as quorum requirements and meeting notices cannot be suspended.[58] Applicable rules from a statute,[59] charter,[60] and parent organization also cannot be suspended.

Governmental meetings sometimes use suspension of the rules in moving ordinances forward.[61] For example, in a reported Missouri case, a city council waived a waiting period so that a bill could immediately be read a third time after its second reading.[62]

In a Pennsylvania case, the court ruled that a city authority entered into a binding lease when it "suspended the standard rules of operation and voted to approve [the lease] which was not on the meeting agenda and not discussed at a prior work session."[63]

---

[1] See, e.g., GEORGE DEMETER, DEMETER'S MANUAL OF PARLIAMENTARY LAW AND PROCEDURE 311 (2001) (asserting that an appeal is among "[t]he most misinterpreted, misunderstood and misapplied proceedings in parliamentary practice").

[2] AMERICAN INSTITUTE OF PARLIAMENTARIANS, STANDARD CODE OF PARLIAMENTARY PROCEDURE 85 (2012) [hereinafter STANDARD CODE].The Standard Code of Parliamentary Procedure lists the following rules for the motion to appeal.

1. Can interrupt a speaker because it must be proposed immediately after the chair's ruling
2. Requires a second
3. Is debatable
4. Cannot be amended
5. Requires a majority vote or a tie vote to sustain the decision of the presiding officer
6. Takes precedence as an incidental motion and must be decided immediately
7. Applies to rulings and decisions of the presiding officer
8. Can have applied to it motions to close debate, to limit debate, and to withdraw
9. Cannot be renewed

[3] In one case, a procedure to "appeal from the decision of the Chair to the meeting without debate immediately after the Chair has decided against him" was included in a labor union's rules of order. George v. Local Union No. 639, 825 F. Supp. 328, 331 (D.D.C. 1993).

4   Sarah Corbin Robert, Henry M. Robert III, William J. Evans, Daniel H. Honemann & Thomas J. Balch, Robert's Rules of Order Newly Revised 255-60 (11th ed. 2011) [hereinafter Robert's Rules]; Hugh Cannon, Cannon's Concise Guide to Rules of Order 40-44 (2001); Floyd M. Riddick & Miriam H. Butcher, Riddick's Rules of Procedure: A Modern Guide to Faster and More Efficient Meetings 22-23 (1985).

5   Rosenberg v. Screen Actors Guild, No. B214056, 2009 WL 3430753, at *8-9 (Cal. Ct. App. Oct. 27, 2009).

6   Town Bd. v. Hallock, 770 N.Y.S.2d 823, 828 (Sup. Ct. 2003).

7   *See, e.g.*, Robert's Rules, *supra* note 4, at 70-71 ("If a pending motion (or a pending amendment) contains two or more parts capable of standing as separate questions, the assembly can vote to treat each part accordingly in succession . . . ."); *see also* Cannon, *supra* note 4, at 99, 112-13.

8   Robert's Rules, *supra* note 4, at 70-71.

9   *Compare id.* at 271 (noting that one member may request a division), *with* Cannon, *supra* note 4, at 112 (recommending that a majority vote is needed rather than allowing one member to make the request).

10   Standard Code, *supra* note 2, at 99.

11   *Id.* at 99.

12   Riddick & Butcher, *supra* note 4, at 88.

13   Robert's Rules, *supra* note 4, 271-72.

14   *Compare id.* at 271 (another speaker cannot be interrupted), *and* Demeter, *supra* note 1, at 44 (only an urgent situation will allow for interruption), *with* Riddick & Butcher, *supra* note 4, at 88 (another speaker can be interrupted).

15   Standard Code, *supra* note 2, at 101.

16   Robert's Rules, *supra* note 4, at 235.

17   Standard Code, *supra* note 2, at 97.

18   Robert's Rules, *supra* note 4, at 296.

19   *Id.* at 297.

20   *Id.*

21   Standard Code, *supra* note 2, at 98.

22   *Id.* But if a motion is withdrawn after the original motion is announced, it is recorded in the minutes. *Id.*

23   Robert's Rules, *supra* note 4, at 469 n.

24   *Id.* at 293.

[25]   *Id.*

[26]   *Id.* at 268.

[27]   CANNON, *supra* note 4, at 99.

[28]   ALICE STURGIS, THE STANDARD CODE OF PARLIAMENTARY PROCEDURE 233 (4th ed., rev. 2001). The American Institute of Parliamentarians Standard Code of Parliamentary Procedure does not mention the motion to object to consideration.

[29]   RIDDICK & BUTCHER, *supra* note 4, at 158-59.

[30]   DEMETER, *supra* note 1, at 142.

[31]   ROBERT'S RULES, *supra* note 4, at 72; *see also* Warburton v. Thomas, 616 A.2d 495, 501 (N.H. 1992) (referring to a parliamentary inquiry in a dispute in a New Hampshire legislature).

[32]   STANDARD CODE, *supra* note 2, at 94.

[33]   ROBERT'S RULES, *supra* note 4, at 450.

[34]   *Compare id.* (making the distinction), *with* RIDDICK & BUTCHER, *supra* note 4, at 138 (stating that "parliamentary inquiry" and "point of information" are used for the same purpose, but "'parliamentary inquiry' is more descriptive and therefore should be used in preference to 'point of information'").

[35]   DEMETER, *supra* note 1, at 125.

[36]   *Compare* STANDARD CODE, *supra* note 2, at 76 (stating a speaker can be interrupted "if it requires immediate decision and action"), *with* RIDDICK & BUTCHER, *supra* note 4, at 139, (noting that the member must either be recognized by the presiding officer or be granted permission by the body).

[37]   *In re* Dupont, 142 S.W.3d 528, 532 (Tex. App. 2004) (citing 59 AM. JUR. 2D *Parliamentary Law* § 5 (2004)). This comment was made in the broader context of the court's role in parliamentary procedure in a meeting.

[38]   STANDARD CODE, *supra* note 2, at 90.

[39]   In one case, a presiding officer ruled that a member who brought "up the issue of" a previous expulsion of a union member was out of order. *See* Howard v. Weathers, 139 F.3d 553, 555 (7th Cir. 1998).

[40]   In a case involving a contentious convention of a state political party, points of order were allegedly disregarded by a chair. Cahill v. Bertuzzi, No. 13-09-00183-CV, 2010 WL 2163136, at *1 (Tex. App. May 27, 2010).

[41]   ROBERT'S RULES, *supra* note 4, at 250.

[42]   *See, e.g., id.* at 252 (stating that it is never too late to raise a point of order alleging an action would deny a right to an individual member such as the right to vote). For an example of a failure to raise a point of order to motions or conduct see, *Dinowitz v. Rivera,* 2008 NY Slip Op 52617U (2008), p. 5.

43   RIDDICK & BUTCHER, *supra* note 4, at 22.

44   STANDARD CODE, *supra* note 2, at 92.

45   Rosenberg v. Screen Actors Guild, No. B214056, 2009 WL 3430753, at *8-9 (Cal. Ct. App. Oct. 27, 2009).

46   *See, e.g.*, George v. Local Union No. 639, 825 F. Supp. 328, 332 (D.D.C. 1993) ("A member speaking out of order may be interrupted and the meeting adjourned . . . even if the adjournment was procedurally improper."); Farrell v. Hellen, 367 F. Supp. 2d 491, 498 (S.D.N.Y. 2005) (alleging points of order were not recognized); Miner v. Local 373, 513 F.3d 854, 859 (8th Cir. 2008) (challenging a document successfully).

47   ROBERT'S RULES, *supra* note 4, at 251-52; RIDDICK & BUTCHER, *supra* note 4, at 91.

48   There was speculation that a point of order would be used by a county commission against an unruly citizen at a meeting. Felphrey v. Cobb Cnty., 448 F. Supp. 2d 1357, 1361 n.6 (N.D. Ga. 2006).

49   Scheub v. Town of Schereville, 617 N.E.2d 585, 585-86 (Ind. Ct. App. 1993); *see also* Timmon v. Wood, 633 F. Supp. 2d 453 (W.D. Mich. 2008) (stating that a council member was allowed to raise a point of order as to whether a citizen's speech was in breach of the rules of decorum).

50   Clark v. City of Hermosa Beach, 56 Cal. Rptr. 2d 223, 229 (Ct. App. 1996).

51   City of King City v. Cmty. Bank, 32 Cal. Rptr. 3d 384, 404 n.18 (Ct. App. 2005).

52   RIDDICK & BUTCHER, *supra* note 4, at 188.

53   *E.g.*, ROBERT'S RULES, *supra* note 4, at 261; STURGIS, *supra* note 28, at 87.

54   *E.g.*, ROBERT'S RULES, *supra* note 4, at 261; STURGIS, *supra* note 28, at 87.

55   *See, e.g.*, RIDDICK & BUTCHER, *supra* note 4, at 188; DEMETER, *supra* note 1, at 133 (commenting on improperly suspended bylaws due to "expediency or strong assembly determination in behalf of a cause or reposition make violations necessary").

56   ROBERT'S RULES, *supra* note 4, at 263; *see also* Jones v. Wilson, 2007-Ohio-6484, at ¶ 31 (suspending of quorum rules at a church's special membership meeting was successful because the court lacked subject matter jurisdiction and would not intervene in an ecclesiastical dispute).

57   ROBERT'S RULES, *supra* note 4, at 263.

58   *Id.*

59   STANDARD CODE, *supra* note 2, at 85.

60   *Id.*

61   *See, e.g.*, *Ex parte* Walter, 829 So. 2d 186, 189 (Ala. 2002) (mentioning that rules of procedure were suspended by a city council to allow for immediate consideration of an amendment to a municipal ordinance).

[62]   Crestwood Commons Redevelopment Corp. v. 66 Drive-In, Inc., 812 S.W.2d 903, 907 (Mo. Ct. App. 1991); *see also* Phillips v. City of Eureka Springs, 847 S.W.2d 21, 22 (Ark. 1993) (motioning to suspend the rules at a city council meeting that allowed for an ordinance to be read a third time); Mollette v. Portsmouth City Council, 2008-Ohio-6342, 902 N.E.2d 515, at ¶ 7 (demonstrating a city council vote to suspend the rules requiring three readings of an ordinance and adopting it after the first reading without objection).

[63]   Beaver Dam Outdoors v. Hazelton City Auth., 944 A.2d 97, 107 (Pa. Commw. Ct. 2008). In an Illinois case, a city council voted to suspend the rules and reconsider a special use (zoning) permit application. Our Savior Evangelical Lutheran Church v. Saville, 922 N.E.2d 1143, 1154 (Ill. App. Ct. 2009).

    In another case, a village council was unable to justify going into executive session and suspending the rules despite declaring an emergency because the executive session did not fall within an enumerated exception to the state's Sunshine law. Myers v. Hensley, No. 6-99-02, 1999 WL 797140, at *2-3 (Ohio Ct. App. 1999).

CHAPTER **6**

Unclassified Motions (No Order of Precedence)

§ 38 MOTION TO RECONSIDER

A motion to reconsider allows an assembly to reconsider a prior vote on a main motion.[1] There is some disagreement as to whether the motion to reconsider must be brought up at the same meeting or if it may be carried forward to the next meeting.[2] Under the <u>Standard Code of Parliamentary Procedure</u>, this motion allows an assembly to set aside a motion taken at the same meeting or convention as if it had not been taken.[3]

The motion is out of order when action has already been taken or to the extent parts of the underlying main motion have been executed such as when someone has been informed of the outcome of a contract.[4] After the motion to reconsider has been adopted all action on the underlying main motion must be suspended.[5] In a reported Connecticut case, after a decision was reached by a zoning board and that decision was published, a motion for reconsideration was improper.[6]

There is considerable disagreement about whether a person who voted on the prevailing side of a motion is the only one eligible to move for its reconsideration.[7] Historically, this was the prevailing view. But opinions have changed. In this writer's opinion anyone should be permitted to move for reconsideration regardless of how he or she previously voted. In a governmental case in Iowa the fact that the person who made the motion for reconsideration had not voted on the prevailing side for an underlying motion at a commission meeting did not negate the motion for reconsideration.[8]

The motion for reconsideration requires a second, cannot be amended, is debatable, can interrupt another speaker if necessary, and takes a majority vote. However, if a motion for reconsideration interrupts another speaker, consideration is deferred to later in the meeting.[9] There is disagreement among parliamentary references on whether the underlying main motion can be debated at the same time as the motion to reconsider. In committee meetings, there is no limit on how often a motion can be reconsidered.[10]

The courts have grappled with this motion in various governmental contexts.[11] For example, in a sample of cases, a court in South Dakota ruled that a motion could not be reconsidered if to do so was in conflict with a statute.[12] In another South Dakota case, reconsideration of a tax levy by a township was authorized when undertaken at a special meeting thereafter.[13] A planning commission in Oregon was able to vote a second time on what was deemed a new motion.[14] A county commission in a Tennessee case was authorized to reconsider the rejection of a development at the commission's next meeting.[15] A commission's attempt to reconsider a hospital's issuance of a certificate of need was rejected.[16] A racing commission in Minnesota was authorized to reconsider an application for a racetrack license sua sponte.[17]

§ 39 MOTION TO RESCIND

A deliberative body may rescind, void or cancel a previously adopted main motion[18] or action.[19] This can be done at any subsequent meeting no matter how much time has intervened.[20] How the moving party voted on the originally adopted motion does not matter.[21]

This motion should be distinguished from the cousin motion to reconsider. Reconsider is offered at the same session in which the motion sought to be undone has been adopted.[22] In contrast, rescission is only offered at a subsequent meeting. Under parliamentary rules, a motion to reconsider does not have to be made before seeking a rescission.[23] There is some disagreement among parliamentary references on what size vote is needed to adopt the motion to rescind.[24] In a North Carolina case, a motion to rescind failed for lack of a second.[25]

By way of illustration, a county board in Wisconsin used the following rule:

> A motion to rescind an action may be made by any member at any time but such motion requires the support of the majority of all supervisors elected, provided, however, that such rescission will not be inconsistent with actions that have been commenced because of the action to be rescinded and will not result in consequences inimical to the interests of the public or the county.[26]

There are situations in which a motion to rescind is improper. First, when a motion to reconsider is available.[27] Second, when something has already taken place on the adopted motion that cannot be undone.[28] And, third, when a person has been notified of his official status as an officer or member.[29]

In a sample of cases, a New York court opinion noted that a city council was authorized to rescind a prior minimum number of firefighters by resolution and by doing so, no contractual rights had been previously created and now breached.[30] County board rules allow for a motion to rescind by a majority vote of the supervisors as long as they are not inconsistent with motions already taken.[31] But an attempt of a city council in Louisiana to rescind their signing of a contract with a labor union was rejected.[32] A county board of education in West Virginia rescinded a decision to grant sick leave to a worker at a subsequent meeting.[33]

A Louisiana court ruled that a motion at a later board meeting which conflicts with another motion at a prior meeting is null and void at a zoning board hearing unless the motion was previously rescinded.[34] A motion to rescind a previously approved budget required the attendance of a quorum.[35]

§ 40 MOTION TO RESUME CONSIDERATION (TAKE FROM THE TABLE)

The purpose of a motion to resume consideration is to return to the assembly consideration of a motion that was previously temporarily postponed.[36] All adhering motions along with the underlying motion are brought back and then decided in the appropriate order.[37] Beyond the allotted period, the motion that was temporarily postponed dies but can be reintroduced later as a new motion.[38]

There is a difference among parliamentary references on how long a period may pass during which this motion can be used. Sturgis limits its use to the same meeting or convention.[39] Demeter limits its use to the same meeting "or at the next session in bodies that meet regularly at least quarterly."[40] RONR says its use is permitted during the same session, at the next meeting if the group will meet again in the same quarter, and "also at the next session after it was laid on the table."[41]

This motion requires a second, is not debatable, not amendable, and takes a majority vote.[42] The proposer of the motion cannot interrupt another speaker, but has priority only over other new main motions.[43]

<hr>

[1] AMERICAN INSTITUTE OF PARLIAMENTARIANS, STANDARD CODE OF PARLIAMENTARY PROCEDURE 44 (2012) [hereinafter STANDARD CODE]. *But see* Howard v. Weathers, 139 F.3d 553, 555-56 (7th Cir. 1998) (disallowing a motion to reconsider a prior expulsion of a union member because under the interpretation of the organization's constitution, membership reinstatement was not permitted).

[2] *See, e.g.,* Irene Neighborhood Ass'n v. Quality Life, LLC, No. W2001-00474-COA-R3-CV, 2002 WL 1050264, at *5 (Tenn. Ct. App. 2002) (allowing a county commission to vote to reconsider a prior rejection of a development at a subsequent meeting because the commission's own procedural rules overrode <u>RONR</u>); *see also* Hirschfield v. Bd. of Cnty. Comm'rs, 944 P.2d 1139, 1144-45 (Wyo. 1997) (allowing a county board to reconsider an action at a later continuation of the same meeting after the measure lost by a tie vote at the initial meeting); Bd. of Cnty. Comm'rs v. Webber, 658 So. 2d 1069, 1072 (Fla. Dist. Ct. App. 1995) (upholding a zoning variance vote when the first vote was reconsidered and revoted at the same session). *But see* Wolfman, Inc. v. City of New Orleans, 2003-0120, p. 7 (La. App. 4 Cir. 4/21/04); 872 So. 2d 261, 264 (finding that under <u>RONR</u> board could only reconsider vote if a motion to consider was made on the same date as the board's vote) (citing ROBERT'S RULES OF ORDER § 37(b)).

[3] STANDARD CODE, *supra* note 1, at 44-45.

[4] GEORGE DEMETER, DEMETER'S MANUAL OF PARLIAMENTARY LAW AND PROCEDURE 158 (2001).

[5] SARAH CORBIN ROBERT, HENRY M. ROBERT III, WILLIAM J. EVANS, DANIEL H. HONEMANN & THOMAS J. BALCH, ROBERT'S RULES OF ORDER NEWLY REVISED 321 (11th ed. 2011) [hereinafter ROBERT'S RULES].
  For example, at a town council's deliberation of a motion to reconsider approval of a zoning matter, a citizen did not have a right to be heard after being heard at a prior meeting. Crispin v. Town of Scarborough, 1999 ME 112, ¶ 22, 736 A.2d 241, 248.

[6] Sharp v. Zoning Bd. of Appeals, 634 A.2d 713 (Conn. App. Ct. 1996).

[7] *Compare* ROBERT'S RULES, *supra* note 5, at 315 (stating the mover of a motion to reconsider must have been on the prevailing side), *with* ALICE STURGIS, THE STANDARD CODE OF PARLIAMENTARY PROCEDURE 40 (4th ed., rev. 2001) (stating a mover of a motion to reconsider does *not* have to be on the prevailing scale), *and* FLOYD M. RIDDICK & MIRIAM H. BUTCHER, RIDDICK'S RULES OF PROCEDURE: A MODERN GUIDE TO FASTER AND MORE EFFICIENT MEETINGS 166 (1985) (same), *and* HUGH CANNON, CANNON'S CONCISE GUIDE TO RULES OF ORDER 127 (2001) (same).
  The contention that the motion to reconsider "could be made only by a member of the majority voting," was made in *Munhall v. Inland Wetlands Commission*, 602 A.2d 566, 567 n.3 (Conn. 1992) (citing ROBERT'S RULES OF ORDER). *See also In re* N. Metro Harness, Inc., 711 N.W.2d 129, 133 (Minn. Ct. App. 2006) (stating that <u>RONR</u> allows an individual on the prevailing side of a vote to move for reconsideration).

[8] State *ex rel.* Miller v. DeCoster, 608 N.W.2d 785, 792 (Iowa 2000). In citing and quoting from its own prior court decision "involving a parliamentary challenge," the court stated:

> Because parliamentary rules are adopted by a council to govern its internal procedures, the procedures may be waived by the council: "The important inquiry always is whether the number required by law have agreed to a particular measure. If this has been done in a way not inconsistent with statutory provisions, it is quite immaterial whether parliamentary procedure has been followed."

Id.

9   STANDARD CODE, *supra* note 1, at 46 (stating the motion to reconsider when it interrupts a speaker "is not considered until the pending business has been handled"); RIDDICK & BUTCHER, *supra* note 7, at 166 (stating a motion to reconsider takes a majority vote, is not amendable and cannot be reconsidered except by unanimous consent); CANNON, *supra* note 7, at 127 (requiring a two-thirds vote if no notice is given and the motion is made beyond the next day); ROBERT'S RULES, *supra* note 5, at 320.

10 *See, e.g.*, RIDDICK & BUTCHER, *supra* note 7, at 167.

11 For example, in a Wisconsin case a county board established seven rules on the use of the motion to reconsider. Olson v. Town of Cottage Grove, 2008 WI 51, ¶ 56, 309 Wis. 2d 365, 749 N.W.2d 211.

12 Cooper v. Hauschild, 527 N.W.2d 908, 910-11 (S.D. 1995) (finding the approval of an application for an alcohol license could not be subsequently reconsidered by a city commission at a later meeting); *see also* Mount St. Scholastica, Inc. v. City of Atchison, 482 F. Supp. 2d 1281, 1289 (D. Kan. 2007) (stating that a request for reconsideration of a denial of a demolition permit for a subsequent meeting was not discussed due to unspecified parliamentary procedures).

13 Zubke v. Melrose Tp., 2007 SD 43, ¶ 9, 731 N.W.2d 918, 921.

14 Gumtow-Farrior v. Crook Cnty., LUBA No. 2003-105, at *3-4 (Or. Land Use Bd. of Appeals Nov. 19, 2003), http://www.oregon.gov/LUBA/docs/opinions/2003/11-03/03105.pdf.

15 Irene Neighborhood Ass'n v. Quality Life, LLC, No. W2001-00474-COA-R3-CV, 2002 WL 1050264, at *5 (Tenn. Ct. App. 2002).

16 Methodist v. Jackson-Madison Cnty. Gen., 129 S.W.3d 57, 67-69 (Tenn. Ct. App. 2003). Under a Tennessee statute, the governmental commission decision to deny or approve an application was final and could not be reconsidered; moreover, no distinction was made between a vote and a decision at a meeting and neither could be reconsidered. *Id.*; *see also* Old Carrolton Neighborhood Ass'n v. City of New Orleans, 2003-0711, p. 8 (La. App. 4 Cir. 1/30/04); 859 So. 2d 713, 717-18 (finding a zoning variance which was denied at a meeting because of a lack of affirmative votes could not be reconsidered and voted on at the next zoning board of adjustments meeting).

17 *In re* N. Metro Harness, Inc., 711 N.W.2d 129, 133 (Minn. Ct. App. 2006).

18 STANDARD CODE, *supra* note 1, at 48. Sturgis also calls this a motion to repeal. STURGIS, *supra* note 7, at 42.

19 RIDDICK & BUTCHER, *supra* note 7, at 173.

20 DEMETER, *supra* note 4, at 165.

21 *Id.*

22 CANNON, *supra* note 7, at 126-27.

23 DEMETER, *supra* note 4, at 166. However, it was noted that for a board of education to alter a previous decision, it first needed a motion to reconsider a decision before a motion for rescission could be offered. Pennycuff v. Fentress Cnty. Bd. of Educ., 206 F. Supp. 2d 911, 913 (M.D. Tenn. 2002) (decided on other grounds).

24   *See* STANDARD CODE, *supra* note 1, at 49 (requiring a majority vote to rescind although a greater vote is needed if the original motion required more than a majority; the same size vote is needed); DEMETER, *supra* note 4, at 165 (requiring two-thirds vote without notice and a majority vote with prior notice); RIDDICK & BUTCHER, *supra* note 7, at 173 (requiring majority vote or the same vote as required to adopt); ROBERT'S RULES, *supra* note 5, at 306. Riddick notes the desirability of prior notice, but does not mandate it unless required in the organization's adopted authority. RIDDICK & BUTCHER, *supra* note 7, at 173.

25   Leete v. Cnty. of Warren, 462 S.E 2d 476, 477 (N.C. 1995).

26   Olson v. Town of Cottage Grove. 2008 WI 51, ¶ 56, 309 Wis. 2d 365, 749 N.W.2d 211.

27   ROBERT'S RULES, *supra* note 5, at 308.

28   *Id.* However, if any aspect of the motion is yet to be done, that part can be rescinded. *Id.*

29   *Id.*

30   Vill. of Johnson City v. Johnson City Firefighters Ass'n, No. 2009-2141, 2010 WL 390931 (N.Y. Sup. Ct. Jan. 21, 2010).

31   *See, e.g., Olson*, 2008 WI 51, ¶ 56, 309 Wis. 2d 365, 749 N.W.2d 211. The court noted that under county board rules a motion to rescind is made on a day sometime after the day when the action to reconsider took place. *Id.* at ¶ 57.

32   City of Pineville v. Am. Fed'n of State, Cnty. & Mun. Emps., 2000-1983, p. 5 (La. 6/29/01); 791 So.2d 609, 613 (finding a mayor had no right to cast a deciding vote to rescind a resolution authorizing a contract at a city council meeting when the tie vote included an abstention causing the tie).

33   Parker v. Summers Cnty. Bd. of Educ., 406 S.E.2d 744, 746 (W. Va. 1991) (decided on other grounds).

34   Old Carrolton Neighborhood Ass'n v. City of New Orleans, 2003-0711, p. 9-10 (La. App. 4 Cir. 1/30/04); 859 So. 2d 713, 718-19 (Decided on other grounds); *see also* Mullin v. Town of Fairhaven, 284 F.3d 31, 33 (1st Cir. 2002) (establishing removal from office for cause when "appointed local officials [were] unwilling to comply with the directive of the Board of Selectmen that they rescind a vote").

35   N.Y. State Corr. Officers & Police Benevolent Ass'n v. Hinman Straub, P.C., 14585/04, 2004 WL 2889761, at *7 (N.Y. Sup. Ct. Oct. 18, 2004).

36   *See, e.g.,* ROBERT'S RULES, *supra* note 5, at 300. Riddick does not specify this motion by name but implies its usage. RIDDICK & BUTCHER, *supra* note 7, at 144. Cannon also declines to identify this motion by name. *See generally* CANNON, *supra* note 7.

37   *See, e.g.,* STURGIS, *supra* note 7, at 45. Note: The AIP Standard Code of Parliamentary Procedure does not include a Motion to Resume Consideration (Take from the Table). However, a majority of the members under the STANDARD Code can return the tabled motion back to the same or a future meeting or convention, at 71.

38   ROBERT'S RULES, *supra* note 5, at 302.

[39]   STURGIS, *supra* note 7, at 44. Note: The Standard Code of Parliamentary Procedure no longer includes a Motion to Resume Consideration (Take from the Table).

[40]   DEMETER, *supra* note 4, at 169. Demeter also allows "tabled motions" to be reintroduced from one annual meeting or convention to another. *Id.*

[41]   ROBERT'S RULES, *supra* note 5, at 301-02.

[42]   STURGIS, *supra* note 7, at 45-46. Note: The Standard Code of Parliamentary Procedure no longer includes a Motion to Resume Consideration (Take from the Table).

[43]   *Id.*

CHAPTER **7**

Debate

§41 DEBATE

A fundamental right of every member of a deliberative assembly is to debate a motion on the floor.[1] All main motions and most secondary motions are debatable. Little or no debate is permitted on other types of motions. The presiding officer should not ordinarily participate in the debate but may turn over the chair on limited occasions to another so he or she can participate.[2]

Healthy, courteous debate is the cornerstone of successful meeting outcomes. Debate follows the introduction of a motion. Other discussion at a meeting is normally limited. The presiding officer should not tolerate negative personal comments or other inappropriate conduct. The assembly has, in this writer's opinion, the authority to vote and have peaceably removed any offending member after sufficient warnings have been issued.

Depending on the need, some organizations adopt rules about debate. These rules can include, for example, the total length of time for debate, how many times one person can speak, and how long a person may speak.[3] The maker of the motion is the first to speak to it.[4] A person should not speak a second time until everyone else who wants to speak gets his or her chance to speak first.[5] Typically, each person can speak up to twice,[6] for up to two minutes each time. Some parliamentary texts grant up to 10 minutes if the organization is silent on the length of time.[7] Other organizations find no need to have fixed debate rules or adopt them as the need arises.

The <u>Standard Code of Parliamentary Procedure</u> categorizes motions into three types based on the extent of their debatability. "1. Motions that are fully debatable 2. Motions that are debatable with restrictions 3. Motions that are not debatable."[8]

Debate rules can be offered before and during a debate by motions. For example, motions to limit or extend debate are available. Such motions require a second and a two-thirds vote for passage since they affect members' rights. The chair should monitor a debate to see if a motion about a debate would be helpful. Sometimes a chair will suggest a suspension of the debate rules by unanimous consent when the need for it seems obvious. For example, if it would best serve the organization to extend it beyond a decided time limit, the presiding officer might approve of additional debate through unanimous consent. Unanimous consent is further discussed in Section 53.

There is a distinction between the right of a voting member to speak in debate compared to a member of the public attending and speaking during the allotted time at a governmental meeting.[9] The "rights" of a member of the public to speak at a governmental meeting are considerably more circumspect and operate under more restrictive rules than the right of a voting member of the governmental body to speak. Much also depends on the nature of the meeting.

Federal labor law allows each member the right "to participate in the deliberations . . . subject to the reasonable rules and regulations in such [labor union's] constitution and by-laws."[10] Under reported cases, a union member has the right to debate a proposed labor contract.[11] One court ruled that a labor union had a duty to provide its membership with a meaningful opportunity to participate in and debate a proposed union contract based on necessary factual information.[12]

§ 42 EXECUTIVE SESSION

Timely use and understanding of executive session is crucial to the overall health and success of many organizations. Executive session takes place when the contents and results of part or all of a meeting are kept strictly confidential.[13] Only members of the assembly are permitted in the meeting during executive session unless non-members are specifically invited.[14] The presiding officer and other attendees should be aware of the need to go into executive session when the agenda is approved or a sensitive subject is anticipated or unexpectedly arises.

Executive sessions are used when there is a compelling reason for secrecy. The discussions that take place within the meeting must remain confidential. The actions taken by the assembly such as adopted motions can either remain confidential or be publicly reported - at the discretion of the assembly.[15] An entire meeting or parts thereof can be held in executive session.

There are a variety of reasons for an organization to enter into executive session. Three common reasons are to discuss a personnel matter,[16] a legal matter, or a disciplinary matter.[17] Other examples could include discussions about intellectual property, the purchase of real estate, and sensitive business matters. The purpose and rules of executive session and the adverse consequences of violating the secrecy rules should be explained to those participating in a meeting.

Statutory law concerning executive sessions must be closely followed for governmental meetings.[18] State open meeting laws must be consulted and these laws generally define how a vote is conducted to go into executive session, what matters will allow for a closed meeting, and what information can be released.[19] A Minnesota court has noted that attorney-client privilege may be recognized to discuss strategy, but not the threat of litigation.[20] There is considerable other case law interpreting the sunshine statutes concerning executive sessions which is beyond the scope of this text.

Minutes taken at executive sessions must be securely stored and remain confidential. They are approved at the next executive session.[21] Competing interests may arise about the secrecy of the minutes in the context of the availability of an organization's records. Making the minutes publicly availably may defeat the purpose of an executive session. In a Wyoming case, the court found the county clerk, although not a county commissioner, had the right to attend commissioner meetings held in executive session in order to take minutes.[22]

A motion to go into executive session is a privileged motion, requires a second, is not debatable, and needs a majority vote for approval.[23] A motion is also needed to leave executive session. It is good practice for an assembly to determine what motions, if any, can be publicly reported out before the executive session ends. Governmental requirements on what is public information will probably differ compared to requirements for nonprofit organizations in this regard.

---

[1] SARAH CORBIN ROBERT, HENRY M. ROBERT III, WILLIAM J. EVANS, DANIEL H. HONEMANN & THOMAS J. BALCH, ROBERT'S RULES OF ORDER NEWLY REVISED 264 (11th ed. 2011) [hereinafter ROBERT'S RULES] (stating all members have the right to debate); HUGH CANNON, CANNON'S CONCISE GUIDE TO RULES OF ORDER 107 (2001) ("Debate is the lifeblood of any meeting . . . ."); FLOYD M. RIDDICK & MIRIAM H. BUTCHER, RIDDICK'S RULES OF PROCEDURE: A MODERN GUIDE TO FASTER AND MORE EFFICIENT MEETINGS 71 (1985) (noting the importance of the role of debate as a "basic principle of parliamentary procedure"); AMERICAN INSTITUTE OF PARLIAMENTARIANS, STANDARD CODE OF PARLIAMENTARY PROCEDURE 126 (2012) [hereinafter STANDARD CODE]; GEORGE DEMETER, DEMETER'S MANUAL OF PARLIAMENTARY LAW AND PROCEDURE 305 (2001) ("The principle of debate connotes *free discussion* before decisions are made and full *unity* afterward.").

[2] In *Mobley v. Tarlini*, 641 F. Supp. 2d 430 (E.D. Pa. 2009), the rights of a councilman to exercise his right to debate at a meeting was partially upheld and partially denied.

[3] For excellent debate rules, see DEMETER, *supra* note 1, at 25-32, RIDDICK & BUTCHER, *supra* note 1, at 71-79, and STANDARD CODE, *supra* note 1, at 126-134.

[4] STANDARD CODE, *supra* note 1, at 127-28.

[5] For example, see *Mobley*, 641 F. Supp. 2d at 434.

[6] ROBERT'S RULES, *supra* note 1, at 43.

[7] *Id.* at 387.

[8] STANDARD CODE, *supra* note 1, at 126.

[9] For example, the chairman at a county board of supervisors meeting acted properly when he found an unruly member of the public out of order, directed that he be seated, and had

him evicted from a public hearing in which the speaker's comments were argumentative and not on the subject. Mannix v. Commonwealth, 522 S.E.2d 885, 887-88 (Va. Ct. App. 2000). However, under a state open meeting law, members of the public could not be deprived of the opportunity to publicly debate a special use permit amendment. Gernatt Asphalt Prods., Inc. v. Town of Sardinia, 622 N.Y.S.2d 395, 400 (App. Div. 1995).

10   Farkas v. Rumore, 881 F. Supp. 884, 888 (S.D.N.Y. 1995) (citing the Labor-Management Reporting and Disclosure Act (LMRDA) § 101(a)(1), 29 U.S.C. § 411(a)(1) (1995)).

11   *See, e.g., id.*

12   Brown v. Int'l Bhd. of Elec. Workers, 936 F.2d 251, 254 (6th Cir. 1991); *accord* Adcox v. Teledyne, Inc., 21 F.3d 1381 (6th Cir. 1994), *overruled on other grounds by,* Winnett v. Caterpillar, Inc., 553 F.3d 1000 (5th Cir. 2009). *But see* George v. Local Union No. 639, 825 F. Supp. 328, 333 (D.D.C. 1993) (upholding the denial of a union member's right to speak when he refused to face the president while speaking).

13   Robert's Rules, *supra* note 1, at 85; Riddick & Butcher, *supra* note 2, at 45. Riddick calls such meetings "closed sessions" and argues the term "executive session" is archaic and does not adequately show the secrecy of such a meeting. Riddick & Butcher, *supra* note 2, at 45. Alice Sturgis, The Standard Code of Parliamentary Procedure 108-09 (4th ed., rev. 2001), also uses the term "Closed Session."

14   Standard Code, *supra* note 1, at 108.

15   Robert's Rules, *supra* note 1, at 95.

16   *See, e.g.,* Kocher v. Larksville Borough, 926 F. Supp. 2d 579, 590, 602 (M.D. Pa. 2013).

17   *See, e.g.,* Peters v. Escobar, No. C060888, 2010 WL 2501495, at *3 (Cal. Ct. App. June 22, 2010).
     For a fuller list of matters that should be taken up in executive session by a governmental board as set forth in the Wyoming Public Meetings Act, see *Fontaine v. Board of County Commissioners,* 4 P.3d 890 (Wyo. 2000) (citing WYO STAT. ANN. § 16-4-405).

18   *See, e.g.,* Warthman v. Genoa Twp. Bd. of Trs., 2011-Ohio-1775 (citing Ohio Rev. Code § 121.22).

19   *See, e.g.,* 65 Pa. Stat. Ann. § 708; N.Y. Pub. Off. §§ 103, 105; N.J. Stat. Ann. § 10:4-12.
     There are numerous legal cases examining the line between open meeting requirements versus closed session. For example, see *Norris v. Monroe City School Board,* 580 So. 2d 425 (La. Ct. App. 1991). A statutory "real property" exception to the open meeting rules was noted in *Allen v. Board of Selectman,* 792 N.E.2d 1000, 1003-04 (Mass. App. Ct. 2003) (quoting Mass. Gen. Laws ch. 39, § 23B). The Massachusetts statute was subsequently amended and relocated. Act of July 1, 2009, ch. 28, § 18, 2009 Mass. Legis. Serv. Ch. 28 (West) (codified as amended at Mass. Gen. Laws ch. 30A, § 18).

20   Prior Lake Am. v. Mader, 642 N.W.2d 729, 739-42 (Minn. 2002).

21   Robert's Rules, *supra* note 1, at 96.

22   *Fontaine,* 4 P.3d at 893-94.

23   Standard Code, *supra* note 1, at 108 (using the term "Closed Meeting").

CHAPTER **8**

Voting
(Generally)

§ 43 RIGHT TO VOTE

Voting is a basic parliamentary right of every member.[1] State nonprofit corporate statutes establish the right to vote by members[2] and directors.[3] However, these same statutes allow for a reduction or elimination of the right to vote by class as long as the organization's articles or bylaws spell this out.[4] Designated classes in the articles of incorporation, or bylaws, or as defined by the organization itself may deprive certain members of the right to vote.[5] Ex-officio members of a board or committee are deemed to have the right to vote unless the organization states otherwise in its bylaws. Thus, an organization should decide when it drafts its bylaws whether to grant an ex-officio member voting rights.

A court in New York has noted that board members can lose their right to vote at a meeting in which they are not personally present if an organization's governing documents fail to explicitly allow for telephone conference call voting.[6] Similarly, a right to vote may be jeopardized if electronic voting is not expressly permitted in state statutes and/or the organization's bylaws. Although more states are modernizing their laws, an organization should not assume that electronic voting is authorized in its state.[7] As stated in the Appendix to this book the state of Michgan is especially progressive in allowing for electronic voting. California has also been very progressive in this manner and other states are following suit.

In a Texas case a class cf members under a country club's bylaws had the exclusive right to vote for the club's dissolution despite opposition from the board composed of non-voting members.[8] In another case, a union's policy to exclude part-time workers from voting on a collective bargaining agreement was upheld as reasonable.[9]

A homeowner's association in a Pennsylvania case lacked authority to amend its bylaws to restrict members' voting rights; the court held that the right to vote is a property right which cannot be reduced without the consent of the party affected.[10] This case illustrates the recognized concept that the right to vote cannot be taken away by those in another membership class or category. However, the case law in a particular state may differ on this point and be open to interpretation.

A member is not compelled to vote[11] and can change his or her vote up to the announcement of the result by the chair.[12] Simply being in arrears on financial obligations does not automatically prevent a member from voting unless the bylaws so state.[13] One commentator has noted that pending disciplinary action may affect the right to vote.[14] The stronger view ir this writer's opinion is that there must first be a formal finding of culpability before the right to vote is taken away. A member's right to vote at any meeting can be challenged and the organization's official list or records then checked.[15] The complete list of members eligible to vote should be available at a meeting of members and if the meeting is held by remote communication the list should reasonably be accessible by electronic network.[16]

Condominium and homeowner associations have their own right-to-vote formulas and the applicable state statute and governing

documents should be consulted. A sample of cases shows the following. In a Delaware case, residents of a condominium had the right
to decide whether to approve a partial sale of their assets after their
condominium board president allegedly led them to believe they had
no such right.[17] In an Alabama case a right to vote as a member of
a cooperative was an individual right that the member had standing
to enforce - not a right for the corporation.[18] In a Delaware case, the
membership of a condominium association was granted the equitable right to vote concerning the sale of real estate although such
authority was vested in the board.[19] It has been held in a California
case that the general rule is that there is one vote per member and
that each homeowner of a lot in a subdivision is entitled to only one
vote even if he or she owns more than one lot.[20]

§ 44 MAJORITY VOTE

A basic principle of parliamentary procedure is that a majority
vote should decide whether to take an action[21] or to decide an election or other matter.[22] State statutes recognize the principle that a
majority vote determines all matters unless the articles, bylaws, or
another statutory provision require otherwise.[23] There are exceptions
as will be noted in Section 45.[24] Parliamentary references also note
that a decision that would be brought about other than by a majority
vote occurs only through a statute, the bylaws, or rules of the organization, or where required under general parliamentary procedure.[25]
One Alabama court noted that a "rule of reasonableness" provided
that only a majority vote was needed at a condominium association
meeting to lease mineral interests.[26]

In order to amend bylaws, a two-thirds or even an 80 percent vote
is typical but not required. A court in Louisiana held that a majority
vote to amend the bylaws was insufficient.[27] In this writer's opinion, a
greater-than-majority vote is preferable given the huge importance of
bylaws and their impact on an organization. However, many organizations prefer a majority vote to amend.

Sometimes an organization is faced with a situation when, as a practical matter, it is unable to secure a required greater-than-majority vote. This puts the organization in a bind. Under these difficult circumstances the court may be petitioned in an effort to reduce a required vote from greater-than-majority to a majority.[28] The author of one article argues that if a quorum cannot be obtained at an annual meeting to amend the bylaws then the quorum requirement should be reduced and that "common sense" should allow for a mail vote even if not ordinarily allowed.[29] Such a course may in this writer's opinion be open to challenge especially in "high stakes" organizations.

Controversy sometimes arises on how to mathematically calculate a majority vote. These situations typically come up when imprecise language is used in the controlling documents. Ordinarily a majority vote means one-half plus one of all members present and actually voting.[30] Abstentions and illegal votes are usually but not always ignored. Specific language is needed by an organization in its documents to determine the basis upon which to count a group of potential voters including whether or not to count abstentions. This topic has been well discussed in parliamentary references[31] and looked at by the courts.

Possibilities for determining a majority include:

1. A majority of a quorum[32]
2. A majority of the members present, voting or not[33]
3. A majority of the members present and voting[34]
4. A majority of the members in good standing
5. A majority of the legal votes cast[35]
6. A majority of the membership, present or absent[36]

How to handle abstentions has been an area of confusion and can affect the result of a vote. Normally abstentions are simply ignored otherwise they would have the effect of a "no" vote. The organization must read its controlling documents to determine how to count abstentions. In an Illinois case a zoning amendment required a majority vote of the entire board; an abstained vote did not count as an affirmative vote.[37] Another court ruled that an abstention may result in the failure to attain a majority if this is what a statute requires statutorily.[38]

§ 45 GREATER-THAN-MAJORITY VOTE

State nonprofit corporation statutes set forth certain situations that require a greater-than-majority vote. An organization's articles or bylaws also may require this. States may provide that in lieu of a meeting, a measure may be adopted by written unanimous vote or consent.[39] State statutes may also provide that the certificate of incorporation or the bylaws can allow for a greater-than-majority vote even if it is more than the vote prescribed in the state statute.[40]

In general, state nonprofit statutes require a two-thirds vote to approve certain types of action such as the sale, lease or other disposition of assets not in the regular course of activities,[41] merger or consolidation,[42] and other significant corporate action.

As noted in Section 44, some statutes allow for an organization to petition the court for relief when a voting requirement is deemed unreasonable.[43] Equitable principles are involved and notice to the membership that the organization is seeking this kind of relief is essential.[44] A California trial court "reduced the percentage required to amend" a homeowner's association declaration of covenants, conditions, and restrictions from 67 percent to a majority of each voting class.[45]

Many parliamentary references consider that greater-than-majority voting, commonly two-thirds, three-fourths, or unanimous, generally violates the parliamentary concept of majority rule.[46] Any exception to majority rule must be specifically required by statute, the bylaws, the charter, or the procedural rules in the adopted parliamentary reference.[47] Special rules of the assembly or organization can also change the principle of majority rule.[48] The parliamentary references may have a different perspective on the benefits of majority rule, which they tend to favor, compared to certain greater-than-majority legal requirements.

There are a number of parliamentary motions which require a two-thirds vote. They are primarily those that affect member rights.[49] Disciplinary actions against an officer, board member or member also typically require a two-thirds vote.[50]

In governmental case opinions, a local government cannot require a greater-than-majority vote unless required by a state statute.[51] The requirement of a "super majority" vote to enact a zoning change was upheld in a New York case when there were protests from neighboring property owners.[52] An ordinance requiring a favorable vote of three members of a board to adopt a zoning change in a Wisconsin case did not need a unanimous vote by all three members, only two of the three.[53]

Housing associations run into controversies about greater-than-majority voting. The state statute governing the condominium or co-op voting must be carefully read to help make that determination. Unanimous consent has been required in some cases.[54] In a New York case, a two-thirds vote was required to terminate certain condominium and co-op contracts with the sponsors and developers of the project.[55]

Uncertainty similar to that on how to determine a majority vote, as cited in Section 44 above,[56] also arises with regard to how to calculate a two-thirds or higher vote.[57] For example, it can mean two-thirds or three-fourths of those who are present at a meeting[58] or it can mean all who are entitled to vote.[59] Abstentions are treated in the same way as with a majority vote. In one Ohio ruling, a unanimous vote requirement for a three-member township board of trustees required all three to vote in the same fashion, not just two trustees when only two trustees were present.[60]

§ 46 CUMULATIVE VOTING

Cumulative voting takes place when a voter has the right to concentrate all of his or her votes for one or some combination of those running for the same position. For example, if five people are running for five board positions, the voter can submit all five of his or her votes for one candidate.

State nonprofit statutes allow for cumulative voting if specifically authorized in the organization's certificate of incorporation or bylaws.[61] Under a state statute, a court in a California case mentioned that a nonprofit corporation offering legal services may not have proxy or cumulative voting.[62] In a California case, when a homeowner's association provided for cumulative voting for a board election, proxy voting was required.[63]

A condominium association in an Illinois case was under no obligation to explain cumulative voting to the voters when the association provided proxy forms to unit owners for board elections.[64] A legal challenge was made against a New York condominium association for amending its bylaws by eliminating cumulative voting for board members; it was asserted that the association must explain to voters the impact of the proposed change.[65]

RONR frowns on cumulative voting "since it violates the fundamental principle of parliamentary law that each member is entitled to one and only one vote on a question."[66] State statutes and case law in general express no similar reservations.

§ 47 PLURALITY VOTE

A plurality vote is the highest number of votes cast for a particular candidate or option when there are more than two choices. The highest vote getter is the winner when there are at least three choices.[67] The winning result may be less than a majority for the successful choice among all the votes cast. Thus, for example, if there are three candidates for an office and one receives 40 votes, one receives 35 votes, and the last receives 25 votes, under plurality voting the candidate who received the 40 votes is the winner even though he or she received less than a majority of the total.

To be valid, plurality voting requires authority from a statute, article of incorporation, bylaw,[68] or special rule of the organization before the vote is taken.[69] Otherwise, a majority vote is usually needed. Plurality voting, notwithstanding its lack of a required majority vote, greatly simplifies the election process since only one vote needs to be taken to obtain a result.

State statutes may provide for plurality election of board members, within each class, unless otherwise provided for in the certificate of incorporation or bylaws.[70] Under RONR, the bylaws must specify an election of officers by plurality vote in order for that vote to be valid.[71]

Ordinarily, a majority vote is required for election under general parliamentary principles. Riddick favors a majority vote to elect a candidate - although sometimes a plurality vote is used in mail balloting to save time and money.[72] Preferential voting is supported by RONR as a better method than a plurality vote to elect officers of an organization.[73]

§ 48 TIE VOTE

A tie vote usually means a motion is defeated.[74] This principle is supported by parliamentary references.[75] The presiding officer usually does not vote under the bylaws or adopted meeting rules. However, he or she can then vote affirmatively to break the tie[76] that would result in the motion passing. Similarly the presiding officer under most rules could defeat a motion which would otherwise pass by one vote by voting in the negative. This would then create a tie.[77]

There are mixed results on how a tie vote is treated at a governmental meeting or hearing. This may be influenced by how a motion is framed and relevant statutory wording. One Tennessee opinion not-ed the ambiguity in a zoning ordinance on how to treat a tie vote on an application and the resulting uncertainty.[78] A tie vote was deemed an affirmative vote in a Tennessee case.[79] More commonly a tie vote at a governmental meeting results in the defeat of the measure.

In a sample of other reported cases, a tie vote at a utility commis-sion meeting in a Pennsylvania case was deemed no action, jurisdic-tion of a matter was retained and the commission was not prohibited from acting again on the matter.[80] A tie vote before an administrative body also in Pennsylvania resulted in a denial of the requested relief and the status quo remained.[81] A provision in Maine allowing for a tie vote for municipal officers to be then decided by lot was invalidated.[82]

§ 49 CHANGING A VOTE

Any voter may change his or her vote prior to the time the presid-ing officer announces a result. After that point the result is final and a voter's attempt to revote is invalid.[83] This should be distinguished from a member calling for a new vote by the entire assembly. An ex-ception is if the entire assembly unanimously allows the member to change his vote.[84]

Any pertinent statute or ordinance must be followed. For exam-ple, in a New York case a utility stockholder had the right to change his vote before an announced result unless there was a controlling bylaw or other binding provision as to the closing of polls.[85]

Zoning boards have looked at this question. Decisions vary. In a Tennessee case, a member may change his vote when the board holds a subsequent meeting on an application because of a lack of overall votes at the prior meeting.[86] In a Connecticut case, a zoning board member could change his vote on an application at a new hearing; the prior hearing was invalid due to defective public notice.[87]

In a New York labor union case, members voting on a labor contract were given the opportunity to change their vote if there was no triable issue about whether the union's conduct was arbitrary, discriminatory, or in bad faith.[88] In a Mississippi local government case, an alderman could revote to correct a clerical or administrative error.[89]

§ 50 CHALLENGING THE VOTE (NOT ELECTIONS)

Any member of the assembly may challenge the validity of a vote.[90] This should be brought up immediately by raising a point of order[91] or similar objection. The chair may make a ruling or first consult the tellers, the credentials committee, or the assembly.[92] An appeal may be taken from the chair's ruling. The entire assembly may be asked to decide if a vote was proper. Members of the assembly can object to the count.[93] The credentials committee may be consulted.[94] In this writer's opinion, short of litigation the assembly holds the ultimate authority in deciding a challenge to a vote.

The reasons to challenge a vote are many. If the number of specific votes challenged would not affect the outcome, in this writer's opinion, such challenge is moot. Thus only a serious error which could affect a result would justify a challenge. In a Massachusetts case, a fax vote to amend the constitution of a college sports league was disallowed when an in-person meeting with notice was required.[95] Other challenges may relate to propriety of the proxy, whether a voter had a conflict of interest,[96] if a voter was not a suspended member,[97] or due to lack of a quorum.[98] A vote by a Florida homeowner's association to amend the declaration allowing for material changes to common elements was disallowed since owners had a vested right in the common elements.[99]

---

[1]   AMERICAN INSTITUTE OF PARLIAMENTARIANS, STANDARD CODE OF PARLIAMENTARY PROCEDURE 147 (2012) [hereinafter STANDARD CODE]; SARAH CORBIN ROBERT, HENRY M. ROBERT III, WILLIAM J. EVANS, DANIEL H. HONEMANN & THOMAS J. BALCH, ROBERT'S RULES OF ORDER NEWLY REVISED 3 (11th ed. 2011) [hereinafter ROBERT'S RULES].

By federal statute, "[e]very member of a labor union [has] equal rights . . . to vote . . . subject to reasonable rules and regulations in such organization's constitution and bylaws." Labor-Management Reporting and Disclosure Act (LMRDA) § 101(a)(1), 29 U.S.C.A. § 411(a)(1) (West 2013)); *see also* Sergeant v. Inlandboatmen's Union of the Pac., 346 F.3d 1196, 1200 (9th Cir. 2003) (citing LMRDA).

2 *E.g.*, Mich. Comp. Laws Ann. § 450.2441 (West 2013); Cal. Corp. Code § 5610 (West 2013 & Supp. 2014); 15 Pa. Stat. Ann. § 5758(a) (West 2013) (every member is entitled to one vote).

3 *E.g.*, N.J. Stat. Ann. § 15A:5-10 (West 2013 & Supp. 2014); 15 Pa. Stat. Ann. § 5729(a) (every director is entitled to one vote).

4 *E.g.*, 15 Pa. Stat. Ann. §§ 5729(a), 5758(a); N.Y. Not-for-Profit Corp. Law § 612 (McKinney 2013); N.J. Stat. Ann. § 15A:5-10; Cal. Corp. Code §§ 5132(c)(2), 5610. For example, under the New Jersey statute,

> The right of the members or classes of members to vote may be limited, enlarged or denied to the extent specified in the certificate of incorporation or bylaws. Unless so limited, enlarged or denied, each member, regardless of class, shall be entitled to one vote on each matter submitted to a vote of members.

N.J. Stat. Ann. § 15A:5-10.

5 Robert's Rules, *supra* note 1, at 3 ("No member can be individually deprived of these basic rights of membership [to vote] . . . . Some organized societies define additional classes of 'membership' that do not entail all of these rights.").

6 *In re* Religious Corps. & Ass'n, No. 206610/2003, 2003 WL 23329273, at *8 (N.Y. Sup. Ct. Sept. 10, 2003). However, most states are now allowing for telephone conference call meetings.

7 At the time of this writing, unlike California, New Jersey and New York do not specifically authorize electronic voting, but this is subject to legislative change. Pennsylvania's statute was recently amended from allowing participation "by means of conference telephone or similar communications equipment" to "by means of conference telephone or other electronic technology" effective September 9, 2013. 2013 Pa. Legis. Serv. Act 2013-67, § 35 (West) (amending 15 Pa. Stat. Ann. § 5708(a)).

8 Baywood Country Club v. Estep, 929 S.W.2d 532, 534 (Tex. Ct. App. 1996).

9 Sergeant v. Inlandboatmen's Union of the Pac., 346 F.3d 1196, 1203 (9th Cir. 2003).

10 Kelso Woods Ass'n v. Swanson, 753 A.2d 894, 901-02 (Pa. Commw. Ct. 2000).

11 Robert's Rules, *supra* note 1, at 407; George Demeter, Demeter's Manual of Parliamentary Law and Procedure 37, 209 (2001).
    The difference between abstaining and recusing from voting was of "no direct concern" to the court in *Town of Sykesville v. West Shore Communications, Inc.*, 677 A.2d 102, 109 (Md. Ct. Spec. App. 1995) ("Mercifully, we have no direct concern with the Byzantine subtleties between abstaining and recusing oneself in response to an ethical dilemma, an exotic problem which, to our knowledge, has not been remotely alluded to in the Maryland case law.").

12 Floyd M. Riddick & Miriam H. Butcher, Riddick's Rules of Procedure: A Modern Guide to Faster and More Efficient Meetings 208 (1985); Demeter, *supra* note 11, at 37.

13 *See, e.g.*, Riddick & Butcher, *supra* note 12, at 198; Robert's Rules, *supra* note 1, at 406; *see also* Chimney Ville Missionary Baptist Church of Garland v. Johnson, 95-819, p. 7 (La. App. 3 Cir. 12/6/95); 665 So. 2d 730, 733 (finding a failure to pay church tithing eliminated the right to vote as a member of a church, but not as a board member); Gordon Props., LLC v. First Owners' Ass'n (*In re* Gordon Props., LLC), 435 B.R. 326, 331 (Bankr. E.D. Va. 2010) (demonstrating a condominium unit owner had a right to vote even if in arrears on condominium fees).

14 Hy Farwell, *Voting—A Right or a Privilege*, Parliamentary J., Vol. XXXIX, No. 1, Jan. 1998. However an adverse final decision for suspension or termination of membership seems more appropriate.

15 N.Y. Not-for-Profit Corp. Law § 607.

16 *E.g.*, Mich. Comp. Laws Ann. § 450.2413. Moreover, if the meeting is held by remote communication, "the information required to access the list shall be provided with the notice of the meeting." *Id.* § 450.2413(1)(c).

17 *E.g.*, Baring v. Watergate E., Inc., No. Civ.A. 192-N, 2004 WL 418007, at *2 (Del. Ch. Feb. 25, 2004).

18 *E.g.*, Baldwin Cnty. Elec. Membership Corp. v. Catrett, 942 So. 2d 337, 346 (Ala. 2006).

19 Baring v. Condrell, No. Civ.A. 516-N, 2004 WL 2340047, *4 (Del Ch. Oct. 18, 2004); *see also* City of Pineville v. Am. Fed'n of State, Cnty. & Mun. Emps., 2000-1983, p. 5 (La. 6/29/01); 791 So.2d 609, 613 (finding a mayor had no right to cast a deciding vote on a resolution at a city council meeting when the tie vote included an abstention causing the tie).
    A court lacked jurisdiction to consider the denial of a woman's right to vote under the bylaws since it was deemed to require consideration of a religious belief, doctrine, custom and practice. Srour v. Bd. of Trs. of the Sephardic Congregation of Har Ha Lebanon, Inc., No. 7044/02, 2004 WL 1261467, *4 (N.Y. Sup. Ct. June 3, 2004).

20 Green Gables Home Owners Ass'n v. Sunlite Homes, 202 P.2d 143, 147 (Cal. Dist. Ct. App. 1949).

21 Standard Code, *supra* note 1, at 135.

22 *E.g.*, Robert's Rules, *supra* note 1, at 4; Demeter, *supra* note 11, at 246.

23 *E.g.*, N.J. Stat. Ann. § 15A:5-11.a; Cal. Corp. Code § 5512(c) (allowing for a vote of a greater number than a majority under certain circumstances); 15 Pa. Stat. Ann. § 5757(a); N.Y. Not-for-Profit Corp. Law § 613(b).

24 *See infra* notes 40-41 and accompanying text.

25 See Standard Code, *supra* note 1, at 135-36, for a discussion on the significance of majority vote and Robert's Rules, *supra* note 1, at 4, for a summary of the exceptions to the rule calling for a majority.

26 Lee-Davis v. Dauphin Surf Club Ass'n, 581 So. 2d 1110, 1112, (Ala. Civ. App. 1991). The court cited a Florida appellate court case which stated "the rule of reasonableness [is] the

touchstone by which the validity of a condominium association's actions should be measured." Hidden Harbour Estates, Inc. v. Basso, 393 So. 2d 637, 639 (Fla. Dist. Ct. App. 1981).

"Absent some indication to the contrary, majority rule is generally employed in the governance of religious societies." Apostolic New Life Church of Elgin v. Dominquez, 686 N.E.2d 1187, 1194 (Ill. App. Ct. 1997) (citing Jones v. Wolf, 443 U.S. 595 (1979)).

27   Lain v. Credit Bureau of Baton Rouge, Inc., 637 So. 2d 1080, 1085 (La. Ct. App. 1994) (finding a lack of notice of the proposed bylaw amendments and noting in passing that under Louisiana state law, a two-thirds vote of the members present is required for passage if the articles are silent on the method of amendment).

28   See, e.g., Blue Lagoon Cmty. Ass'n v. Mitchell, 64 Cal. Rptr. 2d 81, 84 (Ct. App. 1997) ("[T]he purpose of section 1356 [California Civil Code] is to give a property owner's association the ability to amend its governing documents when, because of voter apathy or other reasons, important amendments cannot be approved by the normal procedures authorized by the declaration."). However, in Blue Lagoon, a petition seeking a reduction to amend the governing document from 75 percent of the voters (weighted) to a majority of voters was rejected by the trial court as "unreasonable." Id. at 83.

29   Lorenzo R. Cuesta, Four Unfortunate Misconceptions Promoted by Members, NAT'L PARLIAMENTARIAN, Vol. 72, No. 4, Fourth Quarter 2011 (citing Henry M. Robert, PARLIAMENTARY LAW 452 (Irvington Publishers 1991) (1923)).

30   DEMETER, supra note 11, at 246 ("A majority vote means more than half of the votes cast at a legal meeting with a quorum."); HUGH CANNON, CANNON'S CONCISE GUIDE TO RULES OF ORDER 123 (2001).

For additional complexities for determining whether there was a majority, see Robert M. Peskin, When a Majority Is Not So Simple, PARLIAMENTARY J., Vol. XXXVII, No. 1, Jan. 1996.

31   STANDARD CODE, supra note 1, at 138-40; DEMETER, supra note 11, at 35-36; ROBERT'S RULES, supra note 1, at 400-04.

32   Brown Charter Sch. v. Harrisburg City Sch. Dist., 928 A.2d 1145, 1149-50 (Pa. Commw. Ct. 2007). For an excellent overall discussion, see Dwayne S. Roberts, Determining the Count of the Entire Membership of Fixed-Sized Groups, NAT'L PARLIAMENTARIAN, Vol. 58, Fourth Quarter 1997.

33   State ex rel. Keyes v. Ohio Pub. Emps. Ret. Sys., 123 Ohio St. 3d 913, 2009-Ohio-4052, 913 N.E.2d 972, at ¶ 18; see also CAL. CORP. CODE § 5211(a)(4) (when voting to adjourn a meeting).

34   Diamond v. United Food & Commercial Workers Union Local 881, 768 N.E.2d 865, 868 (Ill. App. Ct. 2002); Lake Cnty. Sheriff's Merit Bd. v. Buncich, 869 N.E.2d 482, 486 (Ind. Ct. App. 2007) (citing IND. CODE § 36-8-10-3(b)).

35   See, e.g., Moriarty v. Mt. Diablo Health Care Dist., No. A112499, 2007 WL 3194805, at *5 (Cal. Ct. App. Oct. 31, 2007).

36   Cnty. of Kankakee v. Anthony, 710 N.E.2d 1242, 1246 (Ill. App. Ct. 1999).

37   Id. at 1246-47.

38   *Id.; see also* Smith-Groh, Inc. v. Planning & Zoning Comm'n, 826 A.2d 249, 256 (Conn. App. Ct. 2003) (finding an abstention did not count as a vote for approval and a 2 - 2 tie vote resulted in a denial of a zoning change).

39   *E.g.*, CAL. CORP. CODE § 5211(b); N.J. STAT. ANN. § 15A: 5-6.a. New York passed the Non-Profit Revitalization Act of 2013, which allows "the consent [to] be sent by electronic mail" if "submitted with, information from which it can reasonably be determined that the transmission was authorized by the member." N.Y. NOT-FOR-PROFIT CORP. LAW § 614(a), *amended by* The Non-Profit Revitalization Act of 2013, 2013 N.Y. Sess. Laws ch. 549, § 65 (McKinney) (effective July 1, 2014).

40   *E.g.*, CAL. CORP. CODE §§ 5152(e), 5034; N.J. STAT. ANN. § 15A:5-12.a; 15 PA. STAT. ANN. § 5757(b); N.Y. NOT-FOR-PROFIT CORP. LAW § 615(a)(2); *see also* ALICE STURGIS, THE STANDARD CODE OF PARLIAMENTARY PROCEDURE 131-32 (4th ed., rev. 2001).
     However, under 15 PA. STAT. ANN. § 5757(6) [and perhaps others] the percentage of members needed to call a special meeting of members or for a petition to amend the articles cannot be increased from that required by the statute.

41   *E.g.*, N.J. STAT. ANN. § 15A:10-11.a; 15 PA. STAT. ANN. § 5546 (purchasing or selling real estate requires a two-thirds vote of the board but only a majority if there are 21 or more directors).

42   *E.g.*, N.Y. NOT-FOR-PROFIT CORP. LAW § 903(a)(2); N.J. STAT. ANN. § 15A:10-4.6. Other commonly required two-thirds votes are for dissolution of a corporation and amending the articles of incorporation. Each state statute must be carefully read to determine if the members must approve of an action and what size vote is required.

43   *See supra* note 27 and accompanying text; *see also* Peak Invs. v. S. Peak Homeowners Ass'n, 44 Cal. Rptr. 3d 892, 896 (Ct. App. 2006).

44   *See, e.g.*, CAL. CIV. CODE § 1356(c)(1) (requiring petitioner to give "not less than 15 days written notice of the court hearing to all members of the association," make "[a] reasonably diligent effort . . . to permit all eligible members to vote on the proposed amendment," and for the amendment to be "reasonable").

45   *See* Mission Shores Ass'n v. Pheil, 83 Cal. Rptr. 3d 108, 112 (Ct. App. 2008) (affirming the decision of the trial court).

46   *E.g.*, STANDARD CODE, *supra* note 1, at 135; ROBERT'S RULES, *supra* note 1, at 4; RIDDICK & BUTCHER, *supra* note 12, at 207 ("Any vote requirement that is greater than a majority is inconsistent with the concept that a majority decides.").

47   STANDARD CODE, *supra* note 1, at 36. Standing or special rules of order may also "require more than a majority vote." *Id.*

48   See ROBERT'S RULES, *supra* note 1, at 4, for three listed exceptions to the principle requiring a majority vote. Briefly, more than a majority vote arises where it is required by law, provided by a special rule of an organization, or when required due to a general parliamentary law that compromises certain member rights.

49   For example, a two-thirds vote is needed to amend an approved agenda; close nominations, limit or extend limits of debate and often to amend bylaws. For an excellent list of actions requiring a two-thirds vote, see ROBERT'S RULES, *supra* note 1, at 44-45 and DEMETER, *supra* note 11, at 174.

50   A Rhode Island court found that, a two-thirds vote was required to remove a member from an assembly. Foster Glocester Reg'l Sch. Bldg. Comm. v. Sette, No. PC/07-6060, 2008 WL 693613 (R.I. Super. Ct. Jan. 16, 2008) ("A member of an organization may be expelled by a two-thirds vote of its membership." (citing ROBERT'S RULES OF ORDER 640 (10th ed.))), aff'd in part, vacated in part 996 A.2d 1120 (R.I. 2010).

51   See, e.g., Ind. Land Co., v. City of Greenwood, 378 F.3d 705, 711 (7th Cir. 2004) (finding that a city council's application of an ordinance requiring a two-thirds vote for approval may have violated state law requiring only a majority vote). Despite finding the ordinance in violation of the state statute, the court in Indiana Land Co. found against appellants because they chose not to seek declaratory relief and only later challenged the application of the ordinance on due process grounds. Id. at 712.

52   See, e.g., Eadie v. Town Bd. 854 N.E.2d 464, 46-68 (N.Y. 2006) (finding that a town law requiring zoning regulations to be approved by a three-fourths vote when owners of twenty percent or more of land within 100 feet of proposed change file a written protest did not apply); Ryan Homes, Inc. v. Town Bd., 791 N.Y.S. 355, 358 (2005) (finding town law requiring three-fourths vote if a written protest is presented by owners of twenty percent or more of land directly opposite a proposal did not apply because property was separated by a large highway); Whitaker v. City of Springfield, 889 S.W.2d 869, 871-72 (Mo. Ct. App. 1994) (finding local ordinance requiring three-fifths vote for zoning change at protest of owners of ten percent or more of adjacent property conflicted with state statute and thus was inapplicable).

53   Greatwood Log Homes, Inc. v. Town Bd., No. 93-3134, 1994 WL 551547, at *5-6 (Wis. Ct. App. Oct. 12, 1994).

54   See, e.g., Sisto v. Am. Condo. Ass'n, 68 A.3d 603 (R.I. 2013) (finding that under the Rhode Island's Condominium Act unanimous consent of all other unit owners was required for owner to change boundary of unit) (citing R.I. GEN. LAWS 34-36.1-2.17(d) (2013)); Bogomolov v. Lake Villas Condo. Ass'n of Apt. Owners, 127 P.3d 762, 771 (Wash. Ct. App. 2006) (requiring unanimous consent under condominium association's declaration because of a change in value of units).

In 1998, the Louisiana Supreme Court found that "[a]mend[ing] existing building restrictions to make them more restrictive" [requires] "unanimous consent of all lot owners." Brier Lake, Inc., v. Jones, 710 So. 2d 1054, 1054 (La. 1998). However, following this decision the Louisiana state legislature enacted Act 309 of 1999, specifically overruling the court's decision in Brier Lake. 1999 La. Sess. Law Serv. 309 (West) (codified as amended LA. CIV. CODE ANN. arts. 776, 780, & 783 (2013)). For a detailed discussion of the Brier Lake decision and subsequent legislation, see James Slaton, Comment, Storming the Castle: Surrendering the Sanctity of the Home to the Will of the Masses—Amending Building Restrictions Under 1999 La. Acts 309, 60 LA. L. REV. 909 (2000).

55   Bleecker Charles Co. v. 350 Bleecker Street Apt. Corp., 327 F.3d 197, 199 (2d Cir. 2003) (referring to the Condominium and Cooperative Conversion Protection and Abuse Act, 15 U.S.C. §§ 3601-16) (decided on other grounds).

56   See supra notes 29-37 and accompanying text.

57   It is essential that precise language be used to avoid ambiguity. See ROBERT'S RULES, supra note 1, at 400-06 or DEMETER, supra note 11, at 35-36, for an excellent guide.

58   For example, in a Nebraska case a three-quarters vote to amend a declaration meant three-quarters of those who chose to vote. Regency Homes Ass'n v. Schrier, 759 N.W.2d 484,

489 (Neb. 2009). *See also* Massaro v. Mainlands Section 1 & 2 Civic Ass'n, 796 F. Supp. 1499, 1504 (S.D. Fla. 1992) (allowing bylaws to be altered by a two-thirds vote of "those members that are present"), *rev'd on other grounds by* 3 F.3d 1472 (11th Cir. 1993).

59   For example, a two-thirds vote of all lot owners was required to amend a building restriction declaration in *McGinty v. Majeste*, 98-30384, p. 3 (La. App. 2 Cir. 4/8/98); 711 So. 2d 333, 334.

60   Black v. Bd. of Mecca Twp. Trs., 2005-Ohio-561.

61   *E.g.*, Cal. Corp. Code § 5616(a); N.J. Stat. Ann. § 15A:5-20.c; N.Y. Not-for-Profit Corp. Law § 617; 15 Pa. Stat. Ann. § 5758(c); Mich. Comp. Laws Ann. § 450.2451; *see also* Assalita v. Chestnut Ridge Homeowners Ass'n, 866 A.2d 1214, 1220 n.17 (Pa. Commw. Ct. 2005) (noting election of directors by cumulative voting in the bylaws is authorized by Pennsylvania statute). In California, a voter must give notice of his intention to cumulate votes. Cal. Corp. Code § 5616(b).

Similarly, parliamentary references provide that cumulative voting is only allowed if specifically permitted by the bylaws. *E.g.*, Riddick & Butcher, *supra* note 12, at 200; Sturgis, *supra* note 40, at 246. Under 15 Pa. Stat. Ann. § 5758(c),

> If a bylaw adopted by the members so provides, in each election of directors of a nonprofit corporation every member entitled to vote shall have the right to multiply the number of votes to which he may be entitled by the total number of directors to be elected in the same election by the members or the class of members to which he belongs, and he may cast the whole number of his votes for one candidate or he may distribute them among any two or more candidate.

In *McSweeney v. City of Cambridge*, 665 N.E.2d 11, 13 (Mass. 1996), cumulative voting was noted as one approved method of filling a vacancy on a city council. The court refers to one variation on "cumulative voting used in selection of some corporate boards of directors in which each elector has as many votes as there are places to be filled and may cast one or more of them for the same candidate, the candidates with the largest number of votes being selected." *Id.* (citing L. Guinier, The Tyranny of the Majority 14-16 (1994)). Cumulative voting was defined by one cooperative apartment housing corporation bylaws as follows: "[E]ach shareholder is entitled to cast as many votes as the shares she owns multiplied by the number of directors to be elected. Each shareholder has the right to cast his or her shares of votes for a single candidate or to distribute them among the number of candidates." Lindkvist v. Honest Ballot Ass'n, No. 113590/2010, 2011 WL 2162806, at *2 (N.Y. Sup. Ct. May 24, 2011).

62   Gafcon, Inc. v. Ponsor & Assocs., 120 Cal. Rptr. 2d 392, 408 n.10 (Ct. App. 2002) (citing Cal. Corp. Code § 10830(c)).

63   Chantiles v. Lake Forest II Master Homeowners Ass'n, 45 Cal. Rptr. 2d 1, 6 (Ct. App. 1995) (citing Cal. Corp. Code §§ 7513(e), 7615).

64   Adams v. Meyers, 620 N.E.2d 1298, 1306-07 (Ill. App. Ct. 1993) (finding the association was "under no obligation to provide a detailed explanation of cumulative voting" under the Illinois Condominium Act) (citing current 765 Ill. Comp. Stat. 605/18 (2013)).

65   Bretton Woods Condo. I v. Bretton Woods Homeowners Ass'n, No 09-36820, 2010 WL 4383411, at *4-5 (N.Y. Sup. Ct. Oct. 25, 2010).

66   Robert's Rules, *supra* note 1, at 444.

67   For a good discussion, see *Brown Charter School v. Harrisburg City School District*, 928 A.2d 1145 (Pa. Commw. Ct. 2007).

68   DEMETER, *supra* note 11, at 246.

69   RIDDICK & BUTCHER, *supra* note 12, at 140.

70   *E.g.*, 15 PA. STAT. ANN. § 5758(b); N.J. STAT. ANN. § 15A: 5-20.d; N.Y. NOT-FOR-PROFIT CORP. LAW § 616 (allowing for plurality voting of board members where voting as a class is provided in the certificate of incorporation or the bylaws).

71   ROBERT'S RULES, *supra* note 1, at 405.

72   RIDDICK & BUTCHER, *supra* note 12, at 140. STURGIS, *supra* note 40, at 135, also contends that a plurality vote in an election is usually inadvisable because a candidate with a minority viewpoint might get elected.

73   ROBERT'S RULES, *supra* note 1, at 405.

74   *See* Hirschfield v. Bd. of Cnty. Comm'rs, 944 P.2d 1139, 1145 (Wyo. 1997); Smith-Groh, Inc. v. Planning & Zoning Comm'n, 826 A.2d 249, 256 (2003) (finding a tie vote rejected a zoning application). A tie vote defeats a motion except in the case of an appeal from a decision of the chair, in which case it supports the decision. CANNON, *supra* note 30, at 7; DEMETER, *supra* note 11, at 35; STURGIS, *supra* note 40, at 136-37.

75   *E.g.*, ROBERT'S RULES, *supra* note 1, at 405; STURGIS, *supra* note 40, at 136-37; CANNON, *supra* note 30, at 7.

76   *E.g.*, ROBERT'S RULES, *supra* note 1, at 405; RIDDICK & BUTCHER, *supra* note 12, at 204; *see also* Cerjack v. Bridgewater Borough, 835 A.2d 845, 848 (Pa. Commw. Ct. 2003) (stating a mayor was authorized to vote and thus break a tie vote to fill a vacancy on a borough council). *But see* City of Pineville v. Am. Fed'n of State, Cnty. & Mun. Emps., 2000-1983, p. 5 (La. 6/29/01); 791 So.2d 609, 613 (finding the mayor could "only vote on resolutions if there is an equal division of board members *present*" and thus could not vote when two members approved, two denied, and one abstained).

77   RIDDICK & BUTCHER, *supra* note 12, at 204.

78   Consolidated Waste Systems, LLC v. Solid Waste Region Bd., No. M2002-00560-COA-R3-CV, 2003 WL 21957137, at *6-7 (Tenn. Ct. App. Jul. 02, 2003).

79   *Id.* at 7.

80   Energy Pipeline Co. v. Pa. Pub. Utility Comm'n, 662 A.2d 641, 643-44 (Pa. 1995).

81   Riverwalk Casino v. Pa. Gaming Control Bd., 926 A.2d 926, 940-41 (Pa. 2007).

82   Sch. Comm. v. Town of York, 626 A.2d 935, 945 n.21 (Me. 1993) (finding that Maine statute required tie votes to be resolved by ballot (citing ME. REV. STAT. tit. 30, § 2528 (1993))).

83   ROBERT'S RULES, *supra* note 1, at 408; RIDDICK & BUTCHER, *supra* note 12, at 208. Under Sturgis, a member can only change a roll call vote if a recording error was made. STURGIS, *supra* note 40, at 149.

84 ROBERT'S RULES, *supra* note 1, at 408.

85 Smith v. Orange & Rockland Utils., Inc., 617 N.Y.S.2d 278, 280 (Sup. Ct. 1994) (citing Salgo v. Matthews, 497 S.W.2d 620 (Tex. Ct. App. 1973)).

86 *See* Lions Head Homeowners' Ass'n v. Metro. Bd. of Zoning Appeals, 968 S.W.2d 296, 302 (Tenn. Ct. App. 1997).

87 Hallier v. Zoning Bd. of Appeals, No. CV054008492S, 2006 WL 280418, at *4 (Conn. Super. Ct. Jan. 11, 2006).

88 Marcoux v. American Airlines, Inc., 645 F. Supp. 2d 68, 97 (E.D.N.Y. 2008).

89 Bridge v. Mayor & Bd. of Alderman, 995 So. 2d 81, 84-85 (Miss. 2008). In *Bridge*, city council members were able to revote to correct an administrative mistake; they could not revote to correct an error of judgment. *Id.*; *see also* Strawn v. City of Albany, Luba No. 90-169, at *9 (Or. Land Use Bd. App. May 13, 1991), http://www.oregon.gov/LUBA/docs/Opinions/1991/05-91/90169.pdf (finding city council could change vote on zoning application after remand by land use board of appeals).

90 RIDDICK & BUTCHER, *supra* note 12, at 205.

91 ROBERT'S RULES, *supra* note 1, at 250-51.

92 RIDDICK & BUTCHER, *supra* note 12, at 205.

93 DEMETER, *Supra* note 11, AT 138.

94 See CANNON, *supra* note 30, at 91-93, for the role of the credentials committee in determining the status of attendees.

95 Trs. of Boston Coll. v. Big East Conference, 18 Mass. L. Rptr. 177 (Super. Ct. 2004). A vote to quickly adjourn an annual meeting sine die without giving a shareholder of a condominium association the opportunity to be recognized to move to adjourn to a set time was improper. Gordon Props., LLC v. First Owners' Ass'n (*In re* Gordon Properties LLC), 435 B.R. 326, 334-37 (Bankr. E.D. Va. 2010) (decided on other grounds).

96 ROBERT'S RULES, *supra* note 1, at 407. RONR states that a member with a conflict of interest cannot be forced not to vote. *Id.* However, state laws prescribe limits and conditions of such voting and the Internal Revenue Service also frowns on such conflict of interest voting by nonprofit board members. For example, under 15 PA. STAT. ANN. § 5828 there are various conditions and limitations for a member who votes on a contract or transaction between him/herself and a non-profit corporation.

97 RIDDICK & BUTCHER, *supra* note 12, at 208.

98 A majority vote to approve a policy was determined to be a majority of the entire board even if two members present recused themselves because of a conflict. Alvarez Family Trust v. Ass'n of Owners, 221 P.3d 452, 462 (Haw. 2009).

99 Wellington Prop. Mgmt. v. Parc Corniche Condo. Ass'n, 755 So. 2d 824, 827-28 (Fla. Dist. Ct. App. 2000).

CHAPTER 9

Voting Methods

§ 51 VOTING METHODS (GENERALLY)

There are many methods by which the chair can determine the winning side of a vote on a motion. These include voice vote, rising (standing) vote, by hand, roll call, ballot, and more recently, electronically. "A 'vote' can be expressed 'by ballot, show of hands, or other types of communication. '"[1] The object, of course, is to obtain an accurate count.

Statutes and bylaw provisions must be followed.[2] Email and other forms of electronic voting are now becoming established both by statute[3] and in actual practice. It has been held "that the use of computers for voting and tallying the results is the functional equivalent of a 'writing.'"[4] However, organizations should exercise caution regarding the use of electronic voting since some state statutes have not kept pace with current technology.[5]

The chair has considerable discretion at arriving at an accurate vote - subject to the concerns of the attendees. If he or she is not sure about the results of a voice vote, he can ask for a show of hands, rising vote, or counted vote. However, a combination of voting methods at the same time can result in a chaotic situation and should be discouraged.[6] Although some larger groups use on-site voting devices to calculate a vote a manual backup plan should be ready in the event of technical difficulties.

A Nebraska court ruled that a vote at a church meeting was effective even when the voters expressed their will in an unconventional fashion.[7] Associations may provide for various voting methods in their bylaws, but must comply with the state statute concerning how to obtain a required percentage vote.[8]

A method of voting may be proposed as an incidental motion while the underlying subject is being considered or as a main motion while no other business is pending. The motion must be seconded, is not debatable, is amendable, cannot interrupt another speaker, and requires a majority vote.[9]

§ 52 VOICE VOTE

Voting on a motion or election[10] by voice vote (also called "viva-voce") is most commonly used at meetings.[11] Those in favor of a motion are first asked to say "aye" or "yes." Those opposed are then asked to say "no" or "nae."[12] Abstentions are not requested by the chair.

The chair can ask for a show of hands but when this produces uncertainty about the outcome, he or she should call for a rising (standing) vote. If a member doubts the correctness of the stated result, he can promptly call for a division and a rising vote must be taken.[13] A request for a division must be honored and does not require a second.[14]

A voice vote most often is used when no more than a majority vote is needed.[15] The outcome of a voice vote may be subject to dispute.[16] This is the least precise method of voting and should not be used when the result of the vote is expected to be close.[17] However, when an item is routine and the voice vote produces an overwhelming vote for one side of a question or the other, voice votes are commonly used even if a two-thirds or greater vote is required.

It should be noted that at governmental meetings use of voice votes is subject to statutory law and may be restricted. For example, in a Tennessee case a board of zoning appeals was required to maintain a public record of their meetings including how individual members voted.[18] An Ohio court mentioned that a voice vote may be invalid when a roll call vote is required by statute.[19] State open meeting statutes provide that if a governmental vote is to go into executive session it [the vote] should be recorded.[20] In this situation - an unrecorded voice vote should be avoided.[21]

§ 53 GENERAL CONSENT

General consent, also called unanimous consent, is used by the presiding officer during a formal business meeting for non-controversial decisions and for decisions in which every attendee is in agreement. With regard to a particular action or item of business, when requesting unanimous consent, the chair first asks if any member has an objection to approving or taking an action. After a pause, if no one objects, the presiding officer may assume that the routine motion or other noncontroversial action is adopted.[22] Thus no formal vote is taken.

This device is thought to save time and expedite the business of a meeting.[23] In a Wyoming case minor violations of parliamentary procedure are excused.[24] If even one person expresses concern or objection, the matter must then be handled like any other motion.[25]

Unanimous consent should not be overused by the chair of a meeting. Thus a member should not be discouraged from seeking to remove an item from unanimous consent. In a California case, a claim of unanimous consent was rejected when a list of nominees was offered by a nominating committee.[26] In a New York case, unanimous consent was used when a two-thirds vote for discipline was required.[27] In this writer's opinion, good practice calls for a vote on disciplinary decisions. If much hinges on an outcome, a full vote should be taken and unanimous consent avoided.[28]

Another similar technique to save time is the grouping of various noncontroversial voting items of business as a bloc near the beginning of an agenda. This is called a consent agenda. The items for consideration are lumped together and voted on all at one time without debate.[29] However, if even one attendee states an objection or wishes to discuss or vote separately on an item, that item must be taken off the consent agenda and individually handled like any other motion outside the consent agenda. This method of consent should never be abused. Members should be informed that any one person can move a consent item off of the list by request.

§ 54 SHOW OF HANDS

A commonly accepted method to count votes is a show of hands,[30] also called a hand vote.[31] It is commonly used by smaller groups such as "boards, committees and small assemblies" but can also be used in larger ones.[32] The goal is to use a show of hands when it results in an accurate count and complies with any applicable statutory or organizational authority.

In an Ohio case, the court mentioned the use of a show of hands when deciding an appeal from a decision of the state retirement system board.[33] However, a show of hands in California was ruled in violation of voters' expectation of privacy when it was proposed for election of candidates at a homeowners' association meeting.[34] A show of hands was deemed an acceptable substitute for a voice vote in a city council meeting in Alabama.[35]

A labor union used a show of hands in a group of 2000 members to determine a majority vote to authorize a strike.[36]

The rule of law rather than a show of hands was sarcastically distinguished in a dissenting opinion by Justice Scalia of the U.S. Supreme Court.[37]

§ 55 ROLL CALL VOTE

In a roll call vote, when there is a proposal on the floor, each member's name is called out and the member verbally casts his or her vote.[38]

A roll call vote may be adopted in the bylaws, or by a motion of the members.[39] The names of voters are called in alphabetical or other appropriate order with the presiding officer being called last.[40] An answering member votes aye, no, or by abstaining by saying present or here.[41] Roll call voting as a practical matter is often used in meetings conducted by telephone but the way each individual voted is not necessarily recorded in the minutes since the vote is not treated as traditional roll call voting.

A motion to take a roll call vote requires a second,[42] is not debatable, is amendable,[43] needs a majority vote, and cannot interrupt a speaker. It is an incidental main motion or an incidental motion.[44] A majority vote is needed to have a vote taken by roll call.[45] The way each person voted in a formal roll call vote is recorded in the minutes.

Roll call voting is most common when others are being represented such as at governmental meetings.[46] An Ohio court noted that constituents are entitled to know how their representatives voted.[47] It is thought by some that the public is only entitled to know how individual members voted at a public meeting if a roll call vote is required.[48] It was held in Virginia that the failure to record in the minutes how each individual voted regarding a town zoning ordinance when a roll call vote was required rendered the ordinance invalid.[49]

Roll call voting is a staple of state open meeting laws. Of course, the applicable statute must be followed. In a Michigan case, a roll call vote (two-thirds) was required for a township board to go into executive session. This type of vote must be entered into the minutes.[50] An Ohio court noted that voice acclamation to vote to go into executive session by a city council would be a violation of the state sunshine law.[51]

In a Georgia case, under the state open meetings act, a city council item concerning amending public comment procedures required public disclosure of how members voted.[52] And, after an executive session took place, under the California sunshine law and a city sunshine ordinance, it was decided that a library commission's roll call vote announcing a candidate's actual appointment must be publicly reported.[53]

§ 56 BALLOT VOTE

Ballot vote is a method by which a voter casts a vote on paper without publically revealing his or her position. When secrecy is desired or required a ballot vote is used.[54] Voting in secret is considered a fundamental parliamentary right and an organization should have in place procedures through which the organization can implement them. A California court noted that a voter casting a ballot for a condominium board member had the right of privacy for his ballot vote which was greater than a board member's right of inspection of corporate records.[55]

Typically, state nonprofit statutes provide that the articles or bylaws can allow for voting on any matter by ballot.[56] Under the California Nonprofit Corporation Law, any action that can be taken at a regular or special meeting of members may use a written ballot.[57]

Unless the bylaws provide otherwise, a requirement for secret ballot cannot be waived or suspended[58] - even unanimously.[59] The presiding officer who otherwise might not vote can vote by secret

ballot because the use of a secret ballot by the presiding officer protects his or her public neutrality.

Certain situations lend themselves to or require a secret ballot.[60]
Sometimes a vote by secret ballot is preferred so that voters can better
vote their true beliefs.[61] Contested elections usually require a ballot
vote.[62] In a federal California case, a secret ballot was not required to
raise union dues.[63] Discipline of a member of an organization is typically voted on by a secret ballet.[64] Under the rules of an international
labor union, it was decided that a final settlement offer had to be
submitted to the membership for a secret ballot vote.[65]

Other situations do not require a ballot or are optional. For example, in one case a secret ballot was not required for an international labor organization to decide on a special assessment.[66] It was
decided that a town meeting in Maine could use secret ballot voting
in lieu of another procedure recommended by a state statute.[67]

If a vote by ballot is not already required by the bylaws, it can be
so moved by a member and ordered by the assembly.[68] This motion
takes a majority vote.[69] In a New York case, it was decided that when
a union membership vote is by secret ballot, anyone can move for
reconsideration of the vote.[70] Since it could not be determined with
a secret ballot how someone voted, anyone could move for reconsideration and not have to be on the winning side of the underlying
motion.

There are numerous detailed rules on how a ballot vote is to be
counted and reported, either by mail or in person. For example, a
name could be misspelled or too many candidates checked off. All
of the rule books referenced in this text offer excellent guidelines on
what to do with questionable ballots. The object is to assure the accuracy of the count and security of the vote.[71]

The combining of ballot votes with other kinds of voting should
be discouraged.[72] A Utah court decided that a mail-in ballot of a

condominium association had to be unanimous to be valid under that state's nonprofit corporation act.[73]

Bullet voting is when a voter can mark his or her ballot with less votes than the maximum allowed. For example, there may be six nominees for four positions and the voter only votes for three. This is normally permissible unless there is a specific rule to the contrary.

§ 57 MAIL VOTE

Mail balloting is commonly used by national and international organizations since membership is usually geographically scattered. State statutes allow for mail balloting of elections[74] and in other matters.[75] Under the California statute, a ballot may be sent by electronic transmission[76] and quorum equivalencies must be met.[77] Clearly, electronic voting is beginning to supplant mail voting but the authority of an organization to do so must be individually determined.

The bylaws must authorize mail voting.[78] It is usually reserved for significant matters such as bylaw amendments,[79] election of officers,[80] and important questions.[81] Some bylaws wisely allow for the use of mail balloting when an in-person meeting is cancelled or cannot complete its business.

Some voting, especially during elections, is secretive and provision should be made to keep the voter's selections confidential. The ballot must be marked, signed and returned as instructed by the required date.[82] Details such as whether or not to use postmark dates should be planned to avoid snafus. In a California case, only valid, official, signed ballots were counted in a taxpayer vote to a governmental authority.[83] Plurality voting to determine an outcome is common with mail balloting (to avoid the need for a second vote) although preferential voting is sometimes used in its place.

The use of mail balloting by labor unions has been a matter of controversy.[84] A mail ballot by a community association in Pennsylvania for a special assessment was found to be lawful and consistent with the bylaws.[85] There is a belief by some that broader membership participation is obtained through the use of mail balloting as compared to in-person voting.

Elections by mail ballot sometimes result in controversy. Specific voting rules and instructions such as whether or not to use post-mark dates and the use of post office addresses by the organization should be anticipated.[86] A court in Alabama noted that when additional nominations for office are made at the time of a shareholders' meeting, a new ballot must be sent to the members for a vote if all members are granted the right to vote under the bylaws.[87] And, a recall election of directors of an electric association in Alaska was deemed legitimately held using mail ballots.[88] A summary of the charges and the directors responses were included with the ballot.[89]

At least one parliamentary reference noted that a vote taken by mail ballot on a proposition cannot be rescinded at a meeting but can only be rescinded by another mail ballot vote.[90]

The combining of mail balloting and in-person voting at a meeting can cause problems and is not recommended.[91] A court in Alabama noted that a mail ballot also must be used after minutes are amended at the meeting when minutes must be approved by all the members under the bylaws.[92]

A preferential ballot is a system in which voters can designate all of their voting priorities in descending order on a single ballot. Its purpose is to avoid the need for further balloting if there is no initial winner. It is a useful technique for national mail-in elections so that additional balloting is not needed and a victor determined with just one vote.

§ 58 RISING VOTE

A rising vote is a vote taken by having members stand to be counted. "[A] 'standing vote' occurs when each voter 'stand[s] up when his or her side of the question is counted.'"[93] In larger groups, it helps when the chair has others take the count and report the result to him or her. When a definite number or a specific proportional vote is needed, a standing vote may be preferred.[94]

All those in favor of a motion are asked by the chair to stand and be counted. They are then seated. Next, all those taking the opposing position are asked to stand by the chair, are counted and then told to be seated.[95]

When the chair is uncertain of an outcome from a voice vote, a rising vote may be used.[96] Voice votes can be inconclusive [97] and lead to a rising vote. Disagreement even with a standing vote can occur.[98]

§ 59 VOTE BY PROXY

A proxy is the granting of written authority by one member to another member to vote in the first member's stead at a meeting of members. The scope of authority and other details of the proxy may vary and should be made specific in the proxy document. For example, the proxy may be limited to one meeting, one motion or issue, one person, a specific time period or it can be unlimited.[99] In an Illinois case a proxy used by a nonprofit corporation may be reusable or irrevocable.[100]

State nonprofit statutes allow for proxy voting at membership meetings if specifically authorized under the articles or bylaws.[101] Many statutes provide that the proxy may be valid up to 11 months and are generally revocable at will.[102] It should be noted that some parliamentary references frown on the use of proxies since it [arguably] compromises the concept of members being personally present and voting at meetings.[103] Proxies cannot be used by directors or others at a directors' meeting.[104] This fiduciary duty cannot be delegated to others.

The applicable state statute should be consulted to see about the authorized use of proxies.[105] In a California case, the state corporate code authorized voting by proxy but only if authorized in the homeowners' association bylaws.[106] In some state statutes proxy voting by members is allowed unless prohibited in the charter or bylaws; while in other states, proxies cannot be used unless authorized in the bylaws.[107]

Proxies are non-transferable.[108] They may be used by the holder to vote on secondary motions that arise at a meeting.[109] The proxy is effective when received by the secretary or other officer or agent authorized to tabulate votes.[110] A Pennsylvania court noted that proxy forms that were not the official ones of the board and not sent out by the board pursuant to the bylaws were properly rejected.[111]

There is some disagreement as to whether proxies are counted in determining the presence of a quorum.[112] One parliamentary reference is of the opinion that proxy votes are not counted in the quorum unless authorized by the documentary authority.[113] Yet it has also been held in a case in Florida that proxies are counted in determining the presence of a quorum.[114] This should be researched in advance by the organization to know how to proceed if the organization expects the presence of a quorum at a meeting to become an issue.

In an Ohio case it was decided that a member waives a question as to the use or validity of a proxy at a membership meeting by not objecting at the time of the meeting.[115] A nonprofit organization cannot arbitrarily impose limits on a member's proxy.[116] In another Ohio case it was decided that proxy voting may not be used to eliminate members unless proxy voting was permitted in a hospital's organizing document.[117] In a California case there is an expectation of privacy with a proxy vote.[118]

Disputes about the validity and effect of proxies are commonly delegated to inspectors of elections for resolution by state statute.[119] In the absence of inspectors of elections that have given this authority the decision on whether to accept a contested proxy ultimately rests with the assembly.

[1] Glad Tidings Assembly of God v. Neb. Dist. Council, 734 N.W.2d 731, 737 (Neb. 2007) (quoting BLACK'S LAW DICTIONARY 1306 (8th ed. 2004)).

At least one parliamentary reference contends that a long established custom on a method of voting must be honored. See GEORGE DEMETER, DEMETER'S MANUAL OF PARLIAMENTARY LAW AND PROCEDURE 134 (2001).

[2] 15 PA. STAT. ANN. § 5758(b) (West 2013) ("The manner of voting on any matter, including changes in the articles or bylaws may be by ballot, mail or any reasonable means provided in a bylaw adopted by the members.").

[3] See, e.g., CAL. CORP. CODE §§ 5510(a), 5510(f) (West 2013 & Supp. 2014). Pennsylvania's statute was amended effective September 9, 2013 to add:

(b) Members.—Except as otherwise provided in the bylaws, the presence or participation, including voting and taking other action, at a meeting of members, or the expression of consent or dissent to corporate action, by a member by conference telephone or other electronic means, including, without limitation, the Internet, shall constitute the presence of, or vote or action by, or consent or dissent of the member for the purposes of this subpart.

2013 Pa. Legis. Serv. Act 2013-67. § 35 (West) (codified at 15 PA. STAT. ANN. § 5708(b)). On December 18th, 2013, New York passed the Non-Profit Revitalization Act of 2013, 2013 N.Y. Sess. Laws ch. 549 (McKinney) (effective July 1, 2014). However, while this act makes many changes, including allowing consents for actions in lieu of a meeting to be provided by electronic mail the legislation did not provide for electronic participation and voting in meetings as permitted under Pennsylvania and California statute. See id. § 65 (to be codified at N.Y. NOT-FOR-PROFIT CORP. LAW § 614). See infra Chapter 1, § 6, for a discussion of measures adopted in lieu of a meeting.

[4] Avila v. Apostolic Assembly of the Faith in Christ Jesus, E046233, 2009 WL 891021, at *6 (Cal. Ct. App. Apr. 3, 2009).

[5] For example, voting by email was not specifically authorized in the bylaws and thus this type of voting by a board of managers was rejected by a New York court. Acad. Twins Condo. by the Bd. of Managers v. Elcordy, No. 105931/10, 2010 WL 3206999, at *8-9 (N.Y. Sup. Ct. July 29, 2010).

[6] Meadows Condo. Unit Owners Ass'n v. Blakey, 2010-Ohio-2437 (6/1/2010).

[7] Glad Tidings, 734 N.W.2d at 736-37 (upholding a congregation's vote when church members showed their support of a measure by "standing, nodding, and verbally responding").

[8] See, e.g., Ass'n of Apt. Owners of Maalaea Kai v. Stillson, 116 P.3d 644, 650-51 (Haw. 2005).

[9] SARAH CORBIN ROBERT, HENRY M. ROBERT III, WILLIAM J. EVANS, DANIEL H. HONEMANN & THOMAS J. BALCH, ROBERT'S RULES OF ORDER NEWLY REVISED 284 (11th ed. 2011) [hereinafter ROBERT'S RULES].

10   If the bylaws require the election to be by ballot, the assembly cannot use a voice vote. FLOYD M. RIDDICK & MIRIAM H. BUTCHER, RIDDICK'S RULES OF PROCEDURE: A MODERN GUIDE TO FASTER AND MORE EFFICIENT MEETINGS 26 (1985) ("If bylaws require elections by ballot, no other method of voting is valid."); *see also* ROBERT'S RULES, *supra* note 9, at 442 ("The viva-voce method of election finds application principally in mass meetings—or when an election is not strongly contested and the bylaws do not require election by ballot.").

11   AMERICAN INSTITUTE OF PARLIAMENTARIANS, STANDARD CODE OF PARLIAMENTARY PROCEDURE 148 (2012) [hereinafter STANDARD CODE]. A voice vote was used at a labor union meeting in *Waldinger Corp. v. NLRB*, 262 F.3d 1213, 1215 (11th Cir. 2001).

12   "[A] 'voice vote' can occur when 'the voters collectively [answer] aloud.'" *Glad Tidings*, 734 N.W.2d at 737 (quoting BLACK'S LAW DICTIONARY 1607 (8th ed. 2004)).

13   STANDARD CODE, *supra* note 11, at 149.

14   Confusion erupted when a chair failed to take a rising vote when the result of a voice vote was challenged. Goshorn v. Bar Ass'n of the D.C., 152 F. Supp. 300 (D.D.C. 1957).

15   RIDDICK & BUTCHER, *supra* note 10, at 205.

16   *See, e.g.*, Marshall v. Local Union No. 6, Brewers & Maltsters & Gen. Labor Dep'ts, 960 F.2d 1360 (8th Cir. 1992) (finding that while a union's constitution and bylaws required secret vote on collective bargaining agreements, voice vote was acceptable because this was not a collective bargaining agreement); Essenberg v. Kresky, 696 N.Y.S.2d 282 (App. Div. 1999) (mentioning that a voice vote was disputed at a state political party meeting) (decided on other grounds); *see also* City of King City v. Cmty. Bank of Cent. Cal., 32 Cal. Rptr. 3d 384, 404 n.18 (Ct. App. 2005) (contrasting a recorded vote with "a *viva voce* (live voice) vote, in which the votes of individual members often cannot be distinguished")

17   RIDDICK & BUTCHER, *supra* note 10, at 205.

18   Lewis v. Bedford Cnty. Bd. of Zoning Appeals, 174 S.W.3d 241, 244 (Tenn. Ct. App. 2004) (a voice vote was recorded in the minutes of a county board of zoning)

19   *See* Myers v. Hensley, 1999-Ohio-877.

20   *See supra* Chapter 1, § 3 for further discussion of Open Meetings Statutes.

21   *See* Greemon v. City of Bossier City, 45-664, p. 8 (La. App. 2 Cir. 11/24/10); 59 So.3d 412, *rev'd on other grounds by*, 2010-2828 (La. 7/1/11); 65 So.3d 1263. ("The statute [Open Meetings Law] allows a public body to hold an executive session only after an affirmative vote of two-thirds of members present, and provides that the vote of each member on the question of holding such an executive session and the reason for holding such an executive session shall be recorded and entered into the minutes of the meeting." (citing LA REV. STAT. ANN. 42:6.1)).

22   ROBERT'S RULES, *supra* note 9, at 54; ALICE STURGIS, THE STANDARD CODE OF PARLIAMENTARY PROCEDURE 241 (4th ed., rev. 2001). In an unreported California case, use of unanimous consent was noted at a session of church trustees to oppose a proposed resolution. Jensen v. Huffman, No. G037860, 2007 WL 2433117, at *2 (Cal. Ct. App. Aug. 29, 2007).

23   HUGH CANNON, CANNON'S CONCISE GUIDE TO RULES OF ORDER 43-44 (2001).

24 *See* Deering v. Bd. of Dirs. of the Cnty. Library, 954 P.2d 1359, 1364 (Wyo. 1998).

25 DEMETER, *supra* note 1, at 309.

26 Olson v. Auto. Club of S. Cal., 44 Cal. Rptr. 3d 1, 4 (Ct. App. 2006).

27 Meer v. Klein, No. 108315-08, 2008 WL 5108134, at *6 (N.Y. Sup. Ct. Nov. 24, 2008).

28 ROBERT'S RULES, *supra* note 9, at 56.

29 RIDDICK & BUTCHER, *supra* note 10. at 56.

30 DEMETER, *supra* note 2, at 32 ("All motions requiring a 2/3 vote (or three-fourths, etc.) are normally put to vote by a hand or standing vote."); STURGIS, *supra* note 22, at 141, 143-44. For example, a show of hands was used in *Wiggins v. United Food & Commercial Workers*, 420 F. Supp. 2d. 357, 361 (D.N.J. 2006). A show of hands followed by a standing court was used in *Wolf v. Town of Mansfield*, 851 N.E.2d 1115, 1117 (Mass. App. Ct. 2006). A standing vote was informally used and upheld to express a vote in *Glad Tidings Assembly of God v. Nebraska District Council*, 734 N.W.2d 731, 734 (Neb. 2007), *Smith v. Dugualla Community, Inc.*, No. 51594-2-I, 2003 WL 22701575, at *1 (Wash. Ct. App. Nov. 17, 2003) (2003) and *Savalle v. Hilzinger*, 1 A.3d 1098, 1100 (Conn. App. Ct. 2010). A show of hands was recognized at a school district meeting in, *Forbis v. Freemont County School District No. 38*, 842 P.2d 1063, 1066 (Wyo. 1992) (Urbigkit, J., dissenting).

31 DEMETER, *supra* note 1, at 32.

32 STANDARD CODE, *supra* note 11, at 149.

33 State *ex rel.* Keyes v. Ohio Pub. Emps. Ret. Sys., 123 Ohio St. 3d 29, 2009-Ohio-4052, 913 N.E.2d 972, at ¶ 21 (quoting ROBERT'S RULES OF ORDER).

34 Chantiles v. Lake Forest II Master Homeowners Ass'n, 45 Cal. Rptr. 2d 1, 6-7 (Ct. App. 1995); *see also* Muhammad v. Islamic Soc'y of Orange Cnty., G036534, 2008 WL 855127, at *3 (Cal. Ct. App. Mar. 28, 2008) (following an election vote by a show of hands with a second vote by secret ballot).

35 Waterworks & Sewer Bd. v. Allen, 3 So.3d 846, 851 (Ala. 2008).

36 Spentonbush/Red Star Cos. v. N.L R.B., 106 F.3d 484, 493 (2d Cir. 1997).

37 Hein v. Freedom from Religion Found., Inc., 551 U. S. 587, 618 (2007) (Scalia, J., concurring) ("If this Court is to decide cases by rule of law rather than show of hands, we must surrender to logic and choose sides . . . .").

38 CANNON, *supra* note 23, at 167. Although considered unusual, elections can be held by roll call. ROBERT'S RULES, *supra* note 9, at 443. During telephone meetings, members may vote by stating their position verbally when their name is called. This is done for practical reasons but is not necessarily considered a roll call vote.

39 STANDARD CODE, *supra* note 11, at 150; RIDDICK & BUTCHER, *supra* note 10, at 202.

40 STANDARD CODE, *supra* note 11, at 150.

41 RIDDICK & BUTCHER, *supra* note 10. at 202.

42   DEMETER, *supra* note 1, at 133, notes the possibility that the bylaws may require more than one second to authorize a ballot or roll call vote.

43   *Id.*

44   ROBERT'S RULES, *supra* note 9, at 283.

45   DEMETER, *supra* note 1, at 310.

46   STANDARD CODE, *supra* note 11, at 150. However, in an Ohio case roll call voting was not a required procedure by a school board voting on a proposed supplemental employment contract. State *ex rel.* Savarese v. Buckeye Local Sch. Dist. Bd. of Edu., 660 N.E.2d 463, 466 (Ohio 1996).

47   *See Savarese*, 660 N.E.2d at 466 ("The reason for such enactments is that the people generally, and particularly the constituency of the municipal legislators, are entitled to know how their representatives vote on important questions." (quoting 56 AM. JUR. 2D *Municipal Corps., Counties, & Other Political Subdivisions* § 346 (1971))).

48   *See, e.g.,* Smith v. Sheriff, 982 S.W.2d 775, 779-80 (Mo. Ct. App. 1998). For an excellent summary of the importance of a "recorded" vote and the accountability of those voting, see City of King City v. Cmty. Bank, 32 Cal. Rptr. 3d. 384 (Ct. App. 2005).

49   Town of Madison, Inc. v. Ford, 498 S.E.2d 235, 238 (Va. 1998). In an Illinois case, the roll call recording of votes by a county board was a factor in determining whether or not a zoning code actually was adopted. Cnty. of Kankakee v. Anthony, 710 N.E.2d 1242, 1246 (Ill. App. Ct. 1999).

50   Willis v. Deerfield Twp., 669 N.W.2d 279, 286 (Mich. Ct. App. 2003); *see also* Myers v. Hensley, 1999-Ohio-877 (stating that a public body may only enter executive session after a motion and a roll call vote authorizing it).

51   Piper v. Celina, 2008-Ohio-2741, at ¶ 18. However, the court found enough credible evidence that a roll call vote was taken in order to go into executive session in compliance with the statute. *Id.* at ¶ 18.

52   Cardinale v. City of Atlanta, 722 S.E.2d 732, 736 (Ga. 2012) (citing GA. CODE ANN. § 50-14-1(e)(2)).

53   Gillespie v. San Francisco Pub. Library Comm'n, 79 Cal. Rptr. 2d 649, 654-55 (Ct. App. 1998).

54   ROBERT'S RULES, *supra* note 9, at 412; STURGIS, *supra* note 22, at 144.

55   Chantiles v. Lake Forest II Master Homeowners Ass'n, 45 Cal. Rptr. 2d 1, 6-7 (Ct. App. 1995).

56   15 PA. STAT. ANN. § 5758(b); N.J. STAT. ANN. § 15A:5-20.a (West 2013 & Supp. 2014) ("Elections of trustees need not be by ballot unless a member demands election by ballot at the election and before the voting begins.").

57   CAL. CORP. CODE §§ 5513(a), 5514(a). The terms proxies and written ballots are used interchangeably.

58   STANDARD CODE, *supra* note 11, at 151.

59   *But see* N.J. Stat. Ann. § 15A:5-20.e (allowing for a waiver of election by ballot for trustees).

60   *See, e.g.,* United States v. Int'l Bhd. of Teamsters, Chauffeurs, Warehousemen & Helpers of Am., 896 F. Supp. 1349, 1356 (S.D.N.Y. 1995). There is a school of thought that a secret ballot by mail "reduces the possibility of voter intimidation or harassment and tends to increase membership participatio᷈ in union elections." *Id.*

61   Robert's Rules, *supra* note 9, at 412.

62   Sturgis, *supra* note 22, at 144.

63   Corns v. Laborers Int'l Union of N. Am., 773 F. Supp. 2d 835, 842 (N.D. Cal. 2011). In another case, a collective bargaining agreement and amendments thereto required a secret ballot vote, but a certain memorandum of understanding did not require a secret ballot vote. Marshall v. Local Union No. 6, 960 F.2d 1360, 1369-70 (8th Cir. 1992).

64   *See, e.g.,* Meer v. Klein, No. 1083᷈5-08, 2008 WL 5108134, at *4 (N.Y. Sup. Ct. Nov. 24, 2008).

65   *See* George, v. Local Union No. 639, 100 F.3d 1008, 1010 n.4 (D. Col. 1996).

66   Corns v. Laborers Int'l Union of N. Am. 709 F.3d 901, 912 (9th Cir. 2013). An intermediate labor body may hold elections by secret ballot of the members "or by labor organization officers representative of such members who have been elected by secret ballot." Harrington v. Chao, 280 F.3d 50, 53, (1st Cir. 2002); *see also* Talley v. Feldman, 941 F. Supp. 501, 511 (E.D. Pa. 1996). Disputes can arise as to whether a labor organization is an intermediate body or a local organization. *See, e.g.,* Harrington v. Chao, 280 F.3d 50 (1st Cir. 2002).

67   Sch. Comm. of Town of York v. Town of York, 626 A.2d 935, 945 (Me. 1993).

68   Standard Code, *supra* note 11, at 151; Robert's Rules, *supra* note 9, at 412.

69   Robert's Rules, *supra* note 9, at 412.

70   Sim v. N.Y. Mailers' Union No. 6, 166 F.3d 465, 470 (2d Cir. 1999) (allowing anyone, not just someone who voted with the majority to move for reconsideration "because it would not be known from a secret ballot who was in the majority").

71   See Demeter, *supra* note 1, at 247-48, for the proper handling of the counting of ballot votes.

72   However, combining a mailed ballot and a ballot brought to an annual meeting in person was without incident in *Nelson v. Big Woods Springs Improvement Ass'n*, 322 S.W.3d 678, 679 (Tex. Ct. App. 2010) (decided on other grounds).

73   Park West Condo. Ass'n v. Deppe, 2006 UT App 507, ¶ 23, 153 P.3d 821.

74   *E.g.,* N.J. Stat. Ann. § 15A:5-20; Cal. Corp. Code § 5513; 15 Pa. Stat. Ann. § 5758(b).

75   *E.g.,* 15 Pa. Stat. Ann. § 5758(b); Cal. Corp. Code § 5513(a).

76   Cal. Corp. Code § 5513(a). After a recent change the statute provides,

> Unless otherwise provided by the articles or bylaws and if approved by the board of directors, that ballot and any related material may be sent by electronic transmission by the corporation (Section 20) and responses may be returned to the corporation by electronic transmission to the corporation (Section 21).

Id.

77 *Id.* § 5513(b).

78 RIDDICK & BUTCHER, *supra* note 10, at 200; ROBERT'S RULES, *supra* note 9, at 424; STURGIS, *supra* note 22, at 145.

79 ROBERT'S RULES, *supra* note 9, at 424.

80 *Id.*

81 STANDARD CODE, *supra* note 11, at 152. An argument was made by a labor union that a vote "by mail is typically used only for simple issues where there is no need to provide an extensive presentation to the members regarding the subject on which they are voting" and that questions which require more careful analysis should be voted on in person. Diamond v. United Food & Commercial Workers Union Local 881, 768 N.E.2d 865, 873 (Ill. App. Ct. 2002).

82 RIDDICK & BUTCHER, *supra* note 10, at 104.

83 Silicon Valley Taxpayers Ass'n v. Santa Clara Cnty. Open Space Auth., 30 Cal. Rptr. 3d 853, 866 (Ct. App. 2005) (citing CAL. GOV'T CODE § 53753), *rev'd on other grounds*, 187 P.3d 37 (Cal. 2008).

84 *See, e.g.*, Shepard Convention Servs., Inc. v. N.L.R.B., 85 F.3d 671 (D.C. Cir. 1996); Purdue Farms, Inc. v. N.L.R.B., 935 F. Supp. 713 (E.D.N.C. 1996).

85 Mulrine v. Pocono Highland Cmty. Ass'n, 616 A.2d 188, 190 (Pa. Commw. Ct. 1997).

86 For a description of some of the things that can go wrong with mail ballots and how to avoid them, see Harry S. Rosenthal, *Avoiding Mail Ballot Snafus*, PARLIAMENTARY JOURNAL, Vol. XXXIX, No. 1, (Jan. 1998). In this writer's opinion, post mark dates should be avoided.

87 Baldwin Cnty. Elec. Membership Corp. v. Catrett, 942 So. 2d 337 (Ala. 2006).

88 *See* Matanuska Elec. Ass'n v. Rewire the Bd., 36 P.3d 685, 689 (Alaska 2001).

89 *Id.*

90 DEMETER, *supra* note 1, at 166.

91 STANDARD CODE, *supra* note 11, at 152.

92 *Catrett*, 942 So. 2d at 345.

93 Glad Tidings Assembly of God v. Neb. Dist. Council, 734 N.W.2d 731, 737 (Neb. 2007) (quoting BLACK'S LAW DICTIONARY 1607 (8th ed. 2004)).

94 STANDARD CODE, *supra* note 11, at 149. For example, standing votes are often used when a two-thirds vote is required. *See, e.g.*, Wolf v. Town of Mansfield, 851 N.E.2d 1115, 1117 (Mass. Ct. App. 2006); Massaro v. Mainlands, Section 1 & 2 Civic Ass'n, 796 F. Supp. 1499, 1504 (S.D. Fla. 1992), *re'vd on other grounds*, 3 F.3d 1472 (11th Cir. 1993).

95 CANNON, *supra* note 23, at 122.

96 Gordon Props., LLC v. First Owners' Ass'n (*In re* Gordon Properties LLC), 435 B.R. 326, 338-39 (Bankr. E.D. Va. 2010) (citing ROBERT'S RULES OF ORDER NEWLY REVISED § 4, 48-49 (Sarah C. Robert et al. eds., De Capo Press, 10th ed. 2000)) (decided on other grounds); *see also* STURGIS, *supra* note 22, at 143.

97 ROBERT'S RULES, *supra* note 9, at 45.

98 *See generally Glad Tidings*, 734 N.W.2d 731.

99 STANDARD CODE, *supra* note 11, at 154-55.

100 Natural Organics, Inc. v. Nat'l Nutritional Foods Ass'n, 706 N.E.2d 975, 979 (Ill. App. Ct. 1998).

101 *E.g.*, 15 PA. STAT. ANN. § 5759(c); N.Y. NOT-FOR-PROFIT CORP. LAW §§ 609(a), 609(a)(1) (McKinney 2012); CAL. CORP. CODE § 5510; N.J. STAT. ANN. § 15A:15-18.a.

102 *E.g.*, 15 PA. STAT. ANN. § 5759(b); CAL. CORP. CODE § 5613(b); N.J. STAT. ANN. § 15A:5-18.a; N.Y. NOT-FOR-PROFIT CORP. LAW § 609(a)(2).
Under a Georgia Electric Membership Corporation statute, every proxy is revocable by the maker and the proxy holder's powers are suspended at a meeting if the maker is present and decides to vote in person. Brown v. Pounds, 711 S.E.2d 646, 648 (Ga. 2011) (citing GA. CODE ANN. § 46-3-268(a)) (decided on other grounds).

103 *See, e.g.*, ROBERT'S RULES, *supra* note 9, at 407, 428-29; RIDDICK & BUTCHER, *supra* note 10, at 155 ("Proxy voting does not belong in ordinary societies unless specifically provided for in the bylaws.").

104 STANDARD CODE, *supra* note 11, at 154; *see In re* Audubon Quartet, Inc., 275 B.R. 783, 787 (Bankr. W.D. Va. 2002) ("The general rule is that directors cannot vote by proxy, but must be physically present to act themselves." (citing FLETCHER CYCLOPEDIA OF CORPORATIONS § 427 (Perm. ed.))); *see also* S.I.S. Enters., Inc. v. Zoning Bd. of Appeals, 635 A.2d 835, 838-39 (1993) (disallowing a zoning board member from voting on an application for a variance by an absentee written vote).

105 ROBERT'S RULES, *supra* note 9, at 428; RIDDICK & BUTCHER, *supra* note 10, at 155. Under the New York Not-For-Profit Corporation law, proxies are authorized for the meeting of members unless the certificate of incorporation or bylaws provide otherwise. *See* Congregation of H.O.P.E.-L.I.F.E. Noah's Ark Church, Inc. v. Ramirez, 2011 NY Slip Op 31518(U), at *14 (N.Y. Sup. Ct. June 1, 2011) (citing N.Y. NOT-FOR-PROFIT CORP. LAW § 609(a)), http://www.courts.state.ny.us/Reporter/pdfs/2011/2011_31518.pdf.

106 Kaplan v. Fairway Oaks Homeowners Ass'n, 120 Cal. Rptr. 2d 158, 160 (Ct. App. 2002) (citing CAL. CORP. CODE § 7613).

107 STANDARD CODE, *supra* note 11, at 154; *see also* Willis v. Most Worshipful Prince Hall Grand Lodge of Mo. & Jurisdiction. 866 S.W.2d 875, 878 (Mo. Ct. App. 1993).

[108] RIDDICK & BUTCHER, *supra* note 10, at 155-56.

[109] DEMETER, *supra* note 1, at 222. A proxy may be exercised by the holders to vote to oppose a motion to adjourn a meeting at a timeshare owners' association meeting. *See* Neumann v. Vill. of Winnipesaukee, 784 A.2d 699, 703 (N.H. 2001).

[110] Glover v. Overstreet, 984 S.W.2d 406, 408 (Ark. 1999) (citing ARK. CODE ANN. § 4-28-212(c)(1) (1996)).

[111] Wymbs v. Conashaugh Lakes Cmty. Ass'n, 616 A.2d 749, 750-51 (Pa. Commw. Ct. 1992).

[112] See *supra* Chapter 2, § 10 of this text for additional discussion.

[113] RIDDICK & BUTCHER, *supra* note 10, at 156.

[114] Chateau DeVille Condo. Ass'n v. Mikhail, 583 So. 2d 358, 360 (Fla. Dist. Ct. App. 1991) (citing FLA. STAT. § 718.122(2)).

[115] Wasser v. Rawiga Country Club, 607 N.E.2d 1106, 1107-08 (Ohio Ct. App. 1992).

[116] *See Glover*, 984 S.W.2d at 408.

[117] Hecker v. White, 688 N.E.2d 289, 291 (Ohio Ct. App. 1996).

[118] Chantiles v. Lake Forest II Master Homeowners Ass'n, 45 Cal. Rptr. 2d 1, 6-7 (Ct. App. 1995).

[119] *See, e.g.,* 15 PA. STAT. ANN. § 5762(3); N.Y. NOT-FOR-PROFIT CORP. LAW § 610(b); N.J. STAT. ANN. § 15A:5-22; CAL. CORP. CODE § 5615(b).

CHAPTER 10

Nominations

§ 60 RIGHT TO NOMINATE

A basic principle of parliamentary procedure is that one member may nominate another eligible member for office.[1] If the bylaws provide for "a fair and reasonable procedure for nominating candidates for any office, only" those candidates are eligible for office.[2] Under federal labor law, a union member is guaranteed equal rights and privileges to nominate and vote for candidates.[3]

Regarding directors who are elected by members under the California statute, "there shall be available to the members reasonable nomination and election procedures given the nature, size and operations of the corporation."[4]

Members have the right to offer nominations from the floor (even if others have been nominated by a nominations committee) unless the bylaws provide otherwise.[5] Nominations from the floor do not require a second[6] unless there is a rule to the contrary. Some organizations provide in their bylaws that a prospective candidate must obtain the signatures of a certain number of members or delegates on a petition in order to run.[7] A member has the right to nominate himself or herself.[8] A member can call out the name of a nominee without being recognized.[9] A member can only nominate one person at a time.

After everyone else has had a chance to make a nomination, the same member can nominate others.[10]

Controversies arise in case law as to whether certain persons in an organization have the right to nominate. In one case, the president of a labor union had the right under the bylaws to nominate officers to fill vacancies "with no restriction on when or how those nominations must be made."[11] In another reported case, a sponsor of a residential condominium had the right to designate a member to the board under the condominium bylaws.[12] In a California case it was decided that a board member may participate in the nomination of a successor for his vacant seat if the resignation doesn't take effect until after the seat is vacated.[13]

§ 61 NOMINATING COMMITTEE

A nominating committee decides who will be a candidate for office. Under the Pennsylvania non-profit statute, "[u]nless the bylaws provide otherwise, directors shall be nominated by a nominating committee or from the floor."[14] A nominating committee cannot elect, only nominate.[15]

The bylaws should, according to one parliamentary reference, describe a nominating committee's process of operation.[16] It also is helpful for an organization to have additional adopted policy on the internal procedure of a nominating committee. In this writer's opinion, unless barred by a state open meetings or other act, the nominating committee should meet in executive session to encourage more open discussion within the committee.

The nominating committee either can be a standing or special committee set up in advance of an election.[17] Even if the president is an ex-officio member of all committees, he or she should not select or participate in any phase of the committee's work.[18] Thus, in many organizations the president is not an ex-officio member of the nominating committee.

Parliamentary references agree that a member of the nominating committee can be nominated for office by the committee.[19] Whether such a nominee should immediately resign from the committee is subject to some disagreement.[20] In this writer's opinion it is good practice for the committee member to resign when nominated. If the bylaws or other rules do not require a single slate for nominees, the committee can select more than one nominee for an office if it wishes.[21] Controversy could be avoided if the bylaws are specific on this point. There are schools of thought on the wisdom of the nominating committee offering more than one candidate for an office.

In a reported Maryland case, it was decided that the board's handling of a nominating process within a nonprofit voluntary membership organization would not be reversed absent fraudulent or arbitrary actions.[22] A meeting in Connecticut of the nominating committee of a library board to select board members to fill vacant seats for president and president-elect was ruled a public meeting that was required to comply with the state's open meeting provisions.[23]

Nominations from the nominating committee cannot be stricken by the assembly;[24] only new names can be added if authorized. In a New York case, it was ruled that a board of a credit union lacked authority under the bylaws to reject the nominating committee's slate of candidates.[25] And, in a Texas ruling all nominating committee members were required to be given fair and adequate notice of their committee meeting.[26]

---

[1]   HUGH CANNON, CANNON'S CONCISE GUIDE TO RULES OF ORDER 129 (2001). Cannon notes an exception to this rule if a bylaw provision holds otherwise. *Id.* In *Solid Rock Baptist Church v. Carlton,* 789 A.2d 149 (N.J. Super. 2002), the validity of nominating rules and floor nominations was challenged but the court lacked jurisdiction because it was an ecclesiastical matter.

[2]   15 PA. STAT. ANN. § 5758(b) (West 2013).

3 *See* McCafferty v. Local 254, 186 F.3d 52, 57 (1st Cir. 1999) (citing 29 U.S.C. § 401(a)).

4 CAL. CORP. CODE § 5520(a) (West 2013 & Supp. 2014). Under CAL. CORP. CODE § §5520(b), if certain other sections of the code are met,

> [T]he nomination and election procedures of that corporation shall be deemed reasonable. However, those sections do not prescribe the exclusive means of making available to the members reasonable procedures for nomination and election of directors. A corporation may make available to the members other reasonable nomination and election procedures given the nature, size and operations of the corporation.

And under CAL. CORP. CODE § 5521,

> A corporation with 500 or more members may provide that . . . a director may be nominated . . . (a) by any method authorized in the bylaws, or if no method is set forth in the bylaws by any method authorized by the board. (b) by petition . . . . (c) if there is a meeting to elect directors, by any member present at the meeting in person or by proxy if proxies are permitted.

Under the Pennsylvania nonprofit law, "Unless the bylaws provide otherwise, directors shall be nominated by a nominating committee." 15 PA. STAT. ANN. § 5725.

5 GEORGE DEMETER, DEMETER'S MANUAL OF PARLIAMENTARY LAW AND PROCEDURE 241 (2001).

6 *Id.* at 238.

7 CANNON, *supra* note 1, at 129.

8 DEMETER, *supra* note 5, at 239.

9 SARAH CORBIN ROBERT, HENRY M. ROBERT III, WILLIAM J. EVANS, DANIEL H. HONEMANN & THOMAS J. BALCH, ROBERT'S RULES OF ORDER NEWLY REVISED 432 (11th ed. 2011) [hereinafter ROBERT'S RULES].

10 DEMETER, *supra* note 5, at 239.

11 Helmer v. Briody, 759 F. Supp. 170 (S.D.N.Y. 1991).

12 Tower Assocs. v. Boulevard Towers Condo., 744 N.Y.S.2d 451, 452 (App. Div. 2002); *see also* Reich v. Local 89, 36 F.3d 1470 (9th Cir. 1994) (finding a second membership meeting at which there were additional nominations had to be run just as openly and democratically as the first meeting).

13 Helmy v. Assaf, No. G041883, 2010 WL 411845, at *6 (Cal. Ct. App. Feb. 4, 2010).

14 15 PA. STAT. ANN. § 5725(e). The same provision is set forth for officers: "Unless the bylaws provide otherwise, officers shall be nominated by a nominating committee or from the floor." *Id.* § 5732(c).

15 *See, e.g.*, Townsend v. Trs. of La. Coll., 2005-1283, p. 5 (La. App. 3 Cir. 4/12/06); 928 So. 2d 715, 719.

16 DEMETER, *supra* note 5, at 240.

17 *Id.* at 240.

18 Robert's Rules, *supra* note 9, at 433. However, <u>Riddick</u> notes the president can offer suggestions for candidates. Floyd M. Riddick & Miriam H. Butcher, Riddick's Rules of Procedure: A Modern Guide to Faster and More Efficient Meetings 122 (1985). As a practical matter, especially in smaller organizations, the president often gets involved in selecting his or her successor.

19 Demeter, *supra* note 5, at 239; Riddick & Butcher, *supra* note 18, at 122.

20 *Compare* Alice Sturgis, The Standard Code of Parliamentary Procedure 154 (4th ed., rev. 2001) (a nominating committee member who is nominated "should resign from the committee immediately."), *with* Riddick & Butcher, *supra* note 19, at 122 (resignation not required).

21 Robert's Rules, *supra* note 9, at 433. A church's bylaws which apparently allowed for unscreened floor nominations without prequalification instead of a slate selected by a nominating committee were the subject of a court challenge. Solid Rock Baptist Church v. Carlton, 789 A.2d 149 (N.J. Super. 2002).

22 Tackney v. U.S. Naval Acad. Alumni Ass'n, 971 A.2d 309, 318 (Md. 2009).

23 Ansonia Library Bd. of Dirs. v. Freedom of Info. Comm'n, 600 A.2d 1058, 1060-61 (Conn. Super. Ct. 1991); *accord* Schmiedicke v. Clare Sch. Bd., 577 N.W.2d 706, 708-09 (Mich. Ct. App. 1998).

24 Demeter, *supra* note 5, at 240.

25 Brantley v. Mun. Credit Union, 879 N.Y.S.2d 395, 397 (App. Div. 2009). However, in one case a hospital governing board retained the power to reject a nominating committee's nominees and then hold a joint meeting to select the nominees. Keane v. St. Francis Hosp., 522 N.W.2d 517 n.5 (Wis. Ct. App. 1994)
    In another case, a nominating committee's decision was challenged because petitioners alleged that the committee expended "corporate funds to finance the mailing of campaign materials in favor of the Nominating Committee's Slate." Cuva v. U.S. Tennis Ass'n E., 3280/06, 2006 WL 2918215, at *5 (N.Y. Sup. Ct. Sept. 18, 2006). However, petitioners failed to prove that the funds were used to support the nominating committee's slate over the other candidate and there was no allegation that such funds would have influence the result. *Id.* at *12.

26 There is excellent discussion concerning proper notice to nominating committee members of an upcoming meeting in *Swonke v. First Colony Community Services Ass'n*, No. 14-09-00019-C, 2010 WL 2361691 (Tex. Ct. App. June 15, 2010), *reh'g denied*, 2010 WL 3583150 (Tex. Ct. App. Sept. 16, 2010). Email notice was deemed inadequate by the court. *Id.* In an odd procedural twist, one justice while concurring with the decision to overrule the rehearing motion, mentions that she has since changed her mind on the court's original decision with regard to the email notice. *See id.* 2010 WL 3583150, at 1-*2.

CHAPTER 11

Elections

§ 62 REGULATION OF ELECTIONS

State nonprofit statutes contain varying degrees of details regulating elections. California requires "reasonable . . . election procedures given the nature, size, and operations of the corporations."[1] The bylaws and standing rules often contain provisions on the regulation of elections[2] because of their importance.[3]

Many organizations use an elections committee to oversee the elections process.[4] A teller's committee can also be used in a more limited form to count votes and issue a report to the assembly.[5] The ultimate internal regulation of and "final judgment on the results of an election" rests with the assembly.[6]

§ 63 ELECTION COMMITTEE

Some associations appoint an election committee[7] or may have one already established in their bylaws. As noted above, sometimes the name of the committee used by the organization overlaps with or is called a teller's committee.[8] This committee conducts the election[9] with varying degrees of responsibility and authority.[10] This may include counting or overseeing the counting of the vote. The appointment of a well-respected elections committee can help avert damaging political squabbles.

State nonprofit corporations statutes typically provide for such a committee and provide for various titles for its members such as inspectors of election.[11] If there is no such standing committee, under the statutes, the board may appoint judges of election or they may be appointed upon the request of a member.[12] Among the many possible statutory duties of these officials are determining the number of members, ruling on the existence of a quorum or validity of proxies, and considering challenges.[13] Some organizations empower an election committee to hear and decide electioneering disputes.

A sample of cases shows the following. In a New York ruling a labor union's election committee was deemed to have the authority to grant a waiver to allow members of two newly chartered unions to elect and send delegates to a convention.[14] In a Massachusetts case, an election committee of an employee's credit union lacked the authority to exclude a candidate based on the fact that the bylaws did not specifically provide for exclusion if a candidate was not a member in good standing.[15] A union election committee decision to reject a candidate because he had not been affiliated with the union for at least one year was rejected by a federal court in Puerto Rico.[16] And, an election committee's recommendation to disqualify two board candidates of a residential cooperative for improper electioneering was mentioned in dicta by a New York court.[17]

In a federal Pennsylvania case, the determination by a labor union's election committee that a petition nominee failed to fax enough signatures to be a candidate was reversed.[18] In a New York case the decision of a fire district election committee to disallow certain write-in ballots which appeared out of the correct column and with differing name variations was overruled.[19] A federal court in New York ruled as unreasonable and unnecessarily strict, an election committee decision to disqualify opposition candidates for union office for failing to submit required information by an undisclosed deadline.[20]

A parliamentary reference asserts that the assembly itself makes the ultimate decision regarding election challenges, [unless litigated], after seeing the work or report of the election or teller's committee.[21] The election committee should be above reproach. A sample of case opinions notes the following: In a contested union election in New York, the election committee must act independently of the union and be easily accessible to all candidates.[22] Another court in New York ruled that after a labor union's election committee tallied ballots for an election and announced the result, a subsequent two-week delay with missing ballots and other election materials did not change the outcome or require a new election.[23] In a South Dakota case, a requirement that a formal notice of protest had to be served personally on all members of an election committee was strictly enforced.[24]

§ 64 TIME AND PLACE OF ELECTIONS

The time and place of elections should be specified in the organization's articles of incorporation or bylaws.[25] Elections often are held at the annual membership meeting[26] or convention. Many national organizations conduct their elections by postal mail or electronically (or both); in those cases the place of election does not literally apply except for gathering and counting of votes and announcing the result.

Mixing the place of election for the annual meeting, for example, with the method of voting such as email or postal mail, can create confusion and should be avoided. Allowing floor nominations when there is a prior electronic or mail vote obviously is incompatible. In an Alabama case the court decided that a board election of an electric utility membership corporation could be successfully challenged when mail voting was conducted prior to a meeting where floor nominations could be made.[27]

If an election is incomplete, an adjourned meeting should be scheduled[28] to complete the election. However, under <u>RONR</u> an election cannot be rescheduled in advance if the bylaws require the election at a specific meeting.[29]

When a vacancy in an office occurs an election to fill the vacancy may take place at any regular meeting.[30] When there has been a removal from office and there is no provision in the bylaws for filling the position, upon notice to the membership, a vacancy can be filled at a special meeting.[31]

§ 65 BALLOTING

Balloting is a form of secret voting by paper method. Voting by secret ballot is essential "to protect the privacy of members in casting their votes."[32] When the bylaws require a ballot vote, that type of vote cannot be taken in any other manner even if the result of the vote is unanimous.[33] Any attempt to undermine a pre-established right to a secret ballot must be rejected. If the bylaws require a ballot vote, a vote to have the secretary cast the one vote even if there is but one candidate is improper.[34]

Balloting also may include use of a voting machine[35] and internet voting if the same safeguards are used as that for casting paper ballots.[36] Electronic voting devices must assure the voter's secrecy.[37]

Under state nonprofit statutes, the articles or bylaws may authorize a vote of members by ballot.[38] Under the California statute, written ballots may not be authorized for an election for directors where cumulative voting is in use.[39] A court in California ruled that use of mail ballots by a concominium owners association to amend governing documents is statutorily allowed - unless expressly disallowed in the organization's governing documents.[40] Another court in Pennsylvania decided that mail balloting by a community association was authorized by the state nonprofit statute and the bylaws.[41]

If not otherwise bound by the articles or bylaws the assembly can decide by motion if it wants to vote on a matter by ballot. A second is required, debate is not available, it is amendable, and a majority is required.[42] In a labor union case, a federal court in California noted that union leadership had the discretion to decide what particular method of balloting should be used to ratify a labor-management contract.[43] Subjects which commonly require a ballot vote are elections and important proposals.[44] Disciplinary matters also commonly require a ballot vote. During a written secret ballot vote, the president can vote.[45]

Ballot voting under some circumstances has been disallowed. A sample of cases include the following. In a California case absentee balloting prior to an actual election for a nonprofit director position is improper since it deprives other candidates of the opportunity to be elected.[46] A Washington court ruled that ballot voting during executive session at a city council meeting was a violation of an open meeting law.[47] Mail-in balloting for a homeowners association attempt to change governing documents in Utah was disallowed when the statute and bylaws required that change take place only at a meeting.[48]

When ballots are received, the tellers or election officials determine the validity, interpretation and possible illegality of ballots.[49] Any uncertainty should be included in the report to the voters. Use of secret balloting should not conflict with applicable state open meeting requirements.

§ 66 VOTE NECESSARY TO ELECT

The bylaws of a nonprofit organization should specify what vote is needed to elect the organization's leaders.[50] Normally, a majority vote is needed for election to office unless the bylaws state otherwise.[51] A New York court noted that a lack of a majority vote prevented the election of a presiding officer without a provision or rules to the contrary.[52] A Texas case cited a portion of the Texas Non-Profit

Corporation Act that required the number of votes necessary to remove a director of a property owners' association was "equal to the vote necessary to elect the director[s]."[53]

Some state statutes provide that unless the articles of incorporation or bylaws state otherwise, the officers can be elected or appointed by the board but the statutes are silent on the number of votes needed.[54]

State statutes may also provide that unless otherwise stated in the articles of incorporation or bylaws, a plurality vote of members is needed to elect directors.[55] The fact that a plurality vote is needed to determine the winner of an election must be stated in the bylaws.[56] See Section 47 for more about plurality voting. In general, a majority vote is needed to elect unless a plurality vote is specifically authorized. This may require multiple balloting to achieve majority votes.

Some parliamentary references frown on plurality voting[57] for leaders except for national and international elections. The thought is that a candidate should receive a majority of votes to be elected. RONR's position is that a majority vote by mail may be impractical in international and national elections and suggests that a better method is preferential voting and this method should be included on the election ballot.[58]

§ 67 CLOSING THE POLLS AND ANNOUNCING THE VOTE

The time of closing of election polls, if not already stated in the bylaws, should be established by an adopted rule or by a motion from the floor.[59] The ballot should "provide a reasonable time within which to return the ballot to the corporation."[60] The presiding officer through general consent can close the polls. Parliamentary references recommend that the presiding officer alert voters that the polls are about to close and those who have not voted should do so.[61] Those who are in the polling place waiting in line can vote even if it is after the time for the polls to close.[62]

The incidental motion to close the polls cannot interrupt another speaker, needs a second, is not debatable, and is amendable.[63] This motion requires a two-thirds vote[64] and is only applicable to ballot voting.[65]

After the polls are closed, the tellers prepare their report stating the vote counts. The teller does not declare the results.[66] The chair is handed the report, reads the teller's report out loud and declares the results.[67] In elections conducted by postal mail and/or electronically, the method to in effect close the polls and announce the result should be pre-established either through the bylaws or by organizational policy. It is good practice to inform all voters of the voting rules on the election ballot itself or on a separate attachment accompanying the election ballot

§ 68 CHALLENGING AN ELECTION

Ideally, the bylaws should include a procedure on how an election can be challenged including the taking a recount.[68] Other than assigning this task to an elections committee, few organizations specify the rules for challenging an election.[69] Demeter asserts that there is a "basic parliamentary right to question an inconclusive or invalid election and thus continue the balloting until a nominee has been duly elected by majority vote."[70] Short of litigation, it is incumbent upon the assembly to handle and decide such challenges.[71] Many state nonprofit statutes assign jurisdiction of a challenged election to the local court upon the filing of a formal complaint by a person with standing.[72] Ballots and other documents used for an election should be retained for a reasonable period of time through the use of established rules or policies. Other organizations routinely use a motion for this purpose.

Any voting member can initiate a challenge by raising a point of order.[73] This challenge can interrupt another speaker.[74] Elections can be challenged on multiple grounds such as having ineligible voters, following unauthorized actions or procedure, gross negligence,[75] and election of unqualified directors.[76] In a New York case, an election of board members in a meeting was invalidated when it was held minutes before another faction of voters could attend and vote.[77]

A challenge must be timely made - during the time of the election or reasonably thereafter.[78] In a South Dakota case a failure to comply with the rules to protest an election will result in a denial of the appeal.[79] A continuing breach of fundamental rules or principles may allow for a later challenge.[30] During a challenge the officials who have been elected take office.[81] A California court commented that after interim appointments are made to fill union officer vacancies, timely elections must be held under the LMRDA.[82]

Courts often grant deference to the organization's internal handling of an election challenge. There is a presumption that an election was held in a fair manner. A sample of cases show the following. Board election procedures of an electric utility in a North Carolina case were upheld in part under the business judgment rule and because those challenging the result could not demonstrate board bad faith.[83] A California opinion noted that there may be statutory provisions for alternate dispute resolutions regarding the challenge of a director's election at a condominium association.[84] A court in Louisiana ruled that even though problems occurred during a court-ordered election, since there was no fraud and no contrary result would have occurred, another election was not necessary.[85]

A court may decline entertaining an election challenge unless the aggrieved person has first exhausted his internal organizational remedies. Another sample of cases noted the following. A court in New York noted that under the LMRDA a union member who disputes an election after exhausting his internal union remedies can file a complaint with the Secretary of Labor.[86] It has been held that when there are "ambiguous constitutional provisions" on how to appeal an election, the complaining union member should be favored, "whose interpretations need only be reasonable under the circumstances."[87] One court mentioned that a party challenging a union election's fairness because of pre-election conduct bore the burden of proof.[88]

---

[1] CAL. CORP. CODE § 5520(a) (West 2013 & Supp. 2014). California also has provisions on such matters as nominations, *id.* § 5521, distribution of election material, *id.* § 5523, mailing of nominee election material, *id.* § 5524, and information about the written ballot, *id.* § 5513.

[2] AMERICAN INSTITUTE OF PARLIAMENTARIANS, STANDARD CODE OF PARLIAMENTARY PROCEDURE 159 (2012) [hereinafter STANDARD CODE].

[3] FLOYD M. RIDDICK & MIRIAM H. BUTCHER, RIDDICK'S RULES OF PROCEDURE: A MODERN GUIDE TO FASTER AND MORE EFFICIENT MEETINGS 92 (1985).

[4] *Id.* at 190-91. *See infra* section 63 of this text.

[5] STANDARD CODE, *supra* note 2, at 167. The Standard Code of Parliamentary Procedure uses the terms "Report of Election Committee or Tellers." *Id.* For a sample report of an election committee or tellers see, STANDARD CODE, *supra* note 2, at 167 and SARAH CORBIN ROBERT, HENRY M. ROBERT III, WILLIAM J. EVANS, DANIEL H. HONEMANN & THOMAS J. BALCH, ROBERT'S RULES OF ORDER NEWLY REVISED 417-18 (11th ed. 2011) [hereinafter ROBERT'S RULES].

[6] HUGH CANNON, CANNON'S CONCISE GUIDE TO RULES OF ORDER 134 (2001).

[7] STANDARD CODE, *supra* note 2, at 164.

[8] CANNON, *supra* note 6, at 133-34.

[9] STANDARD CODE, *supra* note 2, at 164.

[10] *See* Wright v. Prairie Chicken, 1998 SD 46, ¶ 14, 579 N.W.2d 7, 11 (a nonprofit corporation's Election Committee "shall make the final determination on the validity of a Protest").

[11] *See, e.g.* 15 PA. STAT. ANN. § 5762 (West 2013) (called "Judges of election"); N.J. STAT. ANN. § 15A:5-21 (West 2013 & Supp. 2014); CAL. CORP. CODE § 5615; N.Y. NOT-FOR-PROFIT CORP. LAW § 610 (McKinney 2013).

[12] *E.g.*, 15 PA. STAT. ANN. § 5762; N.J. STAT. ANN. § 15A:5-21; CAL. CORP. CODE § 5615(a); N.Y. NOT-FOR-PROFIT CORP. LAW § 610.

[13] *E.g.*, N.J. STAT. ANN. § 15A:5-22; 15 PA. STAT. ANN. § 5762(3); CAL. CORP. CODE § 5615; N.Y. NOT-FOR-PROFIT CORP. LAW § 610.

[14] *See* Mason Tenders Local Union 59 v. Laborers' Int'l Union of N. Am., 924 F. Supp. 528, 545 (S.D.N.Y. 1996) (an elections committee decided disputes about and among candidates).

In one case the role of a union election committee is described when there was a dispute as to whether faxed nomination petitions were received by the elections committee. Sickman v. Commc'ns Workers of Am., No. 99-5582, 1999 WL 1045145, at *1-2, 5 (E.D. Pa. Nov. 16, 1999).

[15] Horan v. MBTA Employees Credit Union, No. 0501221, 2005 WL 1811869, at *1 (Mass. Super. Ct. April 1, 2005). A township election committee was able to disqualify applicants for temporary township board of trustees positions allegedly based on the applicants' prior support to recall officials in that township. Brown v. Twp. of Kochville, No. 09-CV-12076, 2011 WL 281053, at *3 (E.D. Mich. 2011).

[16] Herman v. Sindicato De Equipo Pesado, 34 F. Supp. 2d 91, 96 (D.P.R. 1998) (finding that a requirement of being affiliated with the union for one year when affiliation consists of paying a $100 fee "boils down to a filing fee for candidacy eligibility that needs to be filed over one year before election"). The court found this requirement to be in violation of the Labor-Management Reporting and Disclosure Act ("LMRDA"). Id. (citing 29 U.S.C. § 481(e)).

[17] Cylich v. Riverbay Corp., 904 N.Y.S.2d 39 (App. Div. 2010) (decided on other grounds).

[18] Sickman, 1999 WL 1045145, at *5.

[19] Miller v. Lakeland Fire Dist., 818 N.Y.S.2d 278, 280 (App. Div. 2006). For a case where, due to accident and inexperience, an election committee committed numerous procedural mistakes requiring an election to be set aside, see Reich v. Federation of Catholic Teachers, Inc., 853 F. Supp. 710 (S.D.N.Y. 1994).

[20] Herman v. N.Y. Metro Area Postal Union, 30 F. Supp. 2d 636, 645-46 (S.D.N.Y. 1998) (finding that "[c]ompliance with an insufficiently disclosed requirement is not a 'reasonable qualification' for candidacy that allows union members a 'reasonable opportunity' to run for office" (quoting 29 U.S.C. § 481(e)).

[21] Cannon, supra note 6, at 134.

[22] Reich, 853 F. Supp. at 716 (suggesting the importance of appointing a capable election committee).

[23] Commer v. Dist. Council 37, Local 375, 990 F. Supp. 311, 316-17 (S.D.N.Y. 1998) (decided on other grounds).

[24] Wright v. Prairie Chicken, 1998 SD 46, ¶ 14, 579 N.W.2d 7.

[25] E.g., Cal. Corp. Code § 5151(c)(2) "The bylaws may contain . . . [t]he time [and] place . . . of conducting mail ballots."); 15 Pa. Stat. Ann. § 5732(a).
A church constitution provided that the "Board of Directors, or a committee named by the board, will prepare the program . . . stating the date, time and place of elections. This information will be made known to the church in general with adequate time prior to the elections." Avila v. Apostolic Assembly of the Faith in Christ Jesus, E046233, 2009 WL 891021, at *1 n. 3 (Cal. Ct. App. Apr. 3, 2009).

[26] See, e.g., N.J. Stat. Ann. § 15A:5-2.b; see also Robert's Rules, supra note 5, at 94.

[27] Baldwin Cnty. Elec. Membership Corp. v. Catrett, 942 So. 2d 337 (Ala. 2006).

28   ROBERT'S RULES, *supra* note 5, at 444.

29   *Id.* at 185.

30   RIDDICK & BUTCHER, *supra* note 3, at 93 ("or as determined in documents of authority").

31   GEORGE DEMETER, DEMETER'S MANUAL OF PARLIAMENTARY LAW AND PROCEDURE 180 (2001).

32   STANDARD CODE, *supra* note 2, at 166.

33   DEMETER, *supra* note 31, at 244.

34   RIDDICK & BUTCHER, *supra* note 3, at 203.

35   STANDARD CODE, *supra* note 2, at 150.

36   *Id.* at 144, 146.

37   ROBERT'S RULES, *supra* note 5, at 419.

38   *E.g.*, 15 PA. STAT. ANN. § 5758(b); CAL. CORP. CODE § 5513. *But see* N.J. STAT. ANN. § 15A:5-20(a), which states: "Elections of trustees need not be by ballot unless a member demands election by ballot and before the voting begins. If the bylaws require election by ballot at any meeting, the requirement is waived unless compliance therewith is requested by a member entitled to vote at the meeting."

39   CAL. CORP. CODE § 5513(e).

40   Fourth La Costa Condo. Owners Ass'n v. Seith, 71 Cal. Rptr. 3d 299, 306 (Ct. App. 2008); *see also* Mooney v. Town of Stowe, 2008 VT 19, ¶ 8, 183 Vt. 600, 950 A.2d 1198 (finding a town's residents were authorized to use an Australian ballot for the complete budget but "only if approved in the requisite form by town voters").

41   Mulrine v. Pocono Highland Cmty. Ass'n, 616 A.2d 188, 189-90 (Pa. Commw. Ct. 1992). A California state department of real estate regulation "governing common interest developments [homeowners associations] specifies [that], 'Voting for the governing body shall be by secret written ballot.'" Chantiles v. Lake Forest II Master Homeowners Ass'n, 45 Cal. Rptr. 2d 1, 5-6 (Ct. App. 1995) (quoting CAL. CODE REGS. tit. 10, § 2792.19).

42   ROBERT'S RULES, *supra* note 5, at 283.

43   Ackley v. W. Conference of Teamsters, 958 F.2d 1463, 1478 (9th Cir. 1992).
     It was the opinion of an Election Officer that mail balloting for union elections "reduces the possibility of voter intimidation or harassment and tends to increase membership participation in union elections." United States v. Int'l Bhd. of Teamsters, Chauffeurs, Warehousemen & Helpers of Am., 896 F. Supp. 1349, 1356 (S.D.N.Y. 1995).

44   STANDARD CODE, *supra* note 2, at 151.

45   CANNON, *supra* note 6, at 7-8.

46   *See, e.g.*, McElroy v. Pernell, No. B190293, 2007 WL 2793344, at *7 (Cal Ct. App. Sept. 27, 2007).

47 Miller v. City of Tacoma, 979 F.2d 429, 436 (Wash. 1999) (citing WASH. REV. CODE § 42.30.060(2)).

48 Levanger v. Vincent, 2000 UT App 103, ¶ 16, 3 P.3d 187.

49 DEMETER, *supra* note 31, at 247-48. See ROBERT'S RULES, *supra* note 5, at 415-19 for a description of rules related to ballots.

50 STANDARD CODE, *supra* note 2, at 159.

51 DEMETER, *supra* note 31, at 246; CANNON, *supra* note 6, at 131 (asserting that "[a] basic principal of parliamentary procedure is that a candidate must receive a *majority vote* . . . to be elected"); ALICE STURGIS, THE STANDARD CODE OF PARLIAMENTARY PROCEDURE 159 (4th ed., rev. 2001).

52 Toback v. Schmitt, 809 N.Y.S.2d 172, 173-74 (App. Div. 2006); *accord In re* Burgess, 2006-0958, p. 1 (La. App. 1 Cir. 3/23/07).

53 Wingert v. Scenic Heights Subdivision Prop. Owners Ass'n, No. 03-07-00297-CV, 2008 WL 2778017, at *5 (Tex. Ct. App. July 16, 2008) (citing TEX. REV. CIV. STAT. ANN. art. 1396-2.15(D) (West 2003) (articles 1395-2.11 to 1396-2.20 have since expired))

54 N.J. STAT. ANN. § 15A:6-15; CAL. CORP. CODE § 5213(b); 15 PA. STAT. ANN. § 5732(a) ("The officers and assistant officers shall be elected or appointed at such time, and for such terms as may be fixed by or pursuant to the bylaws." [No mention is made whether this is done by the members or the directors]).

55 N.Y. NOT-FOR-PROFIT CORP. LAW, § 613(a); N.J. STAT. ANN. § 15A:5-20.d; CAL. CORP. CODE § 5616(c). However, 15 PA. STAT. ANN. § 5725(b), leaves this vote determination for the bylaws and is otherwise silent or how "directors may be elected, appointed, designated or otherwise selected."

56 ROBERT'S RULES, *supra* note 5, at 405; *see, e.g.*, Tex. Boll Weevil Eradication Found., Inc. v. Lewellen, 952 S.W.2d 454, 457 (Tex. 1997) (using a plurality vote for the election of board members for state approved foundations); Reich v. Local 89, 36 F.3d 1470, 1476 (9th Cir. 1994) (using a plurality vote to nominate non-incumbent candidate in a labor union nominating committee).

57 *E.g.*, ROBERT'S RULES, *supra* note 5, at 405; RIDDICK & BUTCHER, *supra* note 3, at 140 ("A plurality vote ought never elect general officers of an organization, since it permits a minority to control. Any candidate elected by a plurality may expect opposition from the majority.").

58 ROBERT'S RULES, *supra* note 5, at 405.

59 RIDDICK & BUTCHER, *supra* note 3, at 142.

60 CAL. CORP. CODE § 5513(a).

61 DEMETER, *supra* note 31, at 136; ROBERT'S RULES, *supra* note 5, at 286 (stating that it is best to let the chair close the polls).

62 DEMETER, *supra* note 31, at 136.

[63] ROBERT'S RULES, *supra* note 5, at 284.

[64] *Id.* at 284, 286; RIDDICK & BUTCHER, *supra* note 3, at 143.

[65] ROBERT'S RULES, *supra* note 5, at 286.

[66] *Id.* at 418.

[67] *Id.*; DEMETER, *supra* note 31, at 246.

[68] DEMETER, *supra* note 31, at 249.

[69] Election Committees are covered in section 63 *supra*.

[70] DEMETER, *supra* note 31, at 249.

[71] STANDARD CODE, *supra* note 2, at 171. ("If the meeting or convention is no longer in session, the governing board "decides the matter and takes whatever action seems best." "); CANNON, *supra* note 6, at 134; ROBERT'S RULES, *supra* note 5, at 446 (a bylaw or special rule can take authority away from the assembly to decide election disputes).

[72] *E.g.*, CAL. CORP. CODE § 5617; N.Y. NOT-FOR-PROFIT CORP. LAW § 618. In one case under the New York statute, a non-member of a synagogue lacked standing to challenge the results of an election of trustees and officers. Rosen v. Lebewohl, 2010 WL 3326868, at *14 (N.Y. Sup. Ct. 2010) (citing N.Y. NOT-FOR-PROFIT CORP. LAW § 618).

[73] ROBERT'S RULES, *supra* note 5, at 445.

[74] RIDDICK & BUTCHER, *supra* note 3, at 205.

[75] STANDARD CODE, *supra* note 2, at 171.

[76] For example, in *Hancock v. Bisnar*, 132 P.3d 283 (Ariz. 2006) (en banc), an election was successfully contested on the basis that the elected directors were "not qualified to serve under the statutes governing irrigation districts." *Id.* at 284. The court also noted that, "Proceedings to recall the directors of an irrigation district 'shall be in all respects as provided by the constitution and laws of the state for the recall of county officers.'" *Id.* at 286 (quoting ARIZ. REV. STAT. § 16-674(A)).

[77] Hog v. 384 Grand St. Housing Dev. Fund Co., No. 0101607/2008, 2008 WL 2328934, at *7-9 (N.Y. Sup. Ct. May 19, 2008). The court also noted that "[a] court reviewing an election [under the New York statute] sits as a court of equity." *Id.* at 5-6.

[78] STANDARD CODE, *supra* note 2, at 170; ROBERT'S RULES, *supra* note 5, at 250. DEMETER, *supra* note 31, at 249, allows for a challenge up to the time the contested candidate takes possession of the office.

[79] Wright v. Prairie Chicken, 1998 SD 46, ¶ 14, 579 N.W.2d 7.

[80] ROBERT'S RULES, *supra* note 5, at 251.

[81] STANDARD CODE, *supra* note 2, at 171-72.

[82] Solis v. Nat'l Emergency Med. Servs. Ass'n, No. 1:11-cv-01929 AWI DLB, 2012 WL 1192799, at *7 (E.D. Cal. 2012) (citing 29 C.F.R. § 452.25).

[83] Hammonds v. Lumbee River Elec. Membership Corp., 631 S.E.2d 1, 14 (N.C. Ct. App. 2006).

[84] Chacon v. Brookhurst Vill. Condo. Ass'n, No. G043984, 2011 WL 3250462, at *1 (Cal. Ct. App. July 29, 2011) (citing CAL. CIV. CODE § 1369.520(a)).

[85] Clement v. Four Winds Tribe-Louisiana, 2005-652, p. 3-4 (La. App. 3 Cir. 12/30/05); 921 So. 2d 193.

[86] Ellis v. Chao, 336 F.3d 114, 117 (2d Cir. 2003) (citing 29 U.S.C. § 482(a)), *remanded to* 329 F. Supp. 2d 454 (S.D.N.Y. 2004) (decided on other grounds), *aff'd* 155 Fed. App'x. 18 (2d Cir. 2005); *accord* Petersen v. Dole, 956 F.2d 1219 (D.C. Cir. 1992) (involving a complaint that pertained to the choosing of delegates to attend the national union's convention and the resulting national offices' election); *see also* Bello v. Disabled Am. Veterans, No. 18787/10, 2010 WL 5137915 (N.Y. Sup. Ct. 2010) (noting that before initiating litigation an aggrieved member must first exhaust his available internal remedies when challenging an election).

Under Section 402(a) of the LMRDA,

> A member of a labor organization -
> (1) who has exhausted the remedies available under the constitution and bylaws of such organization and of any parent body, or
> (2) who has invoked such available remedies without obtaining a final decision within three calendar months after their invocation, may file a complaint with the Secretary within one calendar month thereafter alleging the violation of any provision of section 481 of this title . . . .

Labor-Management Reporting and Disclosure Act § 402(a), 29 U.S.C. § 482(a) (2013).

[87] Solis v. Local 234, 585 F.3d 172, 181 (3d Cir. 2009).

[88] Honeyville Grain, Inc. v. N.L.R.B., 444 F.3d 1269, 1274-75 (10th Cir. 2006). The court denied a challenge to the election result based on allegations that inflammatory religious comments were made against the owner of the company. *Id.* at 1276-77.

CHAPTER **12**

Committees

§ 69 COMMITTEES (GENERALLY)

State nonprofit statutes recognize that organizations can create committees either by resolution of the board or within their bylaws[1] and determine how the members of such committees are selected. Parliamentary reference also notes that in addition to creation of specific committees in the bylaws, the bylaws may allow for the president or the board to create a committee.[2] They can also be "created by motion from the floor."[3]

The authority of committees may be specifically limited by state statutes.[4] For example, restrictions on what a committee can do may include actions requiring member approval, the filling of board vacancies, amending board actions, fixing of director compensation, approving the budget, and other actions.

State statutes provide for the methods of committee appointments and their replacements, subject to any requirements contained in the articles or bylaws. Riddick notes the five ways committee membership may be determined.[5] Typically, a committee member serves at the will of the appointing authority and can be removed with or without cause. A Washington state court has noted that a board may suspend a member of a supervising committee with cause.[6] In addition, committee vacancies are filled by the same authority which filled or appointed the original members.[7]

Some committee members may be ex-officio; that is, they are automatically members by virtue of an office or other position or association with the organization.[8] Ex-officio members are not elected or appointed to the committee.[9] An ex-officio appointment is created in the bylaws and should state whether or not that member has the right to vote. Commonly, the president is an ex-officio member of all committees except the nominating committee (and perhaps the disciplinary committee).

A committee is run under the same procedural rules as the board and membership meetings but in a much more relaxed and informal manner.[10] The size and nature of the committee will impact on the formality of its rules. This is further discussed in Section 71.

An important function of a committee is to issue reports of its work to the board and membership at their meetings. Moreover, it is common and helpful for a committee to offer motions as a part of its report. A common mistake is for the assembly to "approve" or "accept" a committee report. Such action literally means that the entire verbatim report is adopted in full. While this is certainly an option, in most cases a committee report is merely received. Parliamentary references generally allow for presentation of a minority report of a committee to the assembly, although the consent to present the minority report may first be required.

Perhaps the area which engenders the most controversy is determining the amount of authority that is held by a committee. "Committees are subject at all times to the direction and control of the board."[11] Riddick notes that, "No committee powers are inherent. Powers are granted by the bylaws or motions adopted by the assembly and may be full or limited."[12] The appointing committee may grant the committee "full power" or "with power."[13] In that case, the committee can move forward to implement a decision to which it was referred without further authority from the initiating body.[14] The power or lack of power granted to a committee should be made clear in advance to avoid misunderstandings.

Architectural committees within homeowners associations sometimes engender committee authority questions. The association's documents should clearly specify how much authority is granted to this type of committee and any rights of appeal from it. A sample of court cases which vary have stated the following: An architectural control committee of a homeowner's association must exercise its general powers "in a fair and reasonable manner."[15] A Texas case noted that the authority of the architectural control committee expires at certain times.[16] An architectural control committee of a homeowners' association in a Mississippi case was an extension of the board of directors and the court ruled that it had the same authority.[17] A Virginia court ruled that both the architectural control committee and the board had the authority to approve architectural requests of members under governing documents of a homeowner's association.[18]

Courts have varied on other authority issues related to committees. For example, in a Georgia case, a committee could consider termination of an employee contract but the final decision rested with the college board of trustees.[19] A court in Louisiana ruled that a search committee for a college president vacancy could be filled by the board of trustees and the trustees were not bound to a selection made by a search committee.[20]

How a committee actually functions, not necessarily its designation as a committee, can have significant impact on how it is legally treated. For example, a court in Texas noted that in general, hospital committees may or may not have certain statutory immunity from liability depending upon the function they are performing.[21] Another court in Texas noted that "[t]he function the [hospital] committee is performing determines the protected status of its activities."[22] Medical facilities fall under certain state and federal statutes and their committees have certain specific duties and immunities. The actual function of the committee and not the committee's name is determative in analyzing if and how it fits into the applicable statute.

§ 70 TYPES OF COMMITTEES

There generally are two types of committees, standing and special. Special committees are also called task forces and ad hoc committees. Standing committees are permanent committees established for a defined ongoing purpose assigned to them.[23] Special committees are established for a specific, one-time purpose after which they cease to exist.[24]

Two kinds of standing committees, audit and executive, are expressly created by state statute. Under the California statute, the board is specifically authorized to appoint an audit committee.[25] An audit committee independently reviews the financial transactions and condition of the organization.[26] State statutes governing nonprofits also typically identify executive committees of the board.[27] Creation of an executive committee requires authority from the bylaws.[28] "The specific composition, powers, and duties of this [Executive] committee should be provided for in the bylaws."[29] Executive committees of a board assume many governing responsibilities between board meetings and the bylaws should be explicit on what is permissible.

There is a wide range of functions and options under which an executive committee (a subset of the board) may operate.[30] The specific authority granted to executive committees and their exercise should be reasonably monitored and overseen by the full board. The minutes of executive committee meetings should be freely available to the full board. Executive committees can serve an important function between board meetings. However, the executive committee must not inadvertently overstep its power between board meetings. The board is ultimately responsible for the actions and decisions of the executive committee.[31] At the very least the executive committee must report and account for its activity to the board on a regular basis. In this writer's opinion, if it is not too late, the board can override decisions of the executive committee. Some organizations provide that the full board must ratify the decisions of the executive committee. In a Georgia case, an executive committee could only recommend to a hospital board that an emergency room physician's privileges be terminated – under the hospital bylaws.[32]

Parliamentary references recognize other types of committees. Riddick identifies committees to act[33] and committees to investigate.[34] Demeter similarly recognizes a committee with "full power" - a committee that can carry out a question "without further authority from the body."[35]

A committee of the whole[36] is recognized as a method by which a large assembly such as a board or a group of delegates can more informally debate a question, setting aside most of the usual procedural rules, and thereby act like a committee.[37] To enter into a committee of the whole takes a motion, a second, debate, and a majority vote. Its advantage is a relaxation of the meeting rules and freer discussion.[38] RONR recognizes several types of committees of the whole.[39] The Committee of the Whole, after ending its deliberations, reports to the assembly. Sometimes this is offered with a recommendation or a proposed motion for the assembly to consider.

The following is a sample of cases: In a Michigan case, it was mentioned that a city council could consider an early retirement program as a committee of the whole and then go into executive session to discuss the presentation.[40] Purported adoption of a report of a committee of the whole by a governmental body in an Illinois case could not substitute for a more formal required action such as an ordinance, resolution, or motion.[41] Another Illinois court mentioned the use of a committee of the whole in a controversy related to a property's zoning classification.[42]

When some hospital medical committees convene, issues arise on whether the committee is functioning in such a manner so as to fall within certain statutory definitions. This will impact on what internal procedures must be followed and if the hospital or other health care facility will enjoy immunity from liability. As previously noted in Section 69, the function served by the committee overrides the terminology and titles that are used for it. An opinion in Illinois noted that a hospital's medical staff's committee must be involved in a peer-review process before it could obtain liability protection under a statute.[43] A quality assurance committee related to a nursing home in a North Carolina case was a type of committee whose internal documents were protected from discovery if the records met certain conditions.[44]

§ 71 MEETINGS OF COMMITTEES

Meetings of committees usually are run in a more relaxed and informal way than other assembly meetings.[45] Larger committees looking at controversial matters[46] or the bylaws or rules of the organization may require more formality. A quorum consisting of a majority of a committee's members is [usually] required in these matters.[47] Smaller boards and committees use more relaxed and less formal rules and procedures.[48] Only members of the committee can make motions.[49] Minutes should be taken and subsequently offered to the committee members for approval.

In a committee meeting where there is more informality, there is no limit on debate, informal discussion is permitted, and any member can move for reconsideration.[50] The chair of the committee can make motions, fully participate in debate, and vote.[51] Follow-up action may be taken without a formal motion when its members have agreed to an action at the committee meeting.

Under state statutes, there may be serious limitations regarding a committee's authority.[52] Subject to these limitations are actions which require members' approval such as filling board vacancies, amendment of bylaws, fixing of compensation of board members, and approval of self-dealing transactions. On that latter point, committee members must be aware that their participation is subject to the same or similar conflict of interest restrictions and considerations that board members are under during board meetings.

Committees sometimes conduct hearings on behalf of the larger organization. Such hearings usually are open to members of the organization.[53] However on sensitive topics during testimony there may be limitations on who can attend.[54] During deliberations, after taking testimony, only the committee members can be present.[55]

Notice of meetings to committee members including the time and place must be reasonable. In one Texas case, email notice of a nominating committee meeting two days before the meeting was inadequate and not authorized in the bylaws.[56] Regarding governmental meetings, sunshine laws must be consulted and followed when applicable.[57] In a Massachusetts case a board created committee of a university was found not subject to a state open meeting law.[58]

In a sample of other case law, a search committee's work in a Louisiana case could be overridden by the board of trustees.[59] Some groups may be called committees but due to their function they operate more like a board - with attendant requirements. A medical executive committee meeting in a Kentucky case was distinguished from the term "committee meeting" where the former served more closely as a board.[60]

Depending on the function it performs, a committee meeting may be required to provide procedural due process and similar safeguards. If important membership rights (especially economic ones) are at stake, rules of fairness should be observed. An Illinois court noted that a meeting with the surgical control committee failed to satisfy the requirement for a due process hearing before the executive committee - regarding suspension of clinical staff privileges.[61]

1   *E.g.*, N.J. Stat. Ann. § 15A:6-9.a (West 2013 & Supp. 2014); 15 Pa. Stat. Ann. § 5731(a) (West 2013); N.Y. Not-for-Profit Corp. Law § 712(a) (McKinney 2013), *amended by* The Non-Profit Revitalization Act of 2013, 2013 N.Y. Sess. Laws ch. 549, § 70 (McKinney) (effective July 1, 2014); Cal. Corp. Code § 5212(a) (West 2013 & Supp. 2014).

2   Floyd M. Riddick & Miriam H. Butcher, Riddick's Rules of Procedure: A Modern Guide to Faster and More Efficient Meetings 50 (1985).

3   *Id.* at 49.

4   *See, e.g.*, Cal. Corp. Code § 5212; N.J. Stat. Ann. § 15A:6-9; 15 Pa. Stat. Ann. § 5731(a) (2); N.Y. Not-for-Profit Corp. Law § 712(a), *amended by* The Non-Profit Revitalization Act of 2013, 2013 N.Y. Sess. Laws ch. 549, § 70 (McKinney) (effective July 1, 2014). *But see* Janssen v. Best & Flanagan, 662 N.W.2d 876, 888 (Minn. 2003) (concluding that "the Minnesota Nonprofit Corporations Act does not prohibit corporations from appointing independent committees with the authority to decide whether the corporation should join a member's derivative suit"). For an in-depth discussion of the *Janssen* ruling and special litigation committees in Minnesota, see Eric J. Moutz, Janssen v. Best & Flanagan: *At Long Last, the Beginning of the End for the* Auerbach *Approach in Minnesota*, 30 Wm. Mitchell L. Rev. 489 (2003).

5   Riddick cites various ways to determine committee membership such as nominations by the president or from the floor, appointment by the president, board of managers or directors, and election by ballot.

    Riddick & Butcher, *supra* note 2, at 50-51.

6   Save Columbia CU Comm. v. Columbia, 206 P.3d 1272, 1276 (Wash. Ct. App. 2009) (citing Wash. Rev. Code § 31.12.285).

7   Sarah Corbin Robert, Henry M. Robert III, William J. Evans, Daniel H. Honemann & Thomas J. Balch, Robert's Rules of Order Newly Revised 177 (11th ed. 2011) [hereinafter Robert's Rules].

8   American Institute of Parliamentarians, Standard Code of Parliamentary Procedure 190 (2012) [hereinafter Standard Code].

9   *Id.*

10   Robert's Rules, *supra* note 7, at 500. See *id.* at 487-88, for a full list of how the procedural rules are relaxed for a committee meeting. For a similar summary see, Alice Sturgis, The Standard Code of Parliamentary Procedure 181 (4th ed., rev. 2001).

11   Janssen v. Best & Flanagan, 662 N.W.2d 876, 884 (Minn. 2003) (quoting Minn. Stat. § 317A.241 (2002))

12   Riddick & Butcher, *supra* note 2, at 53-54.

13   The committee can be given "full power" to act for the society in a specific case and can be authorized to spend money or even to add to its own membership. Robert's Rules, *supra* note 7, at 172, 490. Sturgis calls this a "Committee for Action." Sturgis, *supra* note 10, at 177.

14   George Demeter, Demeter's Manual of Parliamentary Law and Procedure 274-75 (2001).

15   Regency Homes Ass'n v. Schrier, 759 N.W.2d 484, 491 (Neb. 2009) (citing Normandy Square Ass'n, v. Ellis, 327 N.W.2d 101 (Neb. 1982)).

16   *See, e.g.*, Anderson v. New Prop. Owners' Ass'n of Newport, 122 S.W.3d 378, 389-90 (Tex. Ct. App. 2003).

17   Goode v. Vill. of Woodgreen Homeowners Ass'n, 662 So. 2d 1064, 1074-75 (Miss. 1995).

18   Farran v. Olde Belhaven Towne Owners Ass'n, No. CL-2009-11786, at *5 (Va. Cir. Ct. July 8, 2010), *available at* http://valawyersweekly.com/wp-files/pdf/010-8-154.pdf.

19   Savannah Coll. of Art & Design, Inc. v. Nulph, 453 S.E.2d 80, (Ga. Ct. App. 1994), *rev'd on other grounds by*, 460 S.E.2d 792 (Ga. 1995).

20   Townsend v. Trs. of Louisiana College, 2005-1283, p. 5 (La. App. 3 Cir. 4/12/06); 928 So. 2d 715, 719.

21   McAllen Methodist Hosp. v. Ramirez, 855 S.W.2d 195, 199 (Tex. Ct. App. 1993); *accord* Ne. Cmty. Hosp. v. Gregg, 815 S.W.2d 320 (Tex. Ct. App. 1991). In *McAllen* the records and activities of a peer review committee were statutorily protected. 855 S.W.2d at 199. However, that same committee, if considering an application to join a medical staff, was not protected. *Id.*

22   *McAllen*, 855 S.W.2d at 199.

23   HUGH CANNON, CANNON'S CONCISE GUIDE TO RULES OF ORDER 4 (2001).

24   *Id.* In a Minnesota case, a nonprofit corporation had the power to create a special litigation committee, but the special litigation committee had to act with independence and good faith. Janssen v. Best & Flanagan, 662 N.W.2d 876, 888 (Minn. 2003).

      Both standing and special committees are recognized by virtually all of the parliamentary authorities. *See* CANNON, *supra* note 23, at 60; ROBERT'S RULES, *supra* note 7, at 490; STURGIS, *supra* note 10, at 266.

25   CAL. CORP. CODE § 5212(d).

26   California recently recognized in its statute an audit committee - if required by a provision of the California Governmental Code. CAL. CORP. CODE § 5212(d).

27   *See, e.g.*, 15 PA. STAT. ANN. § 5731; N.Y. NOT-FOR-PROFIT CORP. LAW § 712(a); N.J. STAT. ANN. § 15A:6-9.a; *see also* STURGIS, *supra* note 10, at 183.

28   STANDARD CODE, *supra* note 8, at 196.

29   *Id.*

30   For example under the New Jersey statute no committee [including the executive committee] can: " (1) Make, alter or repeal any bylaw; (2) Elect or appoint any trustee, or remove any officer or trustee; (3) Submit to members any action that requires member's approval; or (4) Amend or repeal any resolution previously adopted by the board." N.J. STAT. ANN. § 15A:6-9.a.

31   A decision of the medical staff executive committee concerning a physician was approved by a hospital board of trustees in *Willman v. Heartland Hospital East*, 836 F. Supp. 1522, 1529 (W.D. Mo. 1993).

32 Katz v. Hosp. Auth. of Rabun Cnty., 561 S.E.2d 858 (Ga. Ct. App. 2002).

33 RIDDICK & BUTCHER, *supra* note 2, at 49; *see also* STURGIS, *supra* note 10, at 177 (using the term "committee for action"); DEMETER, *supra* note 14, at 224 (using the term "committee for action").

34 RIDDICK & BUTCHER, *supra* note 2, at 49; *see also* STURGIS, *supra* note 10, at 177 (using the term "Committee For Deliberaticn"); DEMETER, *supra* note 14, at 274 ("committees for deliberation, investigation, or recommendation").

35 DEMETER, *supra* note 14, at 274-75.

36 ROBERT'S RULES, *supra* note 7, at 439-90.

37 *See, e.g.,* I.A. Rana Enters., Inc. v. City of Aurora, 630 F. Supp. 2d 912, 920, 924-25 (N.D. III. 2009).

38 *See id.; see also* Our Savior Evangelical Lutheran v. Saville, 922 N.E.2d 1143, (2009) (noting that a city council met as a committee of the whole to converse among themselves and questioned city staff about a spec al use zoning permit).

39 ROBERT'S RULES, *supra* note 7, at 529-31.

40 McKane v. City of Lansing, 938 F. Supp. 462, 464 (W.D. Mich. 1996) (decided on other grounds).

41 People ex.rel. Hansen v. Phelan, 628 N.E.2d 160, 170 (III. App. Ct. 1993). *But see* Sprint Spectrum, L.P. v. Town of W. Seneca, 659 N.Y.S. 2d 687, 688 (Sup. Ct. 1997) (noting a public hearing referred a zoning matter "to a committee of the whole pending the Town's review of its ordinance"); *I.A. Rana Enters.*, 630 F. Supp. 2d at 924-25 (finding a city council committee of the whole meet ng was not a public forum and members of the public could be properly excluded from speaking).

42 Bank of Waukegan v. Vill. of Vernon Hills, 626 N.E.2d 245, 251 (III. App. Ct. 1993). For another illustration of a committee of a whole used by a city council, see *McCrea v. Flaherty*, 885 N.E.2d 836, 842 (Mass. App. Ct. 2008). A committee of the whole was "for the purpose of discussing and reviewing administrative matters with formal action on those matters to take place at the next 'regular' board meeting." Cathedral of Joy Baptist Church v. Vill. of Hazel Crest, 22 F.3d 713, 715 (7th Cir. 1994).

In an unorthodox use of terms a committee of the whole voted to reject a physician from membership to a hospital's medical staff. Corrigan v. Methodist Hosp., 885 F. Supp. 127 (E.D. Pa. 1995). The court confused the parliamentary use of the term committee of the whole. A committee of the whole only makes recommendations and can make no final decisions. The full medical staff was apparently granted authority to make a decision as a committee - but use of the term committee of the whole was technically incorrect in parliamentary parlance. *Id.*

43 Roach v. Springfield Clinic, 623 N.E.2d 246, 251 (III. 1993).

44 Hayes v. Premier Living, Inc., 641 S.E.2d 316 (N.C. Ct. App. 2007). Certain types of hospital committees such as a medical peer review that evaluates the quality of medical care and some aspects of a credentia ing committee have a statutory privilege protecting their records and operations. *See* McAllen Methodist Hosp. v. Ramirez, 855 S.W.2d 195, 199 (Tex. Ct. App. 1993); *see also* Riverside Hosp., Inc. v. Garza, 894 S.W.2d 850 (Tex. Ct.

App. 1995) (applying medical-committee and medical-peer-review committee privilege).

Also, certain types of university committees concerning research projects are not subject to an "Open Door Law" or a state public records act. *See, e.g.,* Robinson v. Ind. Univ., 638 N.E.2d 435, 437 (Ind. Ct. App. 1994). A committee that does "not derive their authority directly from the governing body" may exclude non-members. *Id.* at 438.

45   ROBERT'S RULES, *supra* note 7, at 500; DEMETER, *supra* note 14, at 275.

46   STANDARD CODE, *supra* note 8, at 193.

47   CANNON, *supra* note 23, at 89.

48   *See, e.g.,* Deering v. Bd. of Dirs. of the Cnty. Library, 954 P.2d 1359, 1364 (Wyo. 1998) (citing THE SCOTT, FORESMAN, ROBERT'S RULES OF ORDER NEWLY REVISED 9 (1990 ed.)).

49   DEMETER, *supra* note 14, at 51.

50   RIDDICK & BUTCHER, *supra* note 2, at 52-53; DEMETER, *supra* note 14, at 273 (no seconding of motions is required in a committee).

51   RIDDICK & BUTCHER, *supra* note 2, at 52.

52   *See, e.g.,* CAL. CORP. CODE § 5212(a) (1)-(8); N.Y. NOT-FOR-PROFIT CORP. LAW § 712(a)(1)-(5); 15 PA. STAT. ANN. § 5731(2)(i)-(v).

53   STANDARD CODE, *supra* note 8, at 194.

54   *Id.*

55   *Id.*

56   Swonke v. First Colony Cmty. Servs. Ass'n, No. 14-09-00019-C, 2010 WL 2361691 (Tex. Ct. App. June 15, 2010)

57   See *supra* Chapter 1, § 3 for further discussion of Open Meetings Statutes also known as 'sunshine laws.'

58   Medlock v. Bd. of Trs. of Univ. of Mass., 580 N.E.2d 387 (Mass. App. Ct. 1991). *But cf.* Ark. Gazette Co. v. Pickens, 522 S.W.2d 350 (Ark. 1975) (permitting newspaper reporters to attend university board of trustee meetings under the Freedom of Information Act).

59   Townsend v. Trs. of Louisiana College, 2005-1283, p. 5 (La. App. 3 Cir. 4/12/06); 928 So. 2d 715, 719. Unless the bylaws provide otherwise, a college president's vacancy can be filled by the board through a floor nomination; the candidate does not have to come from a recommendation of a search committee. *Id.*

Even if a (Breed Standards) Revision Committee was allegedly "manipulated" in a committee vote, a subsequent majority vote of the organization's membership provided a safeguard. Jessup v. American Kennel Club, Inc., 61 F. Supp. 2d 5 (S.D.N.Y. 1999).

60   Smith v. Ashland Hosp. Corp., No. 2002-CA-001245-MR, at *5 (Ky. Ct. App. 2003), *available at* http://162.114.92.72/COA/2002-CA-001245.pdf.

[61] Berry v. Oak Park Hosp., 628 N.E.2d 1159, 1164 (Ill. App. Ct. 1993). A claim that a school district's admission appeals committee meeting failed to provide procedural due process to parents was denied in *Bradshaw v. Cherry Creek School District*, 98 P.3d 886, 890 (Colo. App. 2003).

CHAPTER 13

Officers

§ 72 OFFICERS (GENERALLY)

The bylaws, adopted parliamentary reference, or state statutes, if applicable, should designate a non-profit organization's officers, their duties and qualifications, how they are elected or appointed[1] and other details. Typically, the officers of a nonprofit organization include a president, vice president, secretary and treasurer.[2] Other officers may be appropriate depending upon the needs of the organization.[3] Some organizations have a president-elect in addition to or in place of a vice-president. The bare minimum is a president and a secretary.[4]

State statutes commonly require a least a president, a secretary, and a treasurer.[5] The president should not simultaneously serve as the secretary or treasurer.[6] State statutes further allow the board to select the officers. However, the bylaws may and often do require selection of officers by a vote of the members. Whether the officers are elected by the membership or selected by the board is a choice of the organization. Officers do not necessarily have to be directors.

Many larger organizations hire an executive director or an executive secretary to provide executive and administrative services. In that case, it is advisable to include provision for this hiring in the bylaws - along with details such as whether he or she is a voting or non-voting ex-officio member of the board. In this writer's opinion a hired Executive Director should not have the right to vote in light of the separation of functions and inherent conflicts of interest. Many of the routine duties of officers are delegated to this person.

The authority of an officer is derived from the statutes, the by-laws, charters, and certain implied powers.[7] The duties of the officers should be set forth in the bylaws or as may be determined by the board.[8] Disagreements sometimes arise over the scope of an officer's authority. For example, a New York court noted that union officers had the apparent authority to bind a local labor union to implement the terms of a settlement.[9]

Installation is not usually a requirement to take office - unless there is a legal or bylaw requirement.[10] Officers are entitled to com-plete their full term of office in order to implement the results of an election.[11]

Officers of a local governmental body are subject to the state's open meeting law.[12] In an Alaskan case, the trial court ruled that vil-lage officers were entitled to protection from personal liability that resulted from the umbrella doctrine of sovereign immunity.[13]

Officers are subject to conflict of interest statutes which must be carefully observed. In this writer's opinion, an officer's obligation to protect the organization in the event of a personal conflict of inter-est equals that of a director in Section 80 and 83 of this text. In a California case when an officer of a corporation (church) was openly using the corporation to obtain a benefit for himself, the other parties could not hold the church liable for the action of the officer.[14]

Under RONR, adoption of an officer's report prepared prior to a meeting can be made official or ratified by motion of the assembly.[15] Officers may give their own report to the assembly - usually annually. All such reports are usually for information only. Otherwise, formal adoption or approval of an officer's (or committee's) report means that all of the report's contents constitute the official position of the organization. Some committee reports include proposed motions for consideration by the assembly.

§ 73 PRESIDENT

The presiding officer, also called the chair, "conduct[s] the business of a deliberative assembly."[16] It has been asserted that the presiding officer has a "duty" to know parliamentary law and practice.[17] He or she has a hand in virtually every aspect of a meeting[18] beginning with preparation or input on the initial agenda and calling the meeting to order.[19] A New York court ruled that, when a chair was waiting for a quorum to arrive and be determined, another officer was not authorized to start the meeting.[20] In a Virginia case, it was decided that a chair is without authority to refuse to call a meeting to order.[21] While it is desirable to start a meeting on time, circumstances may justify a reasonable delay.

State nonprofit statutes provide for a president, whether selected by the board or elected by the members.[22] Under the statutes, the organization's bylaws should determine how the president is determined. The authority of the president (like all officers) is set forth in the bylaws and/or by direction of the board.[23]

Among the many other duties at a meeting, the chair recognizes speakers, maintains order, and rules on points of order and questions of privilege. In one legal case, whether a chair of a school committee acted reasonably in evicting another board member for alleged unruly behavior during a meeting raised an issue of fact and resulted in the denial of a motion for summary judgment.[24] In a Pennsylvania case, the court decided that the chair of a city council could properly have and enforce rules for citizen comment periods without violating constitutional rights such as the right of free speech.[25] Another court in Virginia decided that a chair's handling of meeting procedure at a condominium membersh p meeting in effect denied members the right to vote.[26]

As a matter of courtesy, the presiding officer is provided the opportunity to select the parliamentarian if one is desired for a meeting. However, in this writer's opinion, the assembly has the right to make this decision. The parliamentarian is a neutral advisor on meeting procedures but makes no decisions for the assembly.

The chair in larger assemblies and under most parliamentary references does not vote except to create or break a tie. Thus he or she will vote only if it will affect the outcome of a motion. For example, if there is a 5-to-4 vote in the affirmative, the chair could then vote "no", create a tie, and defeat a measure. Or, if there is a 5-to-5 vote, the chair can then vote in the affirmative to pass the motion. The chair also votes when there is a ballot vote.[27] In small boards and committees the chair is active and does get to vote. The chair does not participate by expressing personal opinions while presiding.[28] He or she remains neutral and does not make motions or debate. Many times the chair will offer helpful information during debate and subtly influence a debate by his or her comments. In this writer's opinion, such contributions can be very helpful to an organization and are a positive part of leadership.

The presiding officer also has the option under parliamentary references to step down from the chair in order to participate in a particular debate but this option should be exercised judiciously.

Questions arise about the authority of the president. The president's powers are conferred by statute, the bylaws and board resolutions. Court cases have commented that additional implied authority may arise by virtue of the office.[29] In a Virginia case it was decided that after a person was removed from office as a national party chair, any actions taken by him were without legal effect (ultra vires).[30] Authority issues may arise concerning the authority of the chair vis-à-vis the board.[31]

Some organizations provide for a president-elect in their bylaws.[32] Sometimes this office is in place of a vice president. Normally the president-elect takes office for the president in his or her absence.[33] State statutes surveyed in this text do not make specific reference to a president-elect. If this position is desired the bylaws should provide a description of the duties of the organization's president-elect. For example, a president-elect may be designated the chair of a major committee and a member of the executive committee.

§ 74 VICE PRESIDENT

State nonprofit statutes provide for a vice-president and may also provide some authority to a vice-presidential office.[34] The duties of the vice-president should be assigned in the bylaws.[35] Statutes should be consulted to determine the vice-president's authority and duties at governmental meetings.

The vice-president automatically serves in place of the president unless the bylaws state otherwise or if a president-elect serves in that position.[36] Reasons for a vacancy in the president's office include death, disability, and resignation. A vice-president who assumes the office of the president due to a vacancy may first be subject, under the bylaws, to approval of the members[37] or the board.

A vice-president (and president-elect), who is only an acting president, is unable to alter the rulings of the president, fill vacancies, appoint committee members, or act as an ex-officio in the president's place.[38] The vice-president should take over the running of the meeting if the chair is absent, steps down to participate in debate[39] or is removed.[40]

Upon assuming the office of the president, the vice-president turned president can only be ousted or removed from office in the same manner as any elected president.[41]

§ 75 SECRETARY

The secretary, along with the president, is one of the essential officers for the conduct of business of an organization.[42] The office of secretary is recognized in the state nonprofit corporation statutes.[43] The bylaws should set forth the authority and duties of the secretary and, if these duties are not included in the bylaws, they should be set forth by resolution of the board.[44] The bylaws should further specify if the secretary is elected or appointed, his or her term of office and the required qualifications.

The secretary does not have to be a board member depending upon the organizing documents. The secretary has a long list of corporate functions.[45] Two of the principal duties are the taking of minutes of meetings and the keeping of the organization's records.[46] The secretary provides notices of meetings.[47]

In the absence of the secretary at a meeting, a secretary pro tem (temporary) should be elected.[48] This also occurs when the presiding officer is removed.[49] In a New Jersey case, a secretary pro tem was entitled to indemnification when defending a suit.[50]

In larger organizations with a professional staff, many of the traditional duties of the secretary are handled by others. However, in this writer's opinion, the secretary should oversee such activity given his or her official position and responsibilities.

§ 76 TREASURER

State nonprofit statutes provide for a treasurer.[51] Under the statutes, depending on the articles and/or bylaws, the treasurer can be selected by the board or elected by the members.[52] The authority and duties of the treasurer are set forth in the bylaws and also as may be determined by the board.[53]

The treasurer is responsible for the overall handling of an organization's finances. Among his duties are to give a brief financial report to the membership at each regular membership meeting[54] and a fuller report at the annual meeting or convention.[55] The board should also receive a report at each meeting.[56] The reports of the treasurer submitted at meetings can be made through a verbal statement [57] or in more detailed written form - depending on what the situation requires. No board or assembly approval is taken for these interim unaudited financial reports.

The treasurer's annual financial report should be audited[58] by an outside CPA for larger organizations[59] or by an internal auditing committee composed of at least three respected members for smaller organizations.[60] The formal audited annual report of the treasurer must be submitted to the board or membership for approval. The auditors should be independently selected by the board. The motion for approval of the treasurer's audited financial report requires a second, is debatable, can only be amended for any needed corrections, and requires a majority vote for adoption.[61]

In this writer's opinion, conducting an annual financial audit is very important and both protects the treasurer from potential personal liability and promotes the fiscal well-being of the organization.

As noted above, in a New York case, the treasurer derives his or her authority from statutes, bylaws, and the board. He has no authority by virtue of his office alone.[62] He only can disburse funds that have been budgeted.[63] In a California case, a county treasurer, under a state statute, only had discretionary authority for excess funds and only when he was granted investment authority from the board.[64]

The treasurer does not have the authority on his own to borrow money or issue checks unless authorized by the bylaws or the assembly.[65] Yet in a New York case a chief financial officer of a school district was found to have apparent authority to contractually bind a school district to certain policy loans.[66]

§ 77 OFFICER REMOVAL

Officer suspension and/or removal is a delicate matter. The proper procedure must be carefully researched and followed. Removal is subject to state law, and provisions in the articles and bylaws. It is essential that the organization comply with its own established by-laws, policies and procedures. Under many state statutes, an officer elected or appointed by a board can be removed by the board with or without cause.[67] An officer elected by the members, under many state statutes, may also be removed by a vote of the members with or without cause.[68] Under the New York state statute, an officer elected by the members can be suspended by the board with cause.[69]

An organization has the inherent right to remove an officer upon cause shown.[70] Due to the seriousness of officer suspension or removal, this writer recommends a two-thirds vote be required in the organization's bylaws. The same constituency that elected an officer is the one that can vote to remove that officer.[71] In this writer's opinion, the board has the authority (and at times a duty) to suspend officers - but should only do so for sufficient reason.

Some bylaws list grounds for removal. In addition it is good practice to research case law to determine or confirm the grounds for removal. A federal court has found that under the federal Labor-Management Reporting and Disclosure Act ("LMRDA") that an elected delegate for a labor union cannot be removed from office to suppress dissent within the union, but may be removed for violation of a valid and reasonable rule.[72] Union officers also can only be suspended or removed under certain circumstances; they cannot be deprived of fundamental rights.[73]

A critical element to officer removal for cause is providing the accused with procedural due process. This includes notice of the charges (preferably in writing), time to prepare a defense, an opportunity to appear and defend oneself, and the right to be treated fairly.[74] The accused must be given a meaningful opportunity to defend himself.[75] The organization should consider obtaining outside professional assistance when undertaking formal discipline.

Case opinions have shown that a local union's officers must be afforded full and fair due process.[76] However, in a federal Ohio case union officers are not afforded the same procedural due process rights as union members facing discipline.[77] In the same Ohio case a court decided that an international union president had the authority to remove from office a lower-level union's business manager/financial secretary without procedural requirements.[78] An officer removed from office must first exhaust his internal administrative remedies before seeking help in the courts.[79]

The presiding officer can be censured or suspended by motion from chairing a meeting.[80] A majority vote is needed to censure a presiding officer.[81] Charges can be brought against a president for neglect of duty.[82] A two-thirds vote is usually needed.[83] Under parliamentary references, disciplinary proceedings must be held in executive session.[84] A parliamentary reference recognizes a vote of no confidence[85] and censure.[86] A motion to impeach an officer is a main motion, needs a second, and is debatable and amendable.[87]

An Ohio court has ruled that the executive director of a medical board did not have the requisite authority to accept the resignation of an employee of the board; thus the resigning employee was able to rescind his resignation.[88]

---

[1] SARAH CORBIN ROBERT, HENRY M. ROBERT III, WILLIAM J. EVANS, DANIEL H. HONEMANN & THOMAS J. BALCH, ROBERT'S RULES OF ORDER NEWLY REVISED 572 (11th ed. 2011) [hereinafter ROBERT'S RULES].

[2] HUGH CANNON, CANNON'S CONCISE GUIDE TO RULES OF ORDER 3 (2001).

[3] *Id.*

[4] ROBERT'S RULES, *supra* note 1, at 447.

5   *E.g.*, 15 Pa. Stat. Ann. § 5732(a) (West 2013); N.J. Stat. Ann. § 15A:6-15.a (West 2013 & Supp. 2014); N.Y. Not-for-Profit Corp. Law § 713(a) (McKinney 2013), *amended by* The Non-Profit Revitalization Act of 2013, 2013 N.Y. Sess. Laws ch. 549, § 73 (McKinney) (effective July 1, 2014); Cal. Corp. Code § 5213(a) (West 2013 & Supp. 2014) (identifying a president or a board chair, secretary, a treasurer or a chief financial officer).

6   Cal. Corp. Code § 5213(a) (the president or board chair cannot serve concurrently as secretary or treasurer); N.Y. Not-for-Profit Corp. Law § 713 (the president cannot also serve as secretary), *amended by* The Non-Profit Revitalization Act of 2013, 2013 N.Y. Sess. Laws ch. 549, § 73 (McKinney) (effective July 1, 2014).

7   American Institute of Parliamentarians, Standard Code of Parliamentary Procedure 181-82 (2012) [hereinafter Standard Code].

8   N.J. Stat. Ann. § 15A:6-15.d; 15 Pa. Stat. Ann. § 5732(b); N.Y. Not-for-Profit Corp. Law § 713(e), *amended by* The Non-Profit Revitalization Act of 2013, 2013 N.Y. Sess. Laws ch. 549, § 73 (McKinney) (effective July 1, 2014).

9   United States v. Int'l Bhd. of Teamsters, Chauffeurs, Warehousemen & Helpers of Am., 816 F. Supp. 864, 873 n.3 (S.D.N.Y. 1992). In another case a hospital administrator did not have actual or apparent authority to enter into a certain contract; under the bylaws the authority rested with the board. Pee Dee Nursing Home, Inc. v. Florence Gen. Hosp., 419 S.E.2d 834 (S.C. Ct. App. 1992).
    A New York court concluded, "The authority of a member or an officer of an unincorporated association to bind the association 'will not be presumed or implied from the existence of a general power to attend or transact business, or promote the objects for which the association was formed . . . .'" Barrett v. N.Y. Republican State Comm., 625 N.Y.S.2d 769 (App. Div. 1995).

10 Robert's Rules, *supra* note 1, at 444; George Demeter, Demeter's Manual of Parliamentary Law and Procedure 255 (2001) (if the oath is required to take office, it can be done belatedly).

11 Rogers v. Lucassen, 777 F. Supp. 397 (D.D.C. 1991).

12 *See, e.g.*, Animal Legal Def. Fund, Inc. v. Inst. Animal Care & Use Comm. of Univ. of Vt., 616 A.2d 224, 226 (Vt. 1992).

13 *See* Native Vill. of Tyonek v. Puckett, 957 F.2d 631, 633 (9th Cir. 1992). The appellate court remanded the matter to the district court to obtain facts and evidence on these issues. *Id.* at 635-36. The appellate court called the protection of village officers through the village "derivative sovereign immunity." *Id.* at 635.

14 Saks v. Charity Mission Baptist Church, 110 Cal. Rptr. 2d 45, 72 (Ct. App. 2001).

15 Robert's Rules, *supra* note 1, at 124.

16 Cannon, *supra* note 2, at 166.

17 Demeter, *supra* note 10, at 6.

18 For an excellent listing of the duties of the presiding officer, see Robert's Rules, *supra* note 1, at 449-51 and Demeter, *supra* note 10, at 250-52 (also includes privileges).

[19] Floyd M. Riddick & Miriam H. Butcher, Riddick's Rules of Procedure: A Modern Guide to Faster and More Efficient Meetings 38-39 (1985).

[20] Dinowitz v. Rivera, No. 260448/08, 2008 NY Slip Op 52617(U) (Sup. Ct. Nov. 25, 2008).

[21] Reform Party of U.S. v. Gargan, 89 F. Supp. 2d 751, 759-60 (W.D. Va. 2000).

[22] E.g., Cal. Corp. Code § 5213(a) (stating a corporation can have a board chair or president or both); N.Y. Not-for-Profit Corp. Law § 713, amended by The Non-Profit Revitalization Act of 2013, 2013 N.Y. Sess. Laws ch. 549, § 73 (McKinney) (effective July 1, 2014) (same); N.J. Stat. Ann. § 15A:6-15(a); 15 Pa. Stat. Ann. § 5732(a).

[23] See, e.g., 15 Pa. Stat. Ann. § 5732(b); Cal. Corp. Code § 5213(a) ("The president . . . is the general manager and chief executive officer of the corporation, unless otherwise provided in the articles or bylaws."); N.J. Stat. Ann. § 15A:6-15(d); N.Y. Not-for-Profit Corp. Law § 713(e), N.Y. Not-for-Profit Corp. Law § 713, amended by The Non-Profit Revitalization Act of 2013, 2013 N.Y. Sess. Laws ch. 549, § 73 (McKinney) (effective July 1, 2014).

[24] Vacca v. Barletta, 933 F. 2d 31 (1st Cir. 1991). When the acting chair of a school board attempted to silence and had removed a committee member there were material issues of fact so as to deny summary judgment. Id.
    Mobley v. Tarlini, 641 F. Supp. 2d 430 (E.D. Pa. 2009), contains a detailed discussion on when, how and under what conditions a chair of a township council meeting can limit the comments of another sitting councilman at a meeting. The court framed the case as to "what is the correct balance between free speech rights versus parliamentary rules, including a limitation on comments by a township councilman." Id. at 433.

[25] Galena v. Leone, 711 F. Supp. 2d 440, 455-58 (W.D. Pa. 2010). However, in another case, when the chair of a city council meeting removed a member of the public due to a disturbance that took place during the public comment period, the chair "was not acting in a 'legislative capacity.'" Hansen v. Bennett, 948 F.2d 397, 404 (7th Cir. 1991).

[26] Gordon Props., LLC v. First Owners' Ass'n (In re Gordon Properties LLC), 435 B.R. 326, 337 (Bankr. E.D. Va. 2010) ("The court finds that in light of the growing disorder of the meeting, there was insufficient time within which any member could reasonably have requested a division of the assembly or otherwise objected to the motion [to adjourn] or the ruling of the chair.").

[27] See Alice Sturgis, The Standard Code of Parliamentary Procedure 137 (4th ed., rev. 2001).

[28] Riddick & Butcher, supra note 19, at 40.

[29] For an unusual example of a president who reportedly had the authority under the bylaws to rule with an "iron hand" and a board that had no authority unless the president said it did, see Gideons International, Inc. v. Gideon 300 Ministries, Inc., 94 F. Supp. 2d 566, 575 (E.D. Pa. 1999).

[30] Reform Party of U.S. v. Gargan, 89 F. Supp. 2d 751, 761 (W.D. Va. 2000).

[31] See Cmty. Collaborative of Bridgeport, Inc. v. Ganim, 698 A.2d 245 (Conn. 1997) (finding a president of a nonprofit organization did not have the inherent authority to initiate litigation).

[32] Robert's Rules, supra note 1, at 457; see also Demeter, supra note 10, at 255.

33 *Id.*

34 The New York statute states that he board may elect one or more vice-presidents. N.Y.
Not-for-Profit Corp. Law § 713(a) *amended by* The Non-Profit Revitalization Act of 2013,
2013 N.Y. Sess. Laws ch. 549, § 73 (McKinney) (effective July 1, 2014). It also states,

> The certificate of incorporation or a by-law . . . may provide that all offi-
> cers or that specified officers shall be elected by the members instead of by
> the board, or it may authorize the president to appoint the other officers,
> or some of them, subject to the approval of the board.

N.Y. Not-for-Profit Corp. Law § 713(b), *amended by* The Non-Profit Revitalization Act of
2013, 2013 N.Y. Sess. Laws ch. 549, § 73 (McKinney) (effective July 1, 2014). The California
statue does not specifically identify a vice-president but allows for one if stated in the bylaws
or determined by the board. Cal. Corp. Code § 5213(a). The Pennsylvania statute does not
specifically identify a vice-president but authorizes an election or appointment of "other
officers" which presumably includes vice presidents. 15 Pa. Stat. Ann. § 5732(a).

35 15 Pa. Stat. Ann. § 5732(b) If a description is not found in the bylaws, the board of directors may set out the vice-president's authority and duties.

Cal. Corp. Code § 5214. The vice-president may be able to co-sign legal documents with
another officer.

36 Robert's Rules, *supra* note 1, at 575; Riddick & Butcher, *supra* note 19, at 127.

37 *See* Ferrer v. Int'l Longshoremen's Ass'n, 671 F. Supp. 2d 276, 279 (D.P.R. 2009).

38 Riddick & Butcher, *supra* note 19, at 127.

39 Demeter, *supra* note 10, at 41.

40 Robert's Rules, *supra* note 1, at 633.

41 Demeter, *supra* note 10, at 163.

42 Robert's Rules, *supra* note 1, at 22.

43 *E.g.,* Cal. Corp. Code § 5213(a); N.J. Stat. Ann. § 15A:6-15.a; N.Y. Not-for-Profit Corp.
Law § 713(a), *amended by* The Non-Profit Revitalization Act of 2013, 2013 N.Y. Sess.
Laws ch. 549, § 73 (McKinney) (effective July 1, 2014); 15 Pa. Stat. Ann. § 5732(a).

44 15 Pa. Stat. Ann. § 5732(b); N.J. Stat. Ann. § 15A:6-15.d.
In *Snyder v. Murray City Corp.*, the secretary of the city council had the duty of or-
ganizing and selecting who would deliver an opening prayer. 159 F.3d 1227, 1242 (10th
Cir. 1998). A question was raised about compliance with the Establishment Clause of the
Constitution when a different prayer being offered from a private citizen was denied. *Id.*

45 For three excellent lists of functions, see Robert's Rules, *supra* note 1, at 458-59, Sturgis,
supra note 27, at 166-68, and Demeter, *supra* note 10, at 252 (for recording secretary).

46 Demeter, *supra* note 10, at 221.

47   *See, e.g.,* 15 Pa. Stat. Ann. § 5704(b); *see also* Keystone Plaza Condos. Ass'n v. Eastep, 2004 SD 28, 676 N.W.2d 842 (including a typical bylaw requiring the secretary to mail out notice of meetings); Baldwin Cnty. Elec. Membership Corp. v. Lee, 804 So. 2d 1087, 1090 (Ala. 2001) (noting secretary's duty to send out notice of a special meeting); Memphis Health Ctr., Inc. v. Grant, No. W 2004-02898-COA-R3-CV, at *3 (Tenn. Ct. App. July 28, 2006) (describing the duties of a board secretary in the bylaws as "attending all meetings, recording all votes, keeping minutes of all proceedings, distributing minutes to Board meetings, and giving notice of all board meetings").

48   Robert's Rules, *supra* note 1, at 459-60.

49   *Id.* at 652 n.1.

50   Sahli v. Woodbine Bd. of Educ., 938 A.2d 923, 930 (N.J. 2008).

51   *E.g.,* Cal. Corp. Code § 5213(a); N.J. Stat. Ann. § 15A:6-15.a; N.Y. Not-for-Profit Corp. Law § 713(a), *amended by* The Non-Profit Revitalization Act of 2013, 2013 N.Y. Sess. Laws ch. 549, § 73 (McKinney) (effective July 1, 2014); 15 Pa. Stat. Ann. § 5732(a).

52   *E.g.,* N.Y. Not-for-Profit Corp. Law § 713(a)-(b), *amended by* The Non-Profit Revitalization Act of 2013, 2013 N.Y. Sess. Laws ch. 549, § 73 (McKinney) (effective July 1, 2014) (or the treasurer may be appointed by the president, subject to board approval); 15 Pa. Stat. Ann. § 5732(a); N.J. Stat. Ann. § 15A:6-15.a; Cal. Corp. Code § 5213(b).

53   15 Pa. Stat. Ann. § 5732(b); N.Y. Not-for-Profit Corp. Law § 713(e), *amended by* The Non-Profit Revitalization Act of 2013, 2013 N.Y. Sess. Laws ch. 549, § 73 (McKinney) (effective July 1, 2014); Cal. Corp. Code § 5213(a) (the treasurer is the chief financial officer unless otherwise specified in the articles or the bylaws).

54   Riddick & Butcher, *supra* note 19, at 171; Sturgis, *supra* note 27, at 169.

55   Riddick & Butcher, *supra* note 19, at 171; *see also* 15 Pa. Stat. Ann. § 5554(a) (allowing annual financial report to the members to be "verified by the president and treasurer or by a majority of the directors or members of the other body").

56   Standard Code, *supra* note 7, at 180.

57   Robert's Rules, *supra* note 1, at 477.

58   *Id.*

59   *Id.* at 479.

60   *Id.*

61   Demeter, *supra* note 10, at 253.

62   *See E. Hampton Union Free Sch. Dist. v. Sandpebble Builders, Inc.,* 2009 N.Y. Slip Op. 50572(U), at *8-9 (Sup. Ct. Mar. 16, 2009).

63   *See id.* (stating that under the bylaws of a board of education, the treasurer could only pay and disburse funds after approval by or ordered by a board) (decided on other grounds). In a New Mexico case, a county treasurer had no "authority to file suit to enforce the

personal obligation of owners of real property for the collection of delinquent property taxes," Colfax Cnty. v. Angel Fire Corp., 848 P.2d 532, 533 (N.M. Ct. App. 1993).

[64] Whitmore Union Elementary Sch. Dist. v. Cnty. of Shasta, 104 Cal. Rptr. 2d 227, 229 (Ct. App. 2001).

[65] STURGIS, *supra* note 27, at 168-69.

[66] Bd. of Educ. of Plainedge Union Free Sch. v. Conn. Gen. Life Ins. Co., 309 F. Supp. 2d 416, 425 (E.D.N.Y. 2004). The court stated, "Apparent authority arises from the 'written or spoken words or any conduct of the principal which, reasonably interpreted, causes [a] third person to believe that the principal consents to have [an] act done on [its] behalf by the person purporting to act for him.'" *Id.* at 420-21 (quoting Dinaco, Inc. v. Time Warner, Inc., 346 F. 3d 64, 69 (2d Cir. 2003)).

[67] *E.g.*, 15 PA. STAT. ANN. § 5733; N.Y. NOT-FOR-PROFIT CORP. LAW § 714(a); N.J. STAT. ANN. § 15A:6-16.a; CAL. CORP. CODE § 5213(b). Officers chosen by the board serve at the pleasure of the board. A police chief appointed by a town board of trustees was an employee at will and could be terminated without cause. Lane v. Town of Dover, Okla., 761 F. Supp. 768, 771 (W.D. Okla. 1991).

[68] *E.g.*, N.J. STAT. ANN. § 15A:6-16.a; 15 PA. STAT. ANN. § 5733 ("Unless otherwise provided in the bylaws, any officer or agent of a nonprofit corporation may be removed by the board of directors or other body with or without cause."); N.Y. NOT-FOR-PROFIT CORP. LAW § 714(a).

[69] N.Y. NOT-FOR-PROFIT CORP. LAW § 714(a).

[70] STANDARD CODE, *supra* note 7, at 185-86 (listing valid and invalid reasons for removal); RIDDICK & BUTCHER, *supra* note 19, at 83.

[71] *See* RIDDICK & BUTCHER, *supra* note 19, at 86; STURGIS, *supra* note 27, at 173 (noting the organization has the right to suspend an officer); *see also* CAL. CORP. CODE § 5222(f)(1).

[72] Maddalone v. Local 17, 152 F.3d 178, 184-85 (2d Cir. 1998); Messina v. Local 1199 SEIU, 205 F. Supp. 2d 111, 122-23 (S.D.N.Y. 2002).

[73] Farrell v. Hellen, 367 F. Supp. 2d 491, 502-03 (S.D.N.Y. 2005).

[74] See ROBERT'S RULES, *supra* note 1, at 656, for some suggestions.

[75] Detailed procedures for discipline of an officer can be found in, *id.* at 643-69 and DEMETER, *supra* note 10, at 266-69.

[76] *See, e.g.*, Argentine v. United Steel Workers Ass'n, 23 F. Supp. 2d 808, 818 (S.D. Ohio 1998).

[77] *Id.* at 819.

[78] Murray v. Carroll, 536 F. Supp. 2d 225, 230 (D. Conn. 2008).

[79] Yee v. Wond, 08-814 (La. App. 5th Cir. 3/24/09); 10 So.3d 791; *see also* STURGIS, *supra* note 27, at 174.

[80] RIDDICK & BUTCHER, *supra* note 19, at 85-86.

[81] DEMETER, *supra* note 10, at 263.

[82] *Id.*; ROBERT'S RULES, *supra* note 1, at 650-53.

[83] ROBERT'S RULES, *supra* note 1, at 653, allows for a majority vote with prior notice.

[84] ROBERT'S RULES, *supra* note 1, at 95, 664-65; *see also* RIDDICK & BUTCHER, *supra* note 19, at 86 ("trial . . . *should* be held in closed session") (emphasis added).

[85] DEMETER, *supra* note 10, at 259-60.

[86] *Id.* at 260-264. Censure is also recognized as a form of discipline by RIDDICK & BUTCHER, *supra* note 19, at 40.

[87] DEMETER, *supra* note 10, at 265.

[88] Holben v. Ohio State Med. Bd., 2009-Ohio-6323, 924 N.E.2d 851.

CHAPTER **14**

Directors

§ 78 QUALIFICATION, NOMINATION AND SELECTION OF DIRECTORS

Selection, qualifications and eligibility of directors, including rules of nomination,[1] are determined by statute, the articles of incorporation and the bylaws.[2] "Qualifications for each office" should be set forth in the bylaws.[3]

Required qualifications for office, in this writer's opinion, should not be decided on an ad hoc basis. This creates uncertainty among members about who will be found qualified and can also cause a lack of consistency from year to year. The bylaws can establish "such standards for holding office."[4] Under the New Jersey statute if a by-law adopted by the members provides for a free and reasonable procedure for the nomination and election of candidates for any office (including election of trustee), only candidates who have been duly nominated according to this bylaw should be eligible for election.[5]

Under the California statute larger corporations must allow a nominee "a reasonable opportunity to communicate to the members the nominee's qualifications and the reasons for the nominee's candidacy."[6]

A California court disapproved of an election in which qualifications for a director position for a nonprofit association were so restrictive that only incumbents could serve.[7] In a New Jersey case a board of trustees for a homeowner's association has authority under the bylaws to require additional qualifications for candidates to serve as trustees.[8] In a Louisiana case, an organization's bylaws may be amended to change qualifications of those who seek nomination for office.[9]

Any member can nominate any other eligible member for office.[10] A parliamentary reference states that if the nominated member is in arrears on his dues, he still may be nominated if he has not been suspended from membership or if the bylaws provide otherwise.[11] In a Connecticut case non-members may serve as directors.[12] There are many important advantages to have staggered director terms established in the bylaws such as continuity of leadership.

Directors are commonly elected by members.[13] However, if authorized by the bylaws, directors can be selected or elected by other means[14] such as by a vote of delegates, by being chairs of standing committees,[15] and as ex-officio members.[16] Under the Michigan state nonprofit statute, a distinction may be drawn in the articles between an "entity" organized on either a "membership" or a "directorship basis."[17] If it is the latter, only the directors "vote on the removal of board members or the filling of vacancies on the board."[18]

A sample of cases show varied results regarding what criteria can be used in qualifying for a director position. A labor union rule that nominees were required to submit their social security numbers and addresses during the nominations meeting or be disqualified was ruled illegal by a New York court;[19] moreover, the court stated that qualifying rules must be made readily available.[20] Rules requiring a union member to have attended prior meetings in order to qualify for nomination to office were rejected by a court in Indiana.[21] However, this situation should be carefully researched and evaluated. In a

California case a "qualifying committee" had the discretion on how it wished to weight candidates.[22]

A court ruled in a Kansas case that developers of a condominium were required to relinquish control of the board of directors after a reasonable period of time.[23] A challenger in a New York case had the burden of proof to show that selection of directors was improper.[24]

§ 79 POWERS OF DIRECTORS

State nonprofit statutes declare that "the activities and affairs of the corporation shall be conducted and all corporate powers shall be exercised by or under the ultimate direction of the board."[25] Other titles for boards of directors include board of trustees, board of managers and executive board. The board operates the organization between meetings of the assembly.[26] Under the Pennsylvania state nonprofit statute, the board is specifically granted a lengthy list of general powers also granted to every for-profit corporation, with limitations and restrictions on these powers outlined in the statute or bylaws.[27] Board authority may be limited by the articles, by the bylaws, or by the members.[28]

As noted above, a corporation is managed by its board of directors.[29] For example, it was noted in a university governance bylaw in Connecticut that, "The 'rights, powers and privileges' of the university are vested in a board of trustees."[30] A parliamentary authority has noted that boards have whatever power and authority is given in the bylaws or delegated to it for an individual matter as may be directed by the membership.[31]

Questions arise as to the authority of a board relative to the collective membership. At least one parliamentary reference notes that the assembly can overrule the board on any matter except those powers exclusively given to [a nonprofit] board under the bylaws.[32] Moreover, the board cannot make a decision which alters or conflicts with a prior decision of the assembly.[33] There is a significant school of thought that absent extraordinary circumstances the membership can override a decision of the board even when the board is granted specific authority in the bylaws or articles. Other authorities disagree. Further discussion is beyond the scope of this text.

In an Ohio opinion the court commented that, "An executive board cannot prohibit the membership at large from deciding an issue, especially if that issue has earlier been improperly voted upon by the board. The tail cannot wag the dog."[34] A court in Illinois noted that directors may not remove a clergyman if this power is reserved to members of an organization in the bylaws.[35]

In this writer's opinion, the better view is that the authority of the membership (in membership organizations) overrules that of a board when the entire membership has prior notice of the issue in question and a vote is taken. This of course is dependent on the law of the individual jurisdiction and the facts of the situation.

Boards are given leeway in exercising their powers. Under the "rule of judicial deference," courts will defer to a board's authority and expertise in discretionary matters.[36] In a sample of cases a Tennessee court has noted that the board has the authority to terminate clinical privileges without a due process hearing as a result of the ending of an exclusive provider contract.[37] A California appellate court distinguished between judicial deference under the business judgment rule for a nonprofit corporation compared to judicial deference of the type for homeowners' associations.[38]

There are, of course, limits on board authority.[39] The board's exercise of power must be reasonable. A North Dakota court ruled that imposing a large assessment on a minority of unaffected homeowners was invalid.[40] In an Arizona case, a court is not obligated to defer to the discretion of a board when a suit is brought by a member.[41] An opera board in a Louisiana case could not amend its articles of incorporation when the court decided that such amendment violated the rights of a third party beneficiary.[42]

In a Florida case, a board has the authority to interpret its own bylaws, including amendments, if it is not done in an arbitrary or unreasonable manner.[43] Ambiguous provisions in the bylaws should be interpreted by the board in harmony with the other bylaws. Strained or self-serving interpretation should be avoided. A club's bylaws in a Florida case provided the board with the final interpretation of the bylaws if it was not arbitrary or unreasonable.[44] And, in a District of Columbia case, if the leadership's interpretation of their own constitution and bylaws is believed to be unreasonable and in bad faith, the court will override such interpretation.[45]

The "board can exercise only authority as a collective group."[46] Thus an individual board member outside of a board meeting has no more authority than any other member of the organization. (An exception may be when an individual board member seeks access to corporate records.)

§ 80 DUTIES OF DIRECTORS AND EXECUTIVE COMMITTEES

Virtually all state statutes and common law require directors to comply with a fiduciary duty[47] in exercising their board responsibilities. Directors carry serious responsibilities and duties.[48] Different states use different terms and definitions but they all result in a similar significant obligation to the organization.

For example, the New York not-for-profit corporate statute states that, "Directors and officers shall discharge the duties of their respective positions in good faith and with the care an ordinarily prudent person in a like position would exercise under similar circumstances."[49] State statutes typically add that a director can rely upon the expertise of professionals and [in some cases] committees if such reliance is reasonable.[50]

It has been stated that directors and officers of a nonprofit corporation owe their duty "to the corporation and its members, and shall discharge the duties of their respective positions in good faith, and with that diligence, care, judgment and skill which ordinarily prudent men would exercise under similar circumstances in like positions."[51] A term that is often used to describe a director's duties is the business judgment rule.[52] Another frequently used descriptive term is the "ordinarily prudent person rule."[53]

Under the Louisiana statute, "officers and directors shall be deemed to stand in a fiduciary relation to the corporation and its members, and shall discharge the duties of their respective positions in good faith, and with that diligence, care, judgment and skill which ordinarily prudent men would exercise under similar circumstances in like positions."[54]

The board[55] is expected [and this should be outlined in the bylaws] to make decisions and operate the organization on behalf of the membership in-between membership meetings.[56] The duties, responsibilities, and powers of the board should be specified in the bylaws.[57] There are options on what wording to use in the bylaws to describe the scope and reach of the board's authority and such wording should be carefully considered when the bylaws are drafted.

A fiduciary [director] has the burden in a Kansas case to show a transaction is fair and done in good faith when that transaction is challenged.[58] A South Dakota court decided that hospital directors had a duty to manage the organization and did not have to consult the medical staff to make business decisions.[59]

A board member has a duty to disclose and comply with conflict of interest laws and rules[60] when he or she is voting. This is further discussed in Section 83 of this text. A serious failure of this duty can result in personal liability to the director. Yet mere status as a director does not create individual liability.[61] The IRS tax exempt status of a nonprofit organization can be put at risk by a director's failure to comply with conflict of interest regulations and the organization's acquiescence.[62]

In Pennsylvania, if a director at a meeting feels strongly opposed to a vote or action taken by the rest of the directors, he or she has the right to have his contrary position noted in the minutes or to transmit such adverse position immediately after the meeting in writing to the secretary.[63] This is a matter of good practice in whatever state the meeting takes place.

§ 81 REMOVAL AND RESIGNATION OF DIRECTORS

State nonprofit corporate statutes vary on the requirements for removal of board members. Some require cause,[64] others do not,[65] and some include both options.[66] Each state statute for the applicable venue must be read carefully to see if and when removal of a director requires cause and for similar details. Many of the statutes defer to the organization's bylaws and only a majority vote with the presence of a quorum may be required. Under the Pennsylvania statute the board can declare a board position vacant for an "unsound mind," conviction "of an offense punishable by imprisonment for a term of more than one year," "or for any other proper cause which the bylaws may specify."[67]

There must be sufficient grounds in which to remove a director for cause. These grounds may be specified by statute or in the organization's bylaws. Case law for the particular state should also be consulted. One parliamentary reference lists grounds which it considers valid for removal and lists others which are not valid.[68]

Directors may be removed for failure to attend meetings.[69] A failure to recuse oneself from participating in a matter in which the director has a conflict of interest constitutes just cause for removal from a board position.[70] Under a new California statutory provision, a director may be removed for losing his originally required qualifications.[71] In a Texas case, a threat of a lawsuit against a property owners' association constituted cause.[72] In a Washington case, suspension for cause is a determination within a board's discretion.[73]

Under the New Jersey statute, board members may be suspended by the rest of the board for cause.[74] A court in Washington commented that a nonprofit board may suspend other members of the board for up to 30 days by which time the membership must vote on removal from office.[75]

Critical to an organization is that the bylaws and/or pre-existing official policy set out a fair procedure for the removal or suspension of a director and that the procedure is fairly and closely followed. RONR has a lengthy set of procedures for this purpose.[76] Demeter details in excellent fashion the process including the "trial" phase.[77] To the extent feasible the disciplinary process should be conducted privately.

Elements of due process should be the cornerstone of the disciplinary procedure. This includes informing the accused of the charges[78] (preferably in writing), allowing time to prepare a defense,[79] an opportunity to appear and defend oneself,[80] and the chance to be fairly treated.[81] One view is that the accused has a right to legal counsel for his defense.[82]

As noted above, state statutes often require only a majority vote to remove a director.[83] Normally, directors, officers, and committee members can be removed from office by the same authority that put them in office.[84] In a Florida case, only a majority vote of the voting members with or without cause to recall a sitting board member may be necessary.[85] Under the California statute, a vacancy can be created if a director does not accept office, attend board meetings, or meet "any required qualification that was in effect at the beginning of that director's current term of office."[86] A common clause in bylaws is that failure to attend a certain number of board meetings without justification is grounds for removal.

An officer or director can resign effective immediately or at a later date.[87] If the resignation is effective at a later date and has yet to have been accepted or the date reached, the resignation can be withdrawn.[88] Good practice is for a resignation to be formally voted on for approval but this is usually not required. In a Georgia case, the court decided that a board member could only resign in writing to be removed.[89] If the resignation date has not been reached or the resignation not yet formally accepted, an attempt to rescind the resignation by the maker may be effective.

§ 82 VACANCIES

Vacancies in an officer or board member's position are defined by statute or the bylaws.[90] A vacancy may occur through a variety of reasons including death, resignation, or removal from office.[91] Committee positions can, of course, be vacant as well. Other reasons for vacancy can be ineligibility of an officer, abandonment, prolonged neglect,[92] or inability to act [93] Vacancies should never be hidden or ignored.[94] Vacancies should never be created through deception.[95]

Questions may arise about how and when an officer resigns and if such resignation must be formally accepted. In this writer's opinion, a formal acknowledgement of a resignation is desirable - even if often not required. Under the California statute, a director's resignation is effective upon giving notice unless the notice specifies a later time.[96] In an Ohio court opinion, a school district director was able to rescind her resignation if the resignation had not been formally accepted.[97]

State statutes, as modified by the bylaws[98] determine how a vacancy in a nonprofit corporation is filled. Usually, unless there is a bylaw or other rule to the contrary, vacancies are filled by the same constituency that elected or appointed the person to the position originally.[99] State statutes may also provide that, unless contrary to the articles or bylaws, board vacancies can be filled by the remainder of the board[100] even if no quorum remains. According to one parliamentary reference, if an election is needed to fill a vacancy, prior notice to the voters is required.[101] Bylaws typically provide that the vacancy of the president is filled by the president-elect or the vice-president.[102] However, the bylaws may provide for a special election to fill the opening. Board vacancies cannot be filled by committees.[103]

An Ohio court noted that a quorum is not needed to fill a vacancy if a quorum cannot be obtained.[104]

Applicable state statutes determine the filling of vacancies of governmental organizations. In a Pennsylvania case, a vacancy on a township board of supervisors must be filled by "an affirmative vote of a majority of the *entire* board," not a majority of a quorum.[105]

In another Pennsylvania case, the court ruled that the mayor was allowed "to cast a tie-breaking vote in order to fill a vacancy on Borough Council" based on a section of the Borough Code.[106] In a California case, an appointee was determined eligible to fill a vacancy on a district board only until the person elected at the next general election was qualified to fill that vacancy.[107]

§ 83 CONFLICT OF INTEREST

Board members, including officers, must be very careful in dealing with any matter in which they have business dealings[108] or a pecuniary,[109] or a direct personal interest with the organization.[110] A good illustration is a proposed business contract between a director and the organization he or she serves. These situations create a conflict of interest. "[L]oans by a corporation to its directors or officers" are normally prohibited.[111] The director's interest must be disclosed to the others.[112] In addition to abstaining from voting it may be good practice, although not necessarily mandatory, for the recusing person to have only limited participation in the debate and even leave the meeting room during the taking of the vote.[113] The president should step down from presiding when he or she has a direct personal or pecuniary interest in a motion.[114]

In this writer's opinion, conflict of interest requirements should be explained at the beginning of every board meeting. Those with a conflict or a potential conflict should disclose this at the start of the meeting (if known) and again when the subject comes up. The adverse consequences both to the member and the organization for failing to comply with conflict of interest mandates should be explained at the meeting.

The conflict does not necessarily or automatically prevent the director from engaging in a business relationship with the organization, but the contract or transaction in question must be fair to the organization. The contract or transaction may be subsequently voidable by the organization even if it is deemed fair. However, in this writer's opinion, there are circumstances in which the conflict is one in which the director should not continue to serve in his or her fiduciary capacity - especially in a governmental context. There may also be statutory and other legal requirements or circumstances that prevent such conflicts from being overcome even when they are fully disclosed.

Virtually all state nonprofit statutes provide a procedure for handling such conflicts. Two of the cornerstones are that there be full and complete disclosure of the material facts of the conflict by the director or officer with the conflict and that there be sufficient votes in support of the measure, excluding those with the conflict.[115] Those with a conflict are counted in determining if there is a quorum.[116] As noted above, the transaction must be fair and reasonable to the organization when looked at objectively at the time of the vote.[117]

Courts have noted that a conflict of interest transaction involving a director may be approved by a board provided there are certain safeguards.[118] The conflict of interest may affect the method of determining the outcome of a vote and how it is calculated.[119] Under a Hawaii statute a resident manager of a condominium was ruled eligible to serve on the board although the retroactivity of the law was challenged.[120]

The usual context for a conflict of interest is a transaction or contract between a board member and the nonprofit corporation.[121] The organization's bylaws should have provisions for handling a conflict of interest or alternatively, there should be an adopted policy.[122] The bylaw or policy of the organization should be consistent with the applicable state statute. One parliamentary reference argues that if the bylaws prevent an immediately interested member from voting on a proposition the relevant bylaw is binding.[123]

A failure to comply with the conflict of interest requirements can have serious adverse consequences.[124] In one New York case it was determined that officers of a nonprofit corporation has a duty to comply with the conflicts of interest policy as an inherent fiduciary duty.[125] In an Ohio case, failing to recuse oneself constitutes just cause for removal.[126]

§ 84 INDEMNIFICATION

In the event of a legal claim against an officer or a board member acting within the course of performing his or her duties, the organization may, depending on the individual circumstances, pay for or indemnify the officer or board member for his or her legal fees, financial liabilities and obligations. This is determined on a case by case basis.

This is an area covered in virtually all state nonprofit statutes[127] and sometimes, bylaw provisions, as well. Statutory provisions describe the internal procedure which must be followed.[128] Usually the decision on whether to indemnify an officer or director is made by a majority vote of the disinterested directors to the proceedings, or by a vote of the membership with the persons to be indemnified not voting. Appropriate resolutions should be carefully prepared and a quorum must be present when the vote is taken.

A court ruled in an Alabama case that a majority of the utility company's board had the authority to reimburse a board member for legal fees if the board found that the trustee had met the applicable standard of conduct.[129] However, indemnification of legal fees was discretionary in the Alabama case and the utility chose not to pay the fees.[130]

---

[1] CAL. CORP. CODE § 5520(a) (West 2013 & Supp. 2014) ("As to directors elected by members, there shall be available to the members reasonable nomination and election procedures given the nature, size and operations of the corporation.").
Nominations from the floor usually do not require a second unless required by the organization.

[2] *Id.* § 5521(a) (Nominations may be "[b]y any method authorized by the bylaws, or if no method is set forth in the bylaws, by any method authorized by the board." (California goes on to permit nominations by petition and by a floor nomination.)); 15 PA. STAT. ANN. § 5725(e) (West 2013) ("Unless otherwise provided in the bylaws, directors shall be nominated by a nominating committee or from the floor."); N.Y. NOT-FOR-PROFIT CORP. LAW § 701(a) (McKinney 2013); *see also* Boatmen's First Nat'l Bank of W. Plains v. S. Mo. Dist. Council of the Assemblies of God, 806 S.W.2d 706, 173 (Mo. Ct. App. 1991) ("The bylaws of a not-for-profit corporation may contain any provision for the regulation and management of the corporation which is not inconsistent with law or the corporation's articles of incorporation." (footnote omitted).

[3] AMERICAN INSTITUTE OF PARLIAMENTARIANS, STANDARD CODE OF PARLIAMENTARY PROCEDURE 159 (2012) [hereinafter STANDARD CODE].

[4] HUGH CANNON, CANNON'S CONCISE GUIDE TO RULES OF ORDER 129-30 (2001).

[5] N.J. STAT. ANN. § 15A:5-20.e (West 2013 & Supp. 2014).

[6] CAL. CORP. CODE § 5522(c).

[7] McElroy v. Pernell, No. B190293, 2007 WL 2793344 (Cal. Ct. App. Sept. 27, 2007). Here the challenged bylaw said in part "that no individuals aside from those already serving on the Board were able to be on the ballot for consideration." *Id.*
A typical broadly worded bylaw for qualification of directors is that the director must be a voting member in good standing of an organization. *See, e.g.,* Mueller v. Zimmer, 124 P.3d 340,358 (Wyo. 2005).

8   Mulligan v. Panther Valley Prop. Owners Ass'n, 766 A.2d 1186, 1195 (N.J. Super. Ct. App. Div. 2001).

9   *See* Carter v. Dixie Elect. Membership Corp., 98-30483 (La. App. 2 Cir. 8/21/98) 717 So. 2d 691.

10   CANNON, *supra* note 4, at 129.

11   GEORGE DEMETER, DEMETER'S MANUAL OF PARLIAMENTARY LAW AND PROCEDURE 239 (2001).

12   Bella Vista Condo. Ass'n v. Byars, No. CV03180606, 2005 WL 3292533 (Conn. Super. Ct Nov. 8, 2005). Condominium board members do not all have to be condominium owners if they are elected by the owners. *See* Unrau v. Kidron Bethel Retirement Servs., Inc., 27 P.3d 1 (Kan. 2001).

13   CANNON, *supra* note 4, at 3; DEMETER, *supra* note 11, at 270 (noting that directors are normally elected when officers are elected in conformity with the expiration of their terms); SARAH CORBIN ROBERT, HENRY M. ROBERT III, WILLIAM J. EVANS, DANIEL H. HONEMANN & THOMAS J. BALCH, ROBERT'S RULES OF ORDER NEWLY REVISED 463 (11th ed. 2011) [hereinafter ROBERT'S RULES] (asserting that all directors should be elected).

14   15 PA. STAT. ANN. § 5725(b) ("or in the manner provided in, the bylaw . . . ."); CAL. CORP. CODE § 5520(b) ("If a corporation complies with all of the provisions . . . applicable to a corporation with the same number of members, the nomination and election procedures of that corporation shall be deemed reasonable. However, those sections do not prescribe the exclusive means of making available to the members reasonable procedures for nomination and election of directors. A corporation may make available to the members other reasonable nomination and election procedures given the nature, size, and operations of the corporation.").

       In *First Assembly of God Christian Center of Pittsburg v. Bridgeway*, A121224 (Cal. Ct. App. June 24, 2009), the court's involvement regarding selection of directors was not barred as an ecclesiastical matter; the court relied on the "neutral principles" doctrine. *Id.* "We do not interfere with [the church's] constitutional rights regarding religion if we simply require that it follow the procedures contained in its governing documents based on the application of neutral principles of law." *Id.; accord* Beth Hamedrosh Hagodol Cemetery Ass'n v. Levy, 923 S.W.2d 439, 443 (Mo. Ct. App. 1996).

15   FLOYD M. RIDDICK & MIRIAM H. BUTCHER, RIDDICK'S RULES OF PROCEDURE: A MODERN GUIDE TO FASTER AND MORE EFFICIENT MEETINGS 28 (1985).

16   *Id.*

17   *See, e.g.,* MICH. COMP. LAWS §§ 450.2304, 450.2305 (2013).

18   Mich. Military Moms v. Vanhooser, No. 306553, at *5 (Mich. Ct. App. Jan. 24, 2013), http://publicdocs.courts.mi.gov:81/OPINIONS/FINAL/COA/20130124_C306553_68_306553.OPN.PDF.

19   Herman v. N.Y. Metro Area Postal Union, 30 F. Supp. 2d 636, 644 (S.D.N.Y. 1998).

20   *Id.* at 646.

21   Herman v. Local Union 1011, 59 F. Supp. 2d 770, 779-80 (N.D. Ind. 1999) (finding that an attendance rule which required eight months to qualify was too long when it excluded

90% of the membership); *see also* Local 3489, United Steelworkers of Am. v. Usery, 429 U.S. 305, 310-11 (1977) (finding a qualifying period of eighteen months to be too long).

A claim of age discrimination was recognized by the court for a nominee to a military college's board of visitors. Arnold v. Ass'n of Citadel Men, 523 S.E.2d 757 (S.C. 1999).

[22] Avila v. Apostolic Assembly of the Faith in Christ Jesus, E046233, 2009 WL 891021 (Cal. Ct. App. Apr. 3, 2009). The qualifying committee did not have to nominate the candidates by the majority vote totals in the initial general election. *Id.*

[23] Unrau v. Kidron Bethel Retirement Servs., Inc., 27 P.3d 1 (Kan. 2001).

[24] Mittasch v. Long Island Greyhound Transfer, Inc., 2008 NY Slip Op 31414(U) (Sup. Ct. May 6, 2008).

[25] *E.g.,* CAL. CORP. CODE § 5210; *see also* N.J. STAT. ANN. § 15A:6-1 ("The activities of a corporation, shall be managed by its board . . . ."); N.Y. NOT-FOR-PROFIT CORP. LAW § 701; 15 PA. STAT. ANN. § 5721.

[26] CANNON, *supra* note 4, at 3.

[27] 15 PA. STAT. ANN. § 5721 (referring back to 15 PA. STAT. ANN. § 5502).

[28] *E.g.,* CAL. CORP. CODE § 5210; N.J. STAT. ANN. § 15A:6-1 (certificate of incorporation can limit board management); N.Y. NOT-FOR-PROFIT CORP. LAW § 701; 15 PA. STAT. ANN. § 5721.

[29] *E.g.,* CAL. CORP. CODE § 5210 ("Each corporation shall have a board of directors."); Fla. State Oriental Med. Ass'n v. Slepin, 971 So. 2d 141, 144 (Fla. Dist. Ct. App. 2007) ("A corporation is managed by its board of directors or by its officers acting under the direction and control of the board."); Steeneck v. Univ. of Bridgeport, 668 A.2d 688 (Conn. 1995).

[30] *Steeneck,* 668 A.2d at 690 (quoting the University's bylaws).

[31] ROBERT'S RULES, *supra* note 13, at 482. See DEMETER, *supra* note 11, at 270-71, for insightful comments about board authority.

[32] ROBERT'S RULES, *supra* note 13, at 483.

[33] *Id.*

[34] Tucker v. Nat'l Ass'n of Postal Supervisors, 2003-Ohio-2994, 790 N.E.2d 370, at ¶ 18.

[35] Ervin v. Lilydale Progressive Missionary, 813 N.E.2d 1073, 1078 (Ill. App. Ct. 2004). In another case, the president did not have the authority to sell corporate assets; only the directors and/or the members had such authority. Lensa Corp. v. Poinciana Gardens Ass'n, 765 So. 2d 296 (Fla. Dist. Ct. App. 2000). However in a New York union case, the Executive Board of the union runs its "daily affairs," has the authority to select legal counsel, and no authority for such selection from the assembly is needed. N.Y. State Corr. Officers & Police Benevolent Ass'n v. Hinman Straub, P.C., 14585/04, 2004 WL 2889761 (N.Y. Oct. 18, 2004).

[36] Harvey v. Landing Homeowners Ass'n, 76 Cal. Rptr. 3d 41, 49-50 (Ct. App. 2008) (citing Lamden v. La Jolla Shores Clubdominium Homeowners Ass'n, 980 P.2d 940 (Cal. 1999)).

[37] Cookeville Reg'l Med. Ctr. v. Humphrey, 126 S.W.3d 897 (Tenn. 2004).

38   Scheenstra v. Cal. Dairies, Inc., 213 Cal. App. 4th 370, 386 (2013) (citing *Lamden*, 21 Cal. 4th 249 (1999)).

39   <u>Demeter</u> provides a summary of the limitation of board power,

> A board may not reduce or add to prohibitions fixed in the bylaws. It cannot create an office in the organization, unless expressly so authorized. It cannot censure or otherwise punish any one of its members. Instead, it can propose such action before the assembly. Any action taken by a board not expressly authorized by a bylaw may be reversed by the assembly.

DEMETER, *supra* note 11, at 271.

40   Buckingham v. Weston Vill. Homeowners Ass'n, 1997 ND 237, 571 N.W.2d 842.

41   Johnson v. Pointe Cmty. Ass'n, 73 P.3d 616, (Ariz. Ct. App. 2003).

42   New Orleans Opera Ass'n v. So. Reg'l Opera Endowment Fund, 2007-1373 (La. App. 4 Cir. 8/2708); 993 So. 2d 791.

43   *E.g.*, Susi v. St. Andrew Cntry. Club, 727 So. 2d 1058, 1061-62 (Fla. Dist. Ct. App. 1999); Boca West Club, Inc. v. Levine, 578 So. 2d 14, 15-16 (Fla. Dist. Ct. App. 1991). An executive board has also been found to have the right to reasonably interpret an organization's own constitution and bylaws. Maher v. Int'l Bhd. of Elec. Workers, 15 F.3d 711, 714 (7th Cir. 1994); Air Wisc. Pilots Prot. Comm. v. Sanderson, 909 F.2d 213, 218 (7th Cir. 1990); Local 715 v. Michelin Am. Small Tire, 848 F. Supp. 1400, 1408-09 (N.D. Ind. 1994); Massaro v. Mainlands Section 1 & 2 Civic Ass'n, 796 F. Supp. 1499 (S.D. Fla. 1992).

44   *Boca West Club*, 578 So. 2d at 15-16.

45   Rogers v. Lucassen, 777 F. Supp. 997, 999-1002 (D.D.C. 1991).

46   RIDDICK & BUTCHER, *supra* note 15, at 27; *see also* ALICE STURGIS, THE STANDARD CODE OF PARLIAMENTARY PROCEDURE 182 (4th ed., rev. 2001) (stating a board member can only exercise authority while the board is in session).

47   *E.g.*, N.Y. NOT-FOR-PROFIT CORP. LAW § 717(a); Tucker v. Nat'l Ass'n of Postal Supervisors, 2003-Ohio-2994, 790 N.E.2d 370, at ¶ 19.

48   *See* RIDDICK & BUTCHER, *supra* note 15, at 29.

49   N.Y. NOT-FOR-PROFIT CORP. LAW § 717(a); *see also* CAL. CORP. CODE § 5231(a); N.J. STAT. ANN. § 15A:6-14. 15 PA. STAT. ANN. § 5712(a) states the principle as follows:

> A director of a nonprofit corporation shall stand in a fiduciary relation to the corporation and shall perform his duties as a director, including his duties as a member of any committee of the board upon which he may serve, in good faith, in a manner he reasonably believes to be in the best interests of the corporation and with such care, including reasonable inquiry, skill and diligence, as a person of ordinary prudence would use under similar circumstances.

50   *See, e.g.*, 15 PA. STAT. ANN. § 5712(a)(1)-(3) (stating reliance by the board may include officers or employees, counsel, public accountants, and a committee of the board); N.Y.

NOT-FOR-PROFIT CORP. LAW § 717(b): N.J. STAT. ANN. § 15A:6-14 (the New Jersey statute does not mention Trustee allowance on committees); CAL. CORP. CODE § 5231(b)(1)(2)(3).

51 Mary v. Lupin Found., 609 So. 2d 184, 187 (La. 1992) (quoting LA. REV. STAT. § 12:226(A)).

52 *See* Mueller v. Zimmer, 124 P.3d 340, 358 (Wyo. 2005) ("[W]here 'the board act[s] with due care, good faith, and in the honest belief that they are acting in the best interests of the stockholders . . ., the Court gives great deference to the substance of the directors' decision and will not invalidate the decision, will not examine its reasonableness, and will not substitute [its] views for those of the board if the latter's decision can be attributed to any rational business purpose.'"); Buckingham v. Weston Vill. Homeowners Ass'n, 1997 ND 237, 571 N.W.2d 842; 40 W. 67th St. v. Pullman, 790 N.E.2d 1174 (N.Y. 2003).

53 Davencourt at Pilgrims Landing Homeowners Ass'n v. Davencourt at Pilgrims Landing, LC, 2009 UT 65, ¶ 35, 221 P.3d 234. It was also noted that a real estate "developer owes certain limited duties to an association and its members" while they retain control of an association. *Id.* at ¶ 36 (citing RESTATEMENT (THIRD) OF PROPERTY § 6.20); *see also* Martino v. Bd. of Managers of Heron Pointe on the Beach Condo., 774 N.Y.S.2d 422 (App. Div. 2004).

54 *Mary*, 609 So.2d at 187 (citing LA. REV. STAT. § 12:226(A)).

55 The board is variously called trustees, managers, and other titles. State non-profit corporation statutes offer their own names.

56 STANDARD CODE, *supra* note 3, at 195.

57 *Id.* Riddick describes the function of both corporate and unincorporated boards. RIDDICK & BUTCHER, *supra* note 15, at 28.

58 Unrau v. Kidron Bethel Retirement Servs., Inc., 27 P.3d 1 (Kan. 2001).

59 Mahan v. Avera St. Luke's, 2001 SD 9, ¶ 19, 621 N.W.2d 150, 156.

60 STANDARD CODE, *supra* note 3, at 196-97.

61 Taylor v. Wellington Station Conco. Ass'n, 633 So. 2d 43, 45 (Fla. Dist. Ct. App. 1994).

62 *See* STANDARD CODE, *supra* note 3, at 197; Treas. Reg. § 1.501(c)(3)-1(f)(2)(ii), -(iv) *Examples* (2013) (stating that failure to take safeguards to prevent further excess benefits transactions such as adopting a written conflicts of interest policy can result in loss of tax-exempt status). IRS Form 1023, recommends the use of a Conflict of Interest Policy. *See* Instructions to Form 1023, Appendix A: Sample Conflict of Interest Policy, INTERNAL REVENUE SERVICE, *available at* http://www.irs.gov/instructions/i1023/ar03.html.

63 15 PA. STAT. ANN. § 5714. For further discussion of this provision in Pennsylvania law, see Harry S. Rosenthal, *Voter Protests*, NAT'L PARLIAMENTARIAN, Vol. 59, Fourth Quarter 1998. Demeter asserts that a member can demand his vote be recorded in the minutes, but if there is an objection a majority vote is needed. DEMETER, *supra* note 11, at 23.

64 *E.g.*, N.J. STAT. ANN. § 15A:6-6 (The certificate of incorporation and bylaws must be looked at to see if and when cause is needed.).

65 *E.g.*, CAL. CORP. CODE § 5222; 15 PA. STAT. ANN. § 5726(a).

[66]   *E.g.,* N.Y. Not-for-Profit Corp. Law § 706.

[67]   15 Pa. Stat. Ann. § 5726(b); *see also* Cal. Corp. Code § 5221(a).

[68]   Standard Code, *supra* note 3, at 185-86.

[69]   Moriarty v. Mt. Diablo Health Care Dist., No. A112499, 2007 WL 3194805 (Cal. Ct. App. Oct. 31, 2007).

[70]   The court held that one of a board member's conflicts of interest had to pertain to a personal financial interest to constitute just cause for removal. Pullins v. Holmes, 2007-Ohio-4603, at ¶ 51-53.

[71]   Under Cal. Corp. Code § 5221(b), "The board, by a majority vote of the directors who meet all of the required qualifications to be a director, may declare vacant the office of any director who fails or ceases to meet any required qualification that was in effect at the beginning of that director's current term of office."

[72]   Matzel v. Stonecrest Ranch Prop. Owners' Ass'n, 305 S.W.3d 368, 374 (Tex. Ct. App. 2010).

[73]   Save Columbia CU Comm. v. Columbia Cmty. Credit Union, 206 P.3d 1272, 1276-77 (Wash. Ct. App. 2009).

[74]   N.J. Stat. Ann. § 15A:6-6.a ("The certificate of incorporation or bylaws may provide that the board may remove trustees for cause or to suspend trustees pending a final determination that cause exists for removal.").

[75]   *Save Columbia,* 206 P.3d at 1276 (citing Wash. Rev. Code § 31.12.285); *see also* Glover v. Overstreet, 984 S.W.2d 406, 409 (Ark. 1999) (finding members were required by the "[a]ssociation articles and bylaws to first withdraw or suspend the directors' powers and transfer them to the members before [the members] could rescind the existing board's actions").

[76]   Robert's Rules, *supra* note 13, at 650-69. In the author's opinion, the procedures for director removal in RONR are overly cumbersome, especially for small organizations.

[77]   Demeter, *supra* note 11, at 264-69 (using the term "impeachment").

[78]   Robert's Rules, *supra* note 13, at 656. However, in *Matzel* the association's bylaws did not "require the proposed cause for removal to be stated" in a "circulated petition or meeting minutes" to establish cause for removal. 305 S.W.3d at 368.

[79]   Robert's Rules, *supra* note 13, at 656.

[80]   *Id.*

[81]   *Id.*

[82]   Demeter, *supra* note 11, at 268.

[83]   *See, e.g.,* Martindale Brightwood CDC v. Gore, 878 N.E.2d 1280, 1285 (Ind. Ct. App. 2008) ("The director may be removed only if a majority of the directors then in office votes for the removal." (quoting Ind. Code § 23-17-12-10)).

84   Standard Code, *supra* note 3, at 185.

85   Nero v. Cont'l Country Club R.O., Inc., 979 So. 2d 263, 267 (Fla. Dist. Ct. App. 2007) (citing Fla. Stat. § 617.0808 (2005)). In another Florida case, a minority number of directors lacked authority to take control of a nonprofit corporation and remove the majority number of directors. Fla. State Oriental Med. Ass'n v. Slepin, 971 So. 2d 141, 144 (Fla. Dist. Ct. App. 2007). In an Arizona case, the court noted that a director of an Irrigation and Drainage District, as with a county officer, may be recalled "by the vote of a majority of the qualified electors of the division which he represents." Hancock v. Bisnar, 132 P.3d 283, 285 (Ariz. 2006) (en banc) (quoting Ariz. Rev. Stat. § 48-3024 (2005))

86   Cal. Corp. Code § 5221(b); *see also* 15 Pa. Stat. Ann. § 5726(b) (allowing the board to declare vacant a director's office for a failure to "fulfill the other requirements of qualification as the bylaws may specify").

87   Standard Code, *supra* note 3, at 255.

88   *Id.*

89   Ahn v. Lee, 471 S.E.2d 38, 39 (Ga. Ct. App. 1996) (citing Ga. Code Ann. § 14-3-807). *But see id.* at 40 (Ruffin, J., concurring specially) (noting that "other courts interpreting nearly identical language have found the 'in writing' language to be permissive rather than mandatory," but concurring because a jury should determine whether there was intent to resign).

90   *See, e.g.,* Cal. Corp. Code § 5075 ("'Vacancy' when used with respect to the board means any authorized position of director which is not then filled, whether the vacancy is caused by death, resignation, removal, change in the number of directors authorized in the articles or bylaws (by the board or the members) or otherwise.").

91   *See* Iglesia Evangelica Latina, Inc. v. So. Pac. Latin Am. Dist. of the Assemblies of God, 93 Cal. Rptr. 3d 75 (Ct. App. 2009); Scheipe v. Orlando, 739 A.2d 475 (Pa. 1999).

92   Standard Code, *supra* note 3, at 184.

93   *Id.*

94   *Id.* at 173.

95   *Id.*

96   Cal. Corp. Code § 5224(c) (specifying a written resignation).

97   Gusman v. Strongville Bd. of Educ., 2003-Ohio-7077, ¶ 34.

98   *E.g.,* N.J. Stat. Ann. § 15A:6-17 ("Any vacancy occurring among the officers, however caused, shall be filled in the manner provided in the bylaws."); Cal. Corp. Code § 5224(a) (the method of filling a board vacancy is first determined by the articles or bylaws); 15 Pa. Stat. Ann. § 5725(c) (vacancies are filled as set forth in the bylaws; otherwise as specified in the statute).

99   Robert's Rules, *supra* note 13, at 467; Demeter, *supra* note 11, at 310; *see also* N.Y. Not-for-Profit Corp. Law § 705(b).

100 *See, e.g.*, 15 PA. STAT. ANN. § 5725(c); CAL. CORP. CODE § 5224(a); *see also* West Baptist Church v. Church of God of Garden State, Inc., No. A-5428-07T1 (N.J. Super. Ct. App. Div. Mar. 1, 2010) (finding that under the New Jersey statute, a vacancy on a board may be filled by the remaining trustees, but such trustees must be members, attendees or contributors to the church at the time of their appointments (citing N.J. STAT. ANN. § 16:1-11)).

    Remaining board members may fill a board vacancy on a governmental board (excluding those vacancies filled by appointments). *See* Floyd v. Mayor of Baltimore, 946 A.2d 15, 42 (Md. Ct. Spec. App. 2008).

101 ROBERT'S RULES, *supra* note 13, at 468.

102 *Id.* at 457.

103 *See, e.g.*, N.Y. NOT-FOR-PROFIT CORP. LAW § 712(a)(2), *amended by* The Non-Profit Revitalization Act of 2013, 2013 N.Y. Sess. Laws ch. 549, § 70 (McKinney) (effective July 1, 2014).

104 United Tel. Credit Union v. Roberts, 115 Ohio St. 3d 464, 2007-Ohio-5247, 875 N.E.2d 927, ¶ 9; *see also* Bella Vista Condo. Ass'n v. Byars, No. CV03180606, 2005 WL 3292533 (Conn. Super. Ct Nov. 8, 2005) ("A vacancy [on the board] does not invalidate the action of the board as long as a quorum is present.").

105 Scheipe v. Orlando, 739 A.2d 475 (Pa. 1999).

106 Cerjack v. Bridgewater Borough, 835 A.2d 845 (Pa. Commw. Ct. 2003).

107 Robson v. San Gabriel Valley Mun. Water Dist., 47 Cal. Rptr. 3d 908, 917 (Ct. App. 2006).

108 STANDARD CODE, *supra* note 3, at 196.

109 ROBERT'S RULES, *supra* note 13, at 407; DEMETER, *supra* note 11, at 218.

110 ROBERT'S RULES, *supra* note 13, at 407.

111 *See* Kelsey v. Ray, 723 A.2d 1215, 1216 (D.C. 1999). However, in this case a "Religious Society" was exempt from that prohibition. *Id.* at 1217.

112 STANDARD CODE, *supra* note 3, at 196-97.

113 Harry S. Rosenthal, *Abstaining From Voting: It's in Your Interest*, NAT'L PARLIAMENTARIAN, Vol. 67, Second Quarter 2006.

114 DEMETER, *supra* note 11, at 251.

115 *See, e.g.*, CAL. CORP. CODE § 5234; 15 PA. STAT. ANN. § 5728(a); N.Y. NOT-FOR-PROFIT CORP. LAW § 715, *amended by* The Non-Profit Revitalization Act of 2013, 2013 N.Y. Sess. Laws ch. 549, § 74 (McKinney) (effective July 1, 2014).

116 *See, e.g.*, CAL. CORP. CODE § 5234; 15 PA. STAT. ANN. § 5728(b).

117 *See, e.g.*, CAL. CORP. CODE § 5234; 15 PA. STAT. ANN. § 5728(a); N.Y. NOT-FOR-PROFIT CORP. LAW § 715(a), *amended by* The Non-Profit Revitalization Act of 2013, 2013 N.Y. Sess. Laws ch. 549, § 74 (McKinney) (effective July 1, 2014).

[118] *See, e.g.,* Summers v. Cherokee Children & Family Serv., 112 S.W.3d 486, 505 (Tenn. Ct. App. 2002). Under the Tennessee statute,

> A transaction in which a director or officer of a corporation has a conflict of interest may be approved [by the board] if:
>
> > (1) The material facts of the transaction and the director's or officer's interest were disclosed or known to the board of directors or a committee consisting entirely of members of the board of directors and the board of directors or such committee authorized, approved, or ratified the transaction;
> >
> > (2) The material facts of the transaction and the director's or officer's interest were disclosed or known to the members and they authorized, approved, or ratified the transaction;

TENN. CODE ANN. § 48-58-302(b).

A director may on a limited basis be permitted to participate in debate after full disclosure of his personal interest in a matter under discussion is first made. For a recitation of the California Statute Sec. 7233 on disclosure and voting when there is a conflict, see *Harvey v. Landing Homeowners Ass'n*, 76 Cal. Rptr. 3d 41, 52 n.8 (Ct. App. 2008) (quoting CAL. CORP. CODE § 7233).

[119] Alvarez Family Trust v. Ass'n of Owners, 221 P.3d 452, 463-64 (Haw. 2009).

[120] Taniguchi v. Ass'n of Apartment Owners of King Manor, 155 P.3d 1138, 1149 (Haw. 2007). The Hawaii court may have decided the case differently if it was able to rely on subsequent changes to the state statute. *Id.* at 1149 n.15.

[121] Mueller v. Zimmer, 124 P.3d 340, 358 (Wyo. 2005); Glad Tidings Assembly of God v. Neb. Dist. Council of the Assemblies of God, Inc., 734 N.W.2d 731 (2007) (citing *Mueller*, 124 P.3d 340).

A governmental health board member had a conflict of interest in voting against her own termination when she had a personal financial interest in retaining the position. Moriarty v. Mt. Diablo Health Care Dist., No. A112499 (Cal. Ct. App. Oct. 31, 2007).

[122] New York recently passed the Non-Profit Revitalization Act of 2013, 2013 N.Y. Sess. Laws ch. 549 (McKinney) (effective July 1, 2014), which in part amends the New York Not-for-Profit Corporation statute to require "every corporation [to] adopt a conflict of interest policy to ensure that its directors, officers and key employees act in the corporation's best interest and comply with applicable legal requirements." *See id.* § 75 (to be codified at N.Y. NOT-FOR-PROFIT CORP. LAW § 715-a).

A conflict of interest policy is mentioned in *Armenian Assembly of America, Inc. v. Cafesjian*, 597 F. Supp. 2d 128, 133, 142 (D.D.C. 2009). In another case a conflict of interest policy for a voluntary, nonprofit association in part "prohibited [directors and officers] from using their position of trust and confidence to further their private interests." Koly v. Enney, 508 F. Supp. 2d 1254, 1259 (N.D. Ga. 2007). A school board conflict of interest policy is summarized in *Montrose County School District Re-IJ v. Lambert*, 826 P.2d 349 (Colo. 1992). In part, "the Board declares that conflicts of interest can arise when a Board member will personally derive a significant private benefit that is pecuniary in nature from Board action." *Id.* at 350 n.3.

For a discussion of the role of a conflict of interest policy in maintaining tax exempt status of an organization with the IRS, see *supra* note 62 and accompanying text.

123   DEMETER, *supra* note 11, at 218.

124   Even the tax status of the organization can be put into jeopardy. STURGIS, *supra* note 46, at 184; *see also* Rosenthal, *supra* note 113.

125   *In re* Saint Vincent Catholic Med. Ctrs. of N.Y., No. 05 B 14945 (ASH), at *8 (Bankr. S.D.N.Y. Aug. 29, 2007), *available at* http://www.gpo.gov/fdsys/pkg/USCOURTS-nysb-1_05-bk-14945/pdf/USCOURTS-nysb-1_05-bk-14945-0.pdf.

126   *See* Pullins v. Holmes, 2007-Ohio-4603, at ¶ 43. The court found that an association's board members did not have a conflict of interest to justify her removal from the board. *Id.* at ¶ 51.

127   *See, e.g.,* 15 PA. STAT. ANN. § 5741, et seq; CAL. CORP. CODE § 5238; N.Y. NOT-FOR-PROFIT CORP. LAW §§ 721-726, *amended by* The Non-Profit Revitalization Act of 2013, 2013 N.Y. Sess. Laws ch. 549, § 79-80 (McKinney) (effective July 1, 2014); N.J. STAT. ANN. § 15A:3-4.

128   *E.g.,* 15 PA. STAT. ANN. § 5744(1)-(4) (allowing in part for indemnification upon a determination "by independent legal counsel" with a majority vote of disinterested trustees); N.J. STAT. ANN. § 15A:3-4.e.(1)-(3) (allowing for a determination "by independent legal counsel" if directed by a majority of disinterested directors); N.Y. NOT-FOR-PROFIT CORP. LAW § 721 (allowing resolution of members or directors if authorized in the certificate of incorporation or bylaws); CAL. CORP. CODE § 5238(e)(1)-(3) (including approval of the members excluding those seeking indemnification from the vote).

129   Lee v. Baldwin Cnty. Elec. Membership Corp., 853 So. 2d 946, 955 (Ala. 2003).

130   *Id.* at 955-56.

CHAPTER **15**

Members

§ 85 RIGHTS AND DUTIES OF MEMBERS

Members of an organization have certain basic parliamentary rights. These include "full participation in its proceedings,"[1] and in particular, "the right to *attend meetings*, to *make motions*, to *speak in debate*, and to *vote*."[2] By state statutes, the right to vote may be altered by the articles or bylaws.[3] Unless otherwise provided in "the articles or bylaws, all memberships shall have the same rights, privileges, preferences, restrictions and conditions."[4]

A contract is created by the articles of incorporation and the members themselves.[5] "[P]rovisions of the bylaws" bear directly "on the rights of members within the organization."[6] The bylaws also in theory create a contract between each member and with the organization. When a member joins an organization he or she is entering into the contract as set forth in the bylaws.

Basic membership rights include those "concomitant to them, such as the right to make nominations or to give previous notice of a motion."[7] The <u>Standard Code of Parliamentary Procedure</u> lists and describes other member rights as follows:

1. Individual persons have the right to associate with other persons to promote and pursue their common interests and aspirations.
2. Individual persons or groups have a right to assemble to promote their common interest.
3. All members have equal rights, privileges, and obligations.
4. The majority vote decides.
5. The rights of the minority must be protected.
6. Full and free discussion of every proposition presented for decision is an established right of members.
7. Every member has the right to know the meaning of the question before the assembly and what its effect will be.
8. All meetings must be characterized by fairness and by good faith[8]

Other parliamentary references offer their own lists of member rights.[9]

The court may determine who has the right to vote.[10] A Florida court ruled that members did not have the right to vote to retain a clergyman when the authority to dismiss from employment was granted to the board through the articles of incorporation and the bylaws.[11] Authorities also provide that a member should not vote who has "a direct personal or financial interest" in a matter.[12]

As noted previously in state statutes, the bylaws may establish membership classes which limit rights to certain classes.[13] A critical principle pertains to the protection of a member's contractual rights. These rights cannot be overridden by bylaw amendments. It should be noted (as with the other Sections of this text) that the individual facts, decided case law, and results on this subject vary. In a Florida case, a nonprofit corporation was prohibited from impairing a member's contractual rights through a bylaw amendment.[14] A court in Oregon ruled that an association cannot amend its bylaws so that, for example, a member's fundamental bargain in a license agreement for a designated boat slip with the association is abrogated.[15] A non-profit cooperative association could not amend its bylaws restricting a member's use of a parking spot appurtenant to the residential unit, a Florida court decided.[16] Yet an Indiana court decision noted that an amendment to a nonprofit's constitution could honor a prior (pension) contract.[17]

Rules and qualifications of membership must be reasonable and germane.[18] The determination of who is a member in good standing should be defined in the organization's bylaws. A person is a member if he has his "membership rights in a corporation under its articles or bylaws, regardless of how the person is identified."[19] "[E]ligibility for membership is to be determined by the constitution, bylaws, and other organic documents of governance."[20]

Members can be suspended or expelled but less clear are the rights of a member who is in arrears on dues or assessments. Arrearage alone does not automatically deprive a member of the right to vote unless so stated in the bylaws, according to Demeter.[21] The bylaws should make clear at what point a failure to pay dues affects the rights of membership.

United States statutory labor law has its own definition of a member of a labor union. Under the LMDRA "[A] member" is "any person who has fulfilled the requirements for membership in such [labor] organization, and who neither has voluntarily withdrawn from membership nor has been expelled or suspended from membership."[22]

Courts may be hesitant to intervene in membership issues. For example, in an Ohio case there was a reluctance to second guess academic decisions of colleges and universities with regard to faculty tenure and promotions.[23]

An organization's authority over a member may, depending upon the circumstances, be open to challenge. For example, a court in Colorado noted that the size of special assessments imposed on owners of a property association was limited by the original declaration.[24] A condominium association in a Delaware case lacked authority to impose an assessment against members for windows and door replacements.[25] In this writer's opinion, this Delaware case has only very limited further application. It should be noted (as with the other Sections of this text) that the case law and results vary on these subjects.

The duties of a member include attendance and participation at meetings, being familiar and complying with the organization's rules and accepting the decisions of the majority.[26] Under the New Jersey statute "[T]he members of a nonprofit corporation shall not be personally liable for the debts, liabilities or obligations of the corporation."[27] Generally, members of an unincorporated association are not liable for breach of the nonprofit association contract.[28] However, depending on the factual circumstances and the cause of action asserted liability of individual members of an unincorporated association may be established. In most cases, although not a guarantee of protection, creating and maintaining a corporation is legally advantageous for the members of a nonprofit organization. Further discussion is beyond the scope of this text.

§ 86 ACTIONS THAT NEED MEMBERS' APPROVAL

Certain actions of a nonprofit organization require membership approval.[29] State nonprofit corporation statutes must be consulted to see what is needed. The organization's bylaws and case law must also be taken into account. Each situation must be considered on a case by case basis. In any event, mandated statutory approvals by the members cannot be waived at a membership meeting or by the board of directors.

Amendment of the articles of incorporation commonly requires membership approval.[30] Other "fundamental changes" of the organization also commonly require membership approval. For example, conversion from a nonprofit corporation to a for-profit corporation may need membership approval.[31] Merger of two nonprofits typically requires membership approval of both organizations.[32] Voluntary dissolution of an association (including a church) may require membership approval.[33] The sale, lease away or exchange of all or substantially all of an organization's property typically requires membership and/or board approval.[34] An Oregon court recognized the right of a board to purchase real estate and assess the membership[35] but the pertinent statutes must be consulted in each specific situation. The division of a nonprofit corporation into two or more nonprofit corporations takes membership approval.[36]

Bylaw amendments frequently require membership approval.[37] However, this is subject to the provisions of the state statute, articles of incorporation, and existing bylaws.[38] In many other organizations the board has the authority to amend the bylaws. In some organizations, the membership is first informed before the board amends the bylaws.

A Texas court decided that condominium associations did not need membership approval to impose a special assessment to replace the siding of all condominiums.[39] However, in this writer's opinion other courts could decide this differently.

In a New York labor union case, membership approval was needed for expenditures over $5,000.00,[40] but in an Illinois case, approval was not required for a payment of an outside audit.[41] In many organizations membership approval is needed to approve new members or discipline current members.[42]

§ 87 CLASSES OF MEMBERSHIP

The governing documents of a nonprofit corporation may provide for classes of members under state statutory authority.[43] Voting rights (if any) of each class should be specified in the organization's bylaws, subject to the statutory requirements.[44] This includes class voting procedures to amend the bylaws.[45] Parliamentary references recognizes classes of membership within the bylaws,[46] each with varying rights[47] and obligations.[48]

Bylaw amendments which affect an existing membership category are an area of legal sensitivity. In a California case, it was decided that certain bylaw amendments of a condominium association which affect a class must be approved by the voters of the affected class.[49] An attempt to reduce the voting power of a homeowner's association by amending the bylaws was rejected by a New York court.[50] Former members of a country club formed a class for a class action suit to recover equity contribution from the club in a Missouri case.[51]

Certain circumstances have been held not to create classes. For example, in a New York case, a dissenting opinion noted that if neither the certificate of incorporation nor the bylaws provide for different classes of members a religious corporation had by default one class of members.[52] Another ruling in Mississippi noted that different assessments based on a rational purpose by a country club did not create classes of members.[53]

Differing rights among classes have also been recognized. Eliminating voting rights for certain classes in a nonprofit corporation was upheld in an Arkansas case.[54] In a Pennsylvania case, dues and assessments may be applied differently on different membership classes at a country club.[55] However, a federal appellate court ruled that classes of members in a labor union "shall not be discriminated against in their right to nominate and vote".[56]

§ 88 SUSPENSION AND EXPULSION OF MEMBERS

Organizations have an "inherent right" to expel or otherwise discipline members for serious infractions.[57] State statutes recognize the right of nonprofits to expel a member.[58] Preferably, the organization establishes in its bylaws, and perhaps in supplemental policy, procedural details for expelling or otherwise disciplining a member.[59] However, even without such provisions, discipline still is available even if it is not included in the bylaws.[60]

Grounds for suspension and expulsion are many and ideally the grounds desired by the organization should be set forth in the bylaws. Parliamentary references note many of the potential reasons including "violation of an important duty to the organization, a breach of a fundamental rule or principle of the organization or for any violation stated in the bylaws as a ground for expulsion."[61] Others may be "damaging the good name of the organization, causing embarrassment for its members, or hindering its work, . . . drug abuse, committing a criminal offense, or malfeasance in office."[62]

Still other case law has noted other grounds for member discipline. A sample of cases includes the following. A court in Kansas found that a member may be suspended or expelled for foul language.[63] In a Louisiana case, a nonprofit corporation can expel a person as a member for conduct believed to be detrimental to the corporation's operation.[64] Failure to pay assessments can result in suspension of membership.[65] In a Tennessee case, poor medical practice justified revocation of hospital staff privileges for a physician.[66] Each situation must be evaluated and decided on a case-by-case basis after determining the facts and the appropriate criteria to be used.

Members facing discipline must be afforded procedural due process. Disciplining a member is a delicate process, sometimes necessary, but requiring caution to avoid liability.[67] Some state statutes explicitly identify the requirements for due process.[68] "Any expulsion, suspension or termination must be done in good faith and in a fair and reasonable manner."[69] The California state statute lists in considerable detail the ingredients of a fair and reasonable procedure.[70]

Due process includes notice of charges[71] (preferably in writing), an opportunity to prepare a defense, a fair hearing, and arguably the right to counsel.[72] The doctrine of exhaustion of remedies will, in this writer's opinion, likely apply.

As noted in a Massachusetts case, since a physician's inability to practice medicine results from a suspension, he is entitled to certain pre-termination procedural due-process requirements.[73] Individuals should be protected from arbitrary exclusion or expulsion. An economic interest in retaining membership (especially when this membership affects one's livelihood) adds to the pressure and expectation for an organization to provide meaningful due process. Case law has held that members of a nonprofit association are entitled to due process when their livelihood is affected.[74] However, under one California case, affording due process for members is not limited to matters of exclusion or expulsion.[75]

Courts emphasize the importance of a fair and proper procedure and look to see that the procedure has been followed. Whether or not a member facing discipline has been afforded notice of the meeting imposing discipline and an opportunity to be heard is a factual matter for the trial court to determine.[76] A court decided in an Illinois case that they would not interfere in the internal affairs of a voluntary association unless the association has failed to follow its own rules or denied the member a fair hearing.[77]

"California courts have long recognized a common law right to fair procedure protecting individuals from arbitrary exclusion or expulsion from private organizations which control important economic interests."[78]

Substantial friction is sometimes generated when a health provider organization (such as a hospital) disciplines a physician. Factors include the adverse impact on the physician's livelihood,[79] hospital liability, and patient privacy. An underlying theme is the contractual relationship between the physician and the organization. Once again emphasis is on the presence and following of a fair procedure by the organization.[80]

In a sample of cases, courts have noted that terminating a physician's hospital privileges may be decided by a governing board, and not in a neutral arbitration if so agreed to as a matter of contract in the bylaws.[81] Loss of hospital privileges due to an internal staffing decision did not create due process rights for one losing these privileges in an Illinois case.[82] A Massachusetts court was "reluctant" to review a hospital's restricting of staffing privileges of a physician.[83]

In a sample of other cases: It was ruled in a Connecticut case that the standard used to review whether a hospital met its bylaw obligations "for the purpose of terminating a physician's medical staff privilege" is substantial compliance.[84] In another case, a physician's suspension of medical privileges at a health system was upheld after the state supreme court considered "the totality of the fact-finding process" undertaken by the hospital.[85] Retroactive substantive rule changes that impair a member's livelihood are unreasonable and disfavored according to a California court.[86]

In disciplinary cases involving medical providers, the applicability of state and federal statutes often comes into play. The federal Health Care Quality Improvement Act ("HCQIA")[87] pertaining to hospital peer review and immunity protection from liability may apply.[88] The accused must be given a meaningful opportunity to defend oneself - this must not be just a sham.[89] There is a four-pronged test regarding physician hospital privileges noted in a Third Circuit case.[90]

Labor unions have looked at membership expulsion issues - especially the handling of internal procedures. The federal Labor-Management Reporting and Disclosure Act ("LMRDA") guarantees workers a full and fair hearing and this requires the charging party to provide some evidence at the disciplinary hearing to support the charges made.[91] Reinstatement of membership in a labor union after expulsion requires a specific authorization and procedure.[92] Union disciplinary proceedings in a federal district court case in the District of Columbia were not subject to intensive judicial scrutiny.[93]

Courts may or may not feel authorized, because of the constitutional separation of church and state, to decide disputes related to meetings involving religious organizations. This includes matters of internal procedure. A Georgia court determined that there was a lack of jurisdiction to terminate membership due to ecclesiastic principles.[94] Courts look to certain variables to see if they can enter into a dispute within a religious arena. One such variable is whether "neutral principles" are involved. Greater discussion is beyond the scope of this text.

In a Louisiana case there was no cause of action for damages for wrongful expulsion from a social club.[95] A recent addition to the California Corporation Code provides that an expelled or suspended member is liable for certain charges and expenses incurred by the organization.[96]

---

[1] SARAH CORBIN ROBERT, HENRY M. ROBERT III, WILLIAM J. EVANS, DANIEL H. HONEMANN & THOMAS J. BALCH, ROBERT'S RULES OF ORDER NEWLY REVISED 3 (11th ed. 2011) [hereinafter ROBERT'S RULES].

[2] *Id.*

[3] *E.g.*, N.J. STAT. ANN. § 15A:5-10 (West 2013 & Supp. 2014); 15 PA. STAT. ANN. § 5751(a) (West 2013); CAL. CORP. CODE § 5330 (West 2013 & Supp. 2014); N.Y. NOT-FOR-PROFIT CORP. LAW § 612 (McKinney 2013).

[4] CAL. CORP. CODE § 5331; *see also* N.J. STAT. ANN. § 15A:5-10 ("Unless so limited, enlarged or denied, each member regardless of class, shall be entitled to one vote on each matter, submitted to a vote of members.").

[5] Calvary Temple Church, Inc. v. Paino, 827 N.E.2d 125, 134 (Ind. Ct. App. 2005) (noting further that the contract included the state and the corporation).

[6] ROBERT'S RULES, *supra* note 1, at 14.

[7] *Id.* at 3.

[8] AMERICAN INSTITUTE OF PARLIAMENTARIANS, STANDARD CODE OF PARLIAMENTARY PROCEDURE 7-10 (2012) [hereinafter STANDARD CODE].

[9] Demeter, offers a summary of rights, GEORGE DEMETER, DEMETER'S MANUAL OF PARLIAMENTARY LAW AND PROCEDURE 305 (2001), but notes, that members cannot be compelled to vote. *Id.* at 209. Cannon notes that a member should have the opportunity to add to a meeting agenda. HUGH CANNON, CANNON'S CONCISE GUIDE TO RULES OF ORDER 54-56 (2001). Riddick lists sixteen rights at meetings, all valid, and well conceived. Among them are to introduce and speak in support of a matter, to attend meetings, to speak twice, to vote,

to make nominations, to appeal a chair's ruling, to inspect meeting records, and to hold office if qualified.

Floyd M. Riddick & Miriam H. Butcher, Riddick's Rules of Procedure: A Modern Guide to Faster and More Efficient Meetings 111 (1985).

[10] McGee ex rel. Bridgewood Baptist v. Holmes, 182 S.W.3d 293 (Tenn. Ct. App. 2005); see also Cebular v. Cooper Arms Homeowners Ass'n, 47 Cal. Rptr. 3d 666 (Ct. App. 2006) (discussing in detail the conditions, covenants, and restrictions regarding voting rights of condominium owners).

[11] New Mount Moriah Missionary Baptist Church, Inc. v. Dinkins, 708 So. 2d 972, 974 (Fla. Dist. Ct. App. 1998).
In another case, the chair was authorized to adjourn a membership meeting when a member did not face the chair when speaking. George v. Local Union No. 639, 825 F. Supp. 328, 332-33 (D.D.C. 1993).

[12] Standard Code, supra note 8, at 145; see also Robert's Rules, supra note 1, at 407. Members of a church who were defendants in litigation were disqualified from voting on whether the plaintiff's suit should continue and their votes would not count. McGee, 182 S.W.3d 293.

[13] Robert's Rules, supra note 1, at 3

[14] Feldkamp v. Long Bay Partners, LLC, 773 F. Supp. 2d 1273, 1282 (M.D. Fla. 2011) (citing First Fla. Bank, N.A. v. Fin. Transactions Sys., Inc., 522 So. 2d 891 (Fla. Dist. Ct. App. 1988)).

[15] See, e.g., Rosekrans v. Class Harbor Ass'n, 209 P.3d 411, 422 (Or. Ct. App. 2009).

[16] McAllister v. Breakers Seville Ass'n, 981 So. 2d 566, 573 (Fla. Dist. Ct. App. 2008).

[17] Calvary Temple Church, Inc. v. Paino, 827 N.E.2d 125, 135-37 (Ind. Ct. App. 2005), vacated on other grounds, 841 N.E.2d 1133 (Ind. 2006).

[18] 15 Pa. Stat. Ann. § 5751(a) ("Membership in a nonprofit corporation shall be of such classes, and shall be governed by such rules of admission, retention, suspension and expulsion, prescribed in bylaws adopted by the members, except that the rules shall be reasonable, germane to the purpose or purposes of the corporation and equally enforced as to all members of the same class.").

[19] Gloria Dei Lutheran—Mo. Synod v. Gloria Dei Lutheran Church of Cold Spring, Minn., 513 N.W.2d 488, 490 (Minn. Ct. App. 1994) (decided on other grounds) (citing Minn. Stat. § 317A.011 (1992)).

[20] Mittasch v. Long Island Greyhound Transfer, Inc., 2008 NY Slip Op 31414(U) (Sup. Ct. May 6, 2008) (citing Harris v. Lyke, 629 N.Y.S.2d 911 (App. Div. 1995)).

[21] Demeter, supra note 9, at 306.

[22] Patterson v. IATSE Local 13, 754 F. Supp. 2d 1043, 1045 (D. Minn. 2010) (citing 29 U.S.C. §411(a)(2)). The court also stated that "[t]o determine whether a person has fulfilled the requirements of membership, the court looks to the union's reasonable interpretation of its constitution and bylaws." Id. (citing Allen v. United Transp. Union, 964 F.2d 818, 821 (8th Cir. 1992)).

[23]   *See* Scarnati v. Ohio State Univ., 2003-Ohio-7122. Ordinarily "[a] court ought not intervene in the decision or internal disputes of a voluntary organizations unless there is a showing of fraud, arbitrariness, or collusion." Tucker v. Nat'l Ass'n of Postal Supervisors, 2003-Ohio-2994, 790 N.E.2d 370, at ¶ 13 (citing Lough v. Varsity Bowl, Inc. 243 N.E.2d 61 (Ohio 1968)).

[24]   Quinn v. Castle Park Ranch Prop. Owners Ass'n, 77 P.3d 823, 826 (Colo. Ct. App. 2003).

[25]   Council of the Dorset Condo. Apartments v. Gordon, 801 A.2d 1, 7-8 (Del. 2002).

[26]   For excellent summaries of duties/obligations of members, see RIDDICK & BUTCHER, *supra* note 9, at 110 and DEMETER, *supra* note 9, at 6.

[27]   N.J. STAT. ANN. § 15A:5-25.a; Also note, "b. A member shall be liable to the corporation only to the extent of any unpaid portion of membership dues or assessments which the corporation may have lawfully imposed, or for any other indebtedness owed by the member to the corporation." *Id.* § 15A:5-25.b.

[28]   Mohr v. Kelley, 8 P.3d 543 (Colo. App. 2000) (citing Colorado Uniform Unincorporated Nonprofit Association Act, COLO. REV. STAT. §§ 7-30-101 to -106 (1999)). "While mere membership in an association does not of itself impose liability for the acts of the associates, at least in the absence of participation and knowledge or approval, liability of members of a voluntary, unincorporated association may be established by a public act of the association itself, or by the acts of officers, agents, or members where such acts are known to the membership and actively or passively approved." Garofalo v. Lambda Chi Alpha Fraternity, 616 N.W.2d 647, 657 (Iowa 2000) (Lavorato, J., concurring in part, dissenting in part) (citing 7 C.J.S. *Association* § 30 (1980)).

[29]   *See* Twin Lakes Vill. Prop. Ass'n v. Crowley, 857 P.2d 611, 618 (Idaho 1993) ("Any . . . extraordinary assessments must pass by a two-thirds majority" of the membership.); Goglio v. Star Valley Ass'n, 2002 WY 94, ¶ 27, 48 P.3d 1072, 1082 (requiring two-third membership approval for special assessment for culinary water fee); Wollochet Harbor Club v. Knapp, No. 37512-5-II, 2009 WL 3360223 (Wash. Ct. App. Oct 20, 2009) (starting a lawsuit and assessing the costs to the members required membership approval under the articles of incorporation); Glad Tidings v. Neb. Dist. Council, 734 N.W.2d 731, 736-37 (Neb. 2007) (stating that church members voted to close a church and dispose of the property pursuant to constitution and bylaws).

[30]   *See, e.g.,* 15 PA. STAT. ANN. § 5912(b); CAL. CORP. CODE § 5342(c); N.J. STAT. ANN. §§ 15A:9-2.d(3), 15A:5-11.b; RIDDICK & BUTCHER, *supra* note 9, at 44 (original articles of incorporation are signed by charter members); ALICE STURGIS, THE STANDARD CODE OF PARLIAMENTARY PROCEDURE 203 (4th ed., rev. 2001) (charter amendment by the membership).

[31]   N.Y. NOT-FOR-PROFIT CORP. LAW § 908(b); 15 PA. STAT. ANN. § 5962(b) (incorporating 15 PA. STAT. ANN. § 5924(a)). However, in a Delaware case, the conversion of a nonprofit nonstock corporation to a for-profit stock corporation did not require membership approval unless the certificate of incorporation required such a vote. Farahpour v. DCX, Inc., 635 A.2d 894, 897 (Del. 1993) (citing DEL. CODE ANN. tit. 8, § 242).

[32]   15 PA. STAT. ANN. § 5924(a); N.Y. NOT-FOR-PROFIT CORP. LAW § 903(a)(2); Rural Elec. Convenience Coop. Co. v. Soyland Power Coop., Inc., 606 N.E.2d 1269 (Ill. App. Ct. 1992). The two state statutes of any merging nonprofits have to be examined to see what membership and board approvals must be obtained.

33   15 Pa. Stat. Ann. § 5972(b); N.Y. Not-for-Profit Corp. Law § 1002-a(a), *amended by* The Non-Profit Revitalization Act of 2013, 2013 N.Y. Sess. Laws ch. 549, § 90 (McKinney) (effective July 1, 2014); *see also* Feutz v. Hartford Cmty. Serv., Inc., No. 2006AP861, 2007 WL 754995, at *5-6 (Wis. Ct. App. Mar. 14, 2007) West Baptist Church v. Church of God of Garden State, Inc., No. A-5428-07T1, 2010 WL 680846, at * (N.J. Super. Ct. App. Div. Mar. 1, 2010), ("[A] ny Baptist church incorporated under any law of this state [New Jersey] may dissolve by a two-thirds vote of the members, entitled to vote, present and voting at a meeting held in its meetinghouse or usual place of assembly for worship." (quoting N.J. Stat. Ann. § 16:2-16)).

    At a properly noticed meeting of members, a church was dissolved and its assets transferred to another church after payment of debts and liabilities as provided for in the reversionary clause of the constitution. Cen. Coast Baptist Ass'n v. First Baptist Church of Las Lomas, 65 Cal. Rptr. 3d 100, (Ct. App. 2007).

    Resolutions should be adopted, similar to those calling for bylaw amendments, and with required notices to the membership, which includes appropriate distribution of assets. Robert's Rules, *supra* note 1, at 564. The board's resolutions must inform the members of the plan to dispose assets and prior notice must be given. Riddick & Butcher, *supra* note 9, at 87.

34   15 Pa. Stat. Ann. § 5930(a) (incorporating 15 Pa. Stat. Ann. § 5924(a)); *see also* 15 Pa. Stat. Ann. § 5546; Cal. Corp. Code § 5911(a)(2). However, in a Florida case membership approval was not required in the bylaws for the sale of an association's land, rather the board (and not the president) had the authority. Lensa Corp. v. Poinciana Gardens Ass'n, 765 So. 2d 296 (Fla. Dist. Ct. App. 2000) (the board approved sales contract was nullified for other reasons).

35   Gier's Liquor & Sporting Goods, Inc. v. Ass'n of Unit Owners of Driftwood Shores Surfside Inn Condo., 862 P.2d 560, 563 (Or. Ct. App. 1993).

36   15 Pa. Stat. Ann. § 5952(c) (incorporating 15 Pa. Stat. Ann. § 5924(a)).

37   *See* Robert's Rules, *supra* note 1, at 581; N.J. Stat. Ann. § 15A:5-11.b.

38   *See* United States v. Int'l Bhd. of Teamsters, 981 F. Supp. 233, 237 (S.D.N.Y. 1997).

39   Bosch v. Open Pines Condo. Owners Ass'n, No. 01-09-00507-CV, 2010 WL 4484189, at *6 (Tex. Ct. App. 2010).

40   Charles v. Butler, 2007 NY Slip Op 34298(U) (Sup. Ct. May 11, 2007).

41   Mulligan v. Parker, 805 F. Supp. 592, 596 (N.D. Ill. 1992).

42   For one national association, only the membership convened at a convention could "authorize someone other than the Committee on Infractions to conduct an infractions hearing." Nat'l Collegiate Athletic Ass'n v. Miller, 795 F. Supp.1476, 1484 (D. Nev. 1992).

43   *See, e.g.,* 15 Pa. Stat. Ann. § 5306(a)(6)(ii); N.J. Stat. Ann. §§ 15A:5-11.b, 15A:2-8.a.(4).

44   *See, e.g.,* N.J. Stat. Ann. § 15A:5-11.b; N.Y. Not-for-Profit Corp. Law § 612; Cal. Corp. Code § 5151(e); 15 Pa. Stat. Ann. § 5758(b) (election of directors by class unless otherwise provided in the bylaws).

45   15 Pa. Stat. Ann. § 5504(d); N.J. Stat. Ann. §§ 15A:5-11.b, 15A:9-4.b.(6).

46   Riddick & Butcher, *supra* note 9, at 110.

47   ROBERT'S RULES, *supra* note 1, at 571.

48   RIDDICK & BUTCHER, *supra* note 9, at 110.

49   Lake Arrowhead Chalets Timeshare Owners Ass'n v. Lake Arrowhead Chalets Owners Ass'n, 59 Cal. Rptr. 2d 875, 877 (Ct. App. 1996) (citing CAL. CORP. CODE § 7150(b) (1996)).

50   *See* Bretton Woods Condo. I v. Bretton Woods Homeowners Ass'n, 2010 NY Slip Op 33034, at *2 (Sup. Ct. 2010).

51   Wright v. Country Club of St. Albans, 269 S.W.3d 461 (Mo. Ct. App. 2008) (class action certification was allowed).

52   Blaudziunas v. Egan, 905 N.Y.S.2d 45, 53 (App. Div. 2010) (Catterson, J., dissenting).

53   Longanecker v. Diamonhead Country Club, 760 So. 2d 764, 771 (Miss. 2000); *see also* Shorewood W. Condo. Ass'n v. Sadri, 966 P.2d 372, 376 (Wash. Ct. App. 1998) ("[A] bylaw amendment [in a condominium association] restricting all future leases does not create two classes of members."), *rev'd on other grounds*, 992 P.2d 1008 (Wash. 2000).
       A multiple level dues structure of a condominium association "that differentially assesses association members based upon whether or not a member's lot is improved or unimproved" was upheld and did not create two different classes of members. Ackerman v. Sudden Valley Cmty. Ass'n, 944 P.2d 1045, 1047, 1051 (Wash. Ct. App. 1997).

54   Dunaway v. Garland Cty. Fair & Livestock Show Ass'n, 245 S.W.3d 678, 685-86 (Ark. Ct. App. 2006).

55   Anderson v. Colonial Country Club, 739 A.2d 1118, 1123 (Pa. Commw. Ct. 1999) ("[D]ues or assessments or both, may be imposed upon all members of the same class either alike or in different amounts or proportions, and *upon a different basis upon different classes of members*." (emphasis added) (quoting 15 PA. STAT. ANN. § 5544(a))).

56   Members for a Better Union v. Bevona, 152 F.3d 58, 63 (2d Cir. 1998) (quoting Calhoon v. Harvey, 379 U.S. 134, 139 (1964)); *accord* Local Unions 20 v. United Bhd. of Carpenters & Joiners of Am., 223 F. Supp. 2d 491 (S.D.N.Y. 2002).

57   STANDARD CODE, *supra* note 8, at 263.

58   *E.g.,* N.Y. NOT-FOR-PROFIT CORP. LAW § 601(e); 15 PA. STAT. ANN. § 5769; CAL. CORP. CODE § 5341.

59   The use of disciplinary procedures set forth in <u>RONR</u>, when adopted in the bylaws, was sufficient to expel a member for alleged misconduct. *In re* Meer v. Klein, 2008 NY Slip Op 33171(U) (Sup. Ct. Nov. 24, 2008).

60   STANDARD CODE, *supra* note 8, at 263.

61   *Id.* at 263.

62   RIDDICK & BUTCHER, *supra* note 9, at 193.

63   Pollock v. Crestview Country Club Ass'n, 205 P.3d 1283 (Kan. Ct. App. 2009).

64   White v. St. Elizabeth B.C. Bd. of Dirs., 2010-45,213, p. 7 (La. App. 2 Cir. 6/02/10); 37 So. 3d 1139.

65   Lynn v. Windridge Co-Owners Ass'n, 743 N.E.2d 305, 312-13 (Ind. Ct. App. 2001). In *Boca West Club, Inc. v. Levine*, the board of a country club had wide discretion in determining the application of club rules and regulations and the grounds for discipline of a member. 578 So. 2d 14 (Fla. Dist. Ct. App. 1991) (here the grounds for expulsion were failure to continue to own residential property at the club).

66   Eyring v. Fort Sanders Parkwest Med. Ctr., Inc., 991 S.W.2d 230, 232 (Tenn. 1999) (decided on other grounds).

67   For a discussion, see Harry S. Rosenthal, *Disciplinary Procedures by Associations Require Care*, Vol. 58, No. 4, NAT'L PARLIAMENTARIAN, 1997.

68   *See, e.g.*, CAL. CORP. CODE § 5341; 15 PA. STAT. ANN. § 5769(b).

69   CAL. CORP. CODE § 5341(b); *see also* 15 PA. STAT. ANN. § 5769(b) ("A member shall not be expelled from any nonprofit corporation without notice, trial and conviction, the form of which should be prescribed by the bylaws.").

70   CAL. CORP. CODE § 5341(c) (including "provisions of the procedure have been set forth in the articles or bylaws," "giving of 15 days prior notice of the expulsion, suspension or termination and reasons therefor," "an opportunity for the member to be heard").

71   Revocation of membership as a scoutmaster in the boy scouts was reversed when the accused was denied due process for failure to inform him of the charges and an opportunity to respond to the charges. Gibson v. Boy Scouts of Am., 359 F. Supp. 2d 462, 466-67 (E.D. Va. 2005); *see also* Ashcreek Homeowner's Ass'n v. Smith, 902 S.W.2d 586, 589-90 (Tex. Ct. App. 1995) (finding a member of a homeowner's association must be informed in writing of the provisions [deed restrictions] allegedly violated and given a fair opportunity to present evidence).

72   STANDARD CODE, *supra* note 8, at 264-65, notes six essential steps for imposing discipline on a member: charges, investigation, notification, hearing, decision, and penalty.
     In *Baldonado v. Way of Salvations Church*, a church member was entitled to fair and reasonable due process before expulsion. 185 P.3d 913, 917 (Haw. Ct. App. 2008). The court discussed the "ecclesiastical abstention doctrine," but did not find it applies since church polity, law, or doctrine was not a factor. *Id.* at 917-20.

73   Hamilton v. Baystate Med. Educ. & Research Found., Inc., 866 F. Supp. 51, 55 (D. Mass. 1994).

74   *See, e.g.*, Austin v. Am. Ass'n of Neurological Surgeons, 253 F.3d 967, 969 (7th Cir. 2001). But in an unusual decision a court held "that an employee [a contract college professor] who is terminated for cause is not entitled to full compensatory damages even though the termination may have been procedurally flawed." Savannah Coll. of Art & Design, Inc. v. Nulph, 460 S.E.2d 792, 793 (Ga. 1995).

75   Delta Dental Plan of Cal. v. Banasky, 33 Cal. Rptr. 2d 381, 385 (Ct. App. 1994).

76   Stamford Landing Condo. Ass'n v. Lerman, 951 A.2d 642, 646 (Conn. App. Ct. 2008).

77   Lee v. Snyder, 673 N.E.2d 1136, 1139 (Ill. App. Ct. 1996); *see also* Savannah Coll. of Art & Design, Inc. v. Nulph, 453 S.E.2d 80, 81, *rev'd on other grounds*, 462 S.E.2d 812 (Ga. 1995) (finding a final decision to terminate an employment contract rested with the university's board, not with a committee); Garvey v. Seattle Tennis Club, 808 P.2d 1155, (1991) (finding a private club "may re-try" a member for an alleged violation of its rules even though the member was denied due process in the original action).

78   Rosenbilt v. Superior Court, 282 Cal. Rptr. 819, 825 (Ct. App. 1991) (citing Applebaum v. Bd. of Dirs. of Barton Mem'l Hosp., 163 Cal. Rptr. 831 (Ct. App. 1980)).

79   A court noted that an "important economic interest" must be shown as being jeopardized by a party challenging discipline by a voluntary association. *Austin*, 253 F.3d 967, 972 (7th Cir. 2001) (decided on other grounds). The court in *Austin* noted that, "Where membership is optional, expulsion (or suspension, or denial of admission) is not deemed the invasion of an important economic interest." *Id.* (citing Finn v. Beverly Country Club, 683 N.E.2d 1191, 1192 (Ill. Ct, App. 1997); *Lee*, 673 N.E.2d at 1139).

80   This is illustrated by the following cases: A hospital had a duty to make a "reasonable effort" to obtain the facts of the matter when imposing discipline on a physician. Pamintuan v. Nanticoke Hosp., 192 F.3d 378, 389 (3d Cir. 1999) (citing Mathews v. Lancaster General Hosp., 87 F.3d 624, 637 (3d Cir. 1996)). A physician is entitled to notice and hearing before his hospital privileges can be revoked. Peper v. St. Mary's Hosp. & Med. Ctr., 207 P.3d 881, 887 (Colo. Ct. App. 2008). Due process is required by a hospital pursuing the termination of a physician from hospital medical staff membership and clinical privileges. *Rosenbilt*, 282 Cal. Rptr. at 825. A hospital was required to provide a physician a fair hearing regarding his hospital privileges when it was alleged that the physician was released for being uncooperative. Richter v. Danbury Hosp., 759 A.2d 106, 113-14 (Conn. App. Ct. 2000).

81   Katz v. Children's Hosp. Corp., 602 N.E.2d 598, 598-99 (Mass. App. Ct. 1992) (finding that in a contract dispute between a hospital and a physician, a neutral arbitrator was not required).

82   Garibaldi v. Applebaum, 742 N.E.2d 279, 285-86 (Ill. App. Ct. 2000); *accord* Dutta v. St. Francis Reg'l Med. Ctr., Inc., 867 P.2d 1057 (Kan. 1994); Bartley v. E. Me. Med. Ctr., 617 A.2d 1020 (Me. 1992). *But cf.* Larsen v. Carle Found., 898 N.E.2d 728, 733 (Ill. App. Ct. 2008) (stating that when a physician's medical privileges at a hospital expire "because of his own doing," he is not entitled to fair hearing before a hearing panel as there was no adverse decision).

83   *Katz*, 602 N.E.2d at 600.

84   Owens v. New Britain Gen. Hosp., 643 A.2d 233, 234 (Conn. 1994). A hospital must "substantially" comply with its own bylaws when not reappointing a physician's hospital privileges. *Id.*

85   Summers v. Ardent Health Servs., L.L.C., 257 P.3d 943, 951 (N.M. 2011). The court further noted that the hospital undertook "a fact-finding process that involved a broad and thorough investigation." *Id.* at 952.

86   Nasim v. Los Robles Reg'l Med. Ctr., 82 Cal. Rptr. 3d 58, 62 (Ct. App. 2008). This case involved a retroactive requirement for a physician to become board certified in nephrology in order to remain on a medical staff. *Id.*

87   42 U.S.C. §§ 11101-11157 (2013). Excerpts of the HCQIA are provided in the Appendix.

88   Meyer v. Sunrise Hosp., 22 P.3d 1 42, 1149 (Nev. 2001) (citing Bryan v. James E. Holmes Reg'l Med. Ctr., 33 F.3d 1318 (11th Cir. 1994)). Also see, *Brown v. Presbyterian Healthcare Services*, 101 F.3d 1324 (10th Cir. 1996), for application of the HCQIA.

89   *See Matthews*, 87 F.3d 624, 624 (citing Health Care Quality Improvement Act of 1986, 42 U.S.C. §§ 11101-11157 (1988 & Supp. IV 1992)).

90   Brader v. Allegheny Gen. Hosp., 167 F.3d 832, 839 (3d Cir. 1999) (quoting 42 U.S.C. §§ 11112(a)). The court in *Brader* provided a detailed procedural review of the HQCIA. *Id.*

91   Int'l Bhd. of Boilmakers, Iron Shipbuilders, Blacksmiths Forgers & Helpers v. Hardeman, 401 U. S. 233, 244 (1971).

92   Reinstatement into membership was denied since it was deemed a final action by the union. Howard v. Weathers, 139 F.3d 553 (7th Cir. 1998). The court noted that there was no provision allowing for union membership from expulsion in the union constitution. *Id.*

93   Ricks v. Simons, 759 F. Supp. 918. 920 (D.D.C. 1991).

94   Sreng v. Trairatanaram Temple, Inc., 696 S.E.2d 405 (Ga. Ct. App. 2010) ("Georgia courts are prohibited by the First Amencment of the Constitution of the United States and . . . the 1983 Constitution of Georgia from 'determining issues of expulsion of members, pastors, and the internal procedures of a religious entity.'" (quoting United Baptist Church, Inc v. Holmes, 500 S.E.2d 653, 654 (Ga. Ct. App. 1998))); *see also* Horne v. Andrews, 589 S.E.2d 719 (Ga. Ct. App. 2003).

95   Leary v. Foley, 2007-0751, p. 3-4 (La. App. 4 Cir. 2/13/08); 978 So. 2d 1018, 1020-21.

96   CAL. CORP. CODE § 5341(g) ("A member who is expelled or suspended or whose membership is terminated shall be liable for any charges incurred, services or benefits actually rendered, dues, assessments or fees incurred before the expu sion, suspension or termination or arising from contract or otherwise.").

Appendix

Excerpts from U.S. Labor Law

United States Code - Title 29

SUBCHAPTER II - BILL OF RIGHTS OF MEMBERS OF LABOR
ORGANIZATIONS

(Updated to May 5, 2015)

§ 411. Bill of rights; constitution and bylaws of labor organizations

(a)(1) Equal rights

Every member of a labor organization shall have equal rights and
privileges within such organization to nominate candidates, to vote
in elections or referendums of the labor organization, to attend membership meetings, and to participate in the deliberations and voting
upon the business of such meetings, subject to reasonable rules and
regulations in such organization's constitution and bylaws.

(2) Freedom of speech and assembly

Every member of any labor organization shall have the right to meet
and assemble freely with other members;; and to express any views,
arguments, or opinions; and to express at meetings of the labor organization his views, upon candidates in an election of the labor organization or upon any business properly before the meeting, subject to

the organization's established and reasonable rules pertaining to the conduct of meetings; *Provided*, That nothing herein shall be construed to impair the right of a labor organization to adopt and enforce reasonable rules as the responsibility of every member toward the organization as an institution and to his refraining from conduct that would interfere with its performance of its legal or contractual obligations.

(3) Dues, initiation fees, and assessments

Except in the case of a federation of national or international labor organizations, the rates of dues and initiation fees payable by members of any labor organization in effect on September 14, 1959, shall not be increased, and no general or special assessment shall be levied upon such members, except -

(A) in the case of a local labor organization, (i) by majority vote by secret ballot of the members in good standing voting at a general or special membership meeting, after reasonable notice of the intention to vote upon such question, or (ii) by majority vote of the members in good standing voting in a membership referendum conducted by secret ballot; or

(B) in the case of a labor organization, other than a local labor organization or a federation of national or international labor organizations, (i) by majority vote of the delegates voting at a regular convention, or at a special convention of such labor organization held upon not less than thirty days' written notice to the principal office of each local or constituent labor organization entitled to such notice, or (ii) by majority vote of the members in good standing of such labor organization voting in a membership referendum conducted by secret ballot, or (iii) by majority vote of the members of the executive board or similar governing body of such labor organization, pursuant to express authority contained in the constitution and bylaws of such labor organization: *Provided*, That such action on the part of the executive board or similar governing body shall be effective only until the next regular convention of such labor organization.

(4) Protection of the right to sue

No labor organization shall limit the right of any member thereof to institute an action in any court, or in a proceeding before any administrative agency, irrespective of whether or not the labor organization or its officers are named as defendants or respondents in such action or proceeding, or the right of any member of a labor organization to appear as a witness in any judicial, administrative, or legislative proceeding, or to petition any legislature or to communicate with any legislator; *Provided,* That any such member may be required to exhaust reasonable hearing procedures (but not to exceed a four-month lapse of time) within such organization, before instituting legal or administrative proceedings against such organizations or any officer thereof: *And provided further,* That no interested employer or employer association shall directly or indirectly finance, encourage, or participate in, except as a party, any such action, proceeding, appearance, or petition.

(5) Safeguards against improper disciplinary action

No member of any labor organization may be fined, suspended, expelled, or otherwise disciplined except for nonpayment of dues by such organization or by any officer thereof unless such member has been (A) served with written specific charges; (B) given a reasonable time to prepare his defense; (C) afforded a full and fair hearing.

(b) Invalidity of constitution and bylaws

Any provision of the constitution and bylaws of any labor organization which is inconsistent with the provisions of this section shall be of no force or effect.

SUBCHAPTER V - ELECTIONS

§ 481. Terms of office and election procedures

(a) Officers of national or international labor organizations; manner of election

Every national or international labor organization, except a federation of national or international labor organizations, shall elect its officers not less often than once every five years either by secret ballot among the members in good standing or at a convention of delegates chosen by secret ballot.

(b) Officers of local labor organizations; manner of election

Every local labor organization shall elect its officers not less often than once every three years by secret ballot among the members in good standing.

(c) Requests for distribution of campaign literature; civil action for enforcement; jurisdiction; inspection of membership lists; adequate safeguards to insure fair election

Every national or international labor organization, except a federation of national or international labor organizations, and every local labor organization, and its officers, shall be under a duty, enforceable at the suit of any bona fide candidate for office in such labor organization in the district court of the United States in which such labor organization maintains its principal office, to comply with all reasonable requests of any candidate to distribute by mail or otherwise at the candidate's expense campaign literature in aid of such person's candidacy to all members in good standing of such labor organization and to refrain from discrimination in favor of or against any candidate with respect to the use of lists of members, and whenever such labor organizations or its officers authorize the distribution by mail or otherwise to members of campaign literature on behalf of any candidate or of the labor organization itself with reference to such election, similar distribution at the request of any other bona fide candidate shall be made by such labor organization and its officers, with equal treatment as to the expense of such distribution. Every bona fide candidate shall have the right, once within 30 days prior to an election of a labor organization in which he is a candidate, to inspect a list containing the names and last known addresses of all members of the labor organization who are subject to a collective bargaining agreement requiring membership therein as a condition of employment, which list shall be maintained and kept at the principal office of such labor organization by a designated official thereof. Adequate safeguards to insure a fair election shall be provided, including the right of any candidate to have an observer at the polls and at the counting of the ballots.

(d) Officers of Intermediate bodies; manner of election

Officers of intermediate bodies, such as general committees, system boards, joint boards, or joint councils, shall be elected not less often than once every four years by secret ballot among the members in good standing or by labor organization officers representative of such members who have been elected by secret ballot.

(e) Nomination of candidates; eligibility; notice of election; voting rights; counting and publication of results; preservation of ballots and records

In any election required by this section which is to be held by secret ballot a reasonable opportunity shall be given for the nomination of candidates and every member in good standing shall be eligible to be a candidate and to hold office (subject to section 504 of this title and to reasonable qualifications uniformly imposed) and shall have the right to vote for or otherwise support the candidate or candidates of his choice, without being subject to penalty, discipline, or improper interference or reprisal of any kind by such organization or any member thereof. Not less than fifteen days prior to the election notice thereof shall be mailed to each member at his last known home address. Each member in good standing shall be entitled to one vote. No member whose dues have been withheld by his employer for payment to such organization pursuant to his voluntary authorization provided for in a collective bargaining agreement shall be declared ineligible to vote or be a candidate for office in such organization by reason of alleged delay or default in the payment of dues. The votes cast by members of each local labor organization shall be counted, and the results published, separately. The election officials designated in the constitution and bylaws or the secretary, if no other official is designated, shall preserve for one year the ballots and all other records pertaining to the election. The election shall be conducted in accordance with the constitution and bylaws of such organization insofar as they are not inconsistent with the provisions of this subchapter.

(f) Election of officers by convention of delegates; manner of conducting convention; preservation of records

When officers are chosen by a convention of delegates elected by secret ballot, the convention shall be conducted in accordance with the constitution and bylaws of the labor organization insofar as they are not inconsistent with the provisions of this subchapter. The officials designated in the constitution and bylaws or the secretary, if no other is designated, shall preserve for one year the credentials of the delegates and all minutes and other records of the convention pertaining to the election of officers.

(g) Use of dues, assessments or similar levies and funds of employer for promotion of candidacy of person

No moneys received by any labor organization by way of dues, assessment, or similar levy, and no moneys of an employer shall be contributed or applied to promote the candidacy of any person in any election subject to the provisions of this subchapter. Such moneys of a labor organization may be utilized for notices, factual statements of issues not involving candidates, and other expenses necessary for the holding of an election.

(h) Removal of officers guilty of serious misconduct

If the Secretary, upon application of any member of a local labor organization, finds after hearing in accordance with subchapter II of chapter 5 of Title 5 that the constitution and bylaws of such labor organization do not provide an adequate procedure for the removal of an elected officer guilty of serious misconduct, such officer may be removed, for cause shown and after notice and hearing, by the members in good standing voting in secret ballot, conducted by the officers of such labor organization in accordance with its constitution and bylaws insofar as they are not inconsistent with the provisions of this subchapter.

(i) Rules and regulations for determining adequacy of removal procedures

The Secretary shall promulgate rules and regulations prescribing minimum standards and procedures for determining the adequacy of the removal procedures to which reference is made in subsection (h) of this section.

Excerpts From U.S. Health Care Quality Improvement Act of 1986

42 U.S.C. §11101 - 11157

(Updated to May 5, 2015)

§ 11112. Standards for professional review actions

(a) In general

For purposes of the protection set forth in section 11111(a) of this title, a professional review action must be taken --

(1) in the reasonable belief that the action was in the furtherance of quality health care,

(2) after a reasonable effort to obtain the facts of the matter,

(3) after adequate notice and hearing procedures are afforded to the physician involved or after such other procedures as are fair to the physician under the circumstances, and

(4) in the reasonable belief that the action was warranted by the facts known after such reasonable effort to obtain facts and after meeting the requirement of paragraph (3).

A professional review action shall be presumed to have met the preceding standards necessary for the protection set out in section 11111(a) of this title unless the presumption is rebutted by a preponderance of the evidence.

(b) Adequate notice and hearing

A health care entity is deemed to have met the adequate notice and hearing requirement of subsection (a)(3) of this section with respect to a physician if the following conditions are met (or are waived voluntarily by the physician):

(1) Notice of proposed action

The physician has been given notice stating --

(A)(i) that a professional review action has been proposed to be taken against the physician,

(ii) reasons for the proposed action,

(B)(i) that the physician has the right to request a hearing on the proposed action,

(ii) any time limit (of not less than 30 days) within which to request such a hearing, and

(C) a summary of the rights in the hearing under paragraph (3).

(2) Notice of hearing

If a hearing is requested on a timely basis under paragraph (1)(B), the physician involved must be given notice stating --

(A) the place, time, and date, of the hearing, which date shall not be less than 30 days after the date of the notice, and

(B) a list of the witnesses (if any) expected to testify at the hearing on behalf of the professional review body.

(3) Conduct of hearing and notice

If a hearing is requested on a timely basis under paragraph (1)(B) --

(A) subject to subparagraph (B), the hearing shall be held (as determined by the health care entity)--

(i) before an arbitrator mutually acceptable to the physician and the health care entity,

(ii) before a hearing officer who is appointed by the entity and who is not in direct economic competition with the physician involved, or

(iii) before a panel of individuals who are appointed by the entity and are not in direct economic competition with the physician involved;

(B) the right to the hearing may be forfeited if the physician fails, without good cause, to appear;

(C) in the hearing the physician involved has the right --

(i) to representation by an attorney or other person of the physician's choice,

(ii) to have a record made of the proceedings, copies of which may be obtained by the physician upon payment of any reasonable charges associated with the preparation thereof,

(iii) to call, examine, and cross-examine witnesses,

(iv) to present evidence determined to be relevant by the hearing officer, regardless of its admissibility in a court of law, and

(v) to submit a written statement at the close of the hearing; and

(D) upon completion of the hearing, the physician involved has the right --

(i) to receive the written recommendation of the arbitrator, officer, or panel, including a statement of the basis for the recommendations, and

(ii) to receive a written decision of the health care entity, including a statement of the basis for the decision.

A professional review body's failure to meet the conditions described in this subsection shall not, in itself, constitute failure to meet the standards of subsection (a)(3) of this section.

(c) Adequate procedures in investigations or health emergencies

For purposes of section 11111(a) of this title, nothing in this section shall be construed as --

(1) requiring the procedures referred to in subsection (a)(3) of this section--

(A) where there is no adverse professional review action taken, or

(B) in the case of a suspension or restriction of clinical privileges, for a period of not longer than 14 days, during which an investigation is being conducted to determine the need for a professional review action; or

(2) precluding an immediate suspension or restriction of clinical privileges, subject to subsequent notice and hearing or other adequate procedures, where the failure to take such an action may result in an imminent danger to the health of any individual.

Excerpts from the Michigan Compiled Laws Annotated Updated to May 5, 2015

CAUTION: Each state has its own controlling statute.

Michigan is unusually progressive and I offer it here for informational purposes only.

Section 450.2405 Shareholder, member, or proxy holder participation in meeting by conference telephone or other means of remote communications; conditions; participation as presence in person at meeting; participating and voting by remote communication.

Sec. 405.

(1) Unless otherwise restricted by the articles of incorporation or by-laws, a shareholder, member, or proxy holder may participate in a meeting of shareholders or members by a conference telephone or other means of remote communication that permits all persons that participate in the meeting to communicate with all the other participants. All participants shall be advised of the means of remote communication.

(2) Participation in a meeting under this section constitutes presence in person at the meeting.

(3) Unless otherwise restricted by any provisions of the articles of incorporation or bylaws, the board of directors may hold a meeting of shareholders or members that is conducted solely by means of remote communication.

(4) Subject to any guidelines and procedures adopted by the board of directors, shareholders, members and proxy holders that are not physically present at a meeting of shareholders or members may

participate in the meeting by a means of remote communication and are considered present in person and may vote at the meeting if all of the following are met:

(a) The corporation implements reasonable measures to verify that each person that is considered present and permitted to vote at the meeting by means of remote communication is a shareholder, member, or proxy holder.

(b) The corporation implements reasonable measures to provide each shareholder, member, or proxy holder a reasonable opportunity to participate in the meeting and to vote on matters submitted to the shareholders or members, including an opportunity to read or hear the proceedings of the meeting substantially concurrently with the proceedings.

(c) If any shareholder, member, or proxy holder votes or takes other action at the meeting by means of remote communication, a record of the vote or other action is maintained by the corporation.

450.2406a. Notice: electronic transmission: effectiveness

Sec. 406a. In addition to any other form of notice to a shareholder or member permitted by the articles of incorporation, the bylaws, or this chapter, any notice given to a shareholder or member by a form of electronic transmission to which the shareholder or member has consented is effective.

450.2407. Taking corporate action without a meeting; consent; notice; statement on filed certificate; consent by electronic transmission; delivery.

Sec. 407. (1) The articles of incorporation may provide that any action the shareholders or members are required or permitted by this act to take at an annual or special meeting may be taken without a meeting, without prior notice, and without a vote, if written consents, setting forth the action taken, are signed and dated by the holders of outstanding shares or members or their proxies that have not less than the minimum number of votes that is necessary to authorize or take the action at a meeting at which all shares or members entitled to vote on the action were present and voted. The corporation shall give prompt notice of any corporate action taken without a meeting by less than unanimous written consent to those shareholders or members that did not consent to the action in writing.

(2) If the shareholders or members take an action by written consent under subsection (1) that would require filing of a certificate under any other section of this act if the action had been taken at a meeting of the shareholders or members, the certificate filed under that other section shall state, in lieu of any statement required by that section concerning a vote of shareholders or members, that both written consent and written notice have been given as provided in subsection (1).

(3) Any action the shareholders or members are required or permitted by this act to take at an annual or special meeting may be taken without a meeting, without prior notice, and without a vote, if before or after the action all the shareholders or members entitled to vote on the action or their proxies consent to the action in writing. If the shareholders or members take an action by written consent under this subsection that requires filing of a certificate under any other section of this act if the action had been taken at a meeting, the certification filed under the other section shall state, in lieu of any statement required by that section concerning a vote of the shareholders or members, that written consent has been given as provided in this subsection.

(4) An electronic transmission that consents to an action that is transmitted by a shareholder, member, or proxy holder, or by a person authorized to act for the shareholder, member, or proxy holder is written, signed, and dated for the purposes of this section if the electronic transmission is delivered with information from which the corporation can determine that the electronic transmission was

transmitted by the shareholder, member, or proxy holder, or by a person authorized to act for the shareholder, member , or proxy holder, and the date on which the electronic transmission was transmitted. The date on which an electronic transmission is transmitted is the date on which the consent was signed for purposes of this section. A consent given by electronic transmission is not delivered until it is reproduced in paper form and the paper form is delivered to the corporation by delivery to its registered office in this state, its principal office in this state, or an officer or agent of the corporation that has custody of the book in which proceedings of meetings of shareholders or members are recorded. Delivery to a corporation's registered office shall be made by hand or by certified or registered mail, return receipt requested. Delivery to a corporation's principal office in this state or to an officer or agent of the corporation that has custody of the book in which proceedings of meetings of shareholders or members are recorded shall be made by hand, by certified or registered mail, return receipt requested, or in any other manner provided in the articles of incorporation or bylaws or by resolution of the board of directors of the corporation.

Index of Subjects

Committees
    generally, §§ 69-71
    agenda, place of reports on, § 12
    architectural, § 69
    election, § 63
    executive committee, § 70
    nominations by, § 61
    refer to committee, motion to, § 28
    types, § 70
Committee of the whole, § 70
Conflict of interest of director of organization, § 83
Consent, voting by general, § 53
Contracts
    Bylaw amendments effecting, § 16
    members, contractual relation among, § 85
    officer or director and organization, contracts between, § 83
Correction of minutes, procedure for, §§ 13, 20
Counting votes, election committee's duties regarding, § 63
Courtesy in debate, §41
Courts
    election, presumption of fairness accorded, § 68
    member, judicial review of expulsion or suspension of, § 88
Cumulative voting, § 46
Customs for conducting meetings, § 11

D

De facto position held by one elected during challenge, § 68
Debate
    generally, § 41
    close debate, motion to. § 25
    limit or extend, motion to, § 26
    reconsider, motion to, § 38
    rescind, motion to, § 39
    resume consideration, motion to, § 38

M

About The Author

Harry S. Rosenthal, JD, PRP is both a lawyer and parliamentarian located in the Philadelphia, Pennsylvania area. He has been a member of the National Association of Parliamentarians for 15 years having attained the status of Professional Registered Parliamentarian (PRP). A member of the Pennsylvania Bar for many years, the author holds a Juris Doctor degree from Temple University School of Law. Mr. Rosenthal has served as a professional parliamentarian for many national organizations and has written numerous articles on the subject. He may be contacted in Greater Philadelphia at Lawhsr@gmail.com.